39 YEARS
OF
SHORT-TERM
MEMORY
LOSS

TOM DAVIS

GROVE PRESS

NEW YORK

Thanks to: Morgan Entrekin, total freedom. Andrew Robinton. Manuscript management Dara Price; editing Michael Hornburg, Lindsay Brice; Rock Brenner, good advice. Mike Bosze at Broadway Video. Additional thanks to Deb Seager, Mark Malkoff, Michael Streeter.

Copyright © 2009 by Tom Davis

Cast photo on dust jacket cover © 1975 Peter M. Fine
Photo of Tom Davis on title page © 1977 Edie Baskin. All Rights Reserved
Excerpt from *Timothy Leary: A Biography*
copyright © 2006 by Robert Greenfield,
reprinted by permission of Houghton Mifflin Harcourt Publishing Company.
Searching for the Sound by Phil Lesh
copyright © 2005 by Phil Lesh,
by permission of Little Brown & Company.
Lyrics to "Casey Jones" by Robert Hunter
copyright © Ice Nine Publishing Company. Used with Permission.
Brief text as submitted ["The show's announcer,
Don Pardo . . . O'Donoghue's time on the show."] from *Mr. Mike: The Life and Work of Michael O'Donoghue* by Dennis Perrin. Copyright © 1999 by Dennis Perrin. Reprinted by permission of HarperCollins Publishers.
Brief text as submitted [It was Tom Davis and Bill Murray
. . . Bill Murray's mouth."]
from *Dark Star: An Oral Biography of Jerry Garcia*
by Robert Greenfield. Copyright © 1996 by Robert Greenfield. Reprinted by permission of HarperCollins Publishers.
From *A Long Strange Trip: The Inside History of the Grateful Dead*
by Dennis McNally, copyright © 2002 by Dennis McNally.
Used by permission of Broadway Books, a division of Random House, Inc.

Published simultaneously in Canada
Printed in the United States of America

ISBN-13: 978-0-8021-4456-0

Grove Press
an imprint of Grove/Atlantic Inc.
841 Broadway
New York, NY 10003
Distributed by Publishers Group West
www.groveatlantic.com

10 11 12   10 9 8 7 6 5 4 3 2 1

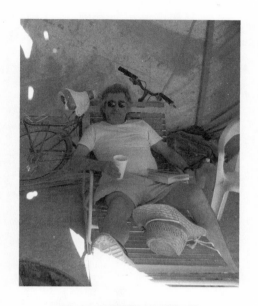

39 YEARS
OF
SHORT-TERM
MEMORY
LOSS

Cross, Country, III, IV, V; Track, IV, V; Publications, IV, V, VI; B-Club, III, IV, V, VI; Union, VI; Debate, III, IV, V, VI; Dramatics, V, VI; Service Comm., IV, V, VI; Dance Comm., V, VI; V Form Speech Contest; Teen Corps member, 6 wks; Don't forget Son of True Grit, (Allen and I co-authored, co-directed, co-starred and shared ego gratification).

Thomas James Davis
T.D., Tom, Tommy ... talent unbounded ... energy ... his eyes sparkle ... enthusiasm with long hair ... he really didn't want a senior article, so we'll stop.

CONTENTS

FOREWORD

When Tom told me he was writing a memoir, I was skeptical. Don't get me wrong, Tom's had a fascinating life, as you will soon find out. But it was my experience that he did not possess, as the title suggests, much of a memory—which seemed to me an essential ingredient in writing a memoir.

Tom asked if he could, from time to time, ask me to refresh his memory, and, of course, I agreed. I was running for the Senate in our home state of Minnesota at the time and reliving some old times, even a few painful ones, would be a welcome distraction from the serious business of campaigning.

Soon we were trading e-mails about some very memorable moments from our lives and careers that Tom was pretty hazy about. "When we did *The Comedy Team that Weighs the Same* on

Letterman—what was that about?" "Remember when you broke your heel jumping into an orchestra pit because some idiot had lowered the pit fifteen feet between rehearsal and the show? Was that an hydraulic orchestra pit? And what college were we playing?" "When Lorne cut your parents from the show—what was that about?"

But it turns out that Tom has a pretty good memory. We might disagree on a few fine or not-so-fine points, but in this book he vividly recollects a life that at once captures the experience of so many baby boomers and yet is unique to Tom Davis, a suburban Minneapolis boy of the 50s and 60s who went on to disappoint his uptight father by running away to show business and the company of everyone from Dan Aykroyd to John Belushi, Jerry Garcia, and Timothy Leary.

Tom does seem to remember every drug he took. Anyone who reads just a few chapters won't be surprised when they find out that it was Tom's drug and alcohol use that broke us up as a team. Tom writes here that he hated my *SNL* character, Stuart Smalley, the codependent host of the fictional twelve-step cable access show, *Daily Affirmations*. Of course, he did. In no small part, it was about him and me. And it was a literal threat to his drinking and drugging. Of course, he hated Stuart.

Tom and I had been best friends and partners for over twenty years, and our breakup was a painful one. I'll give you an idea how close we were. My daughter, born in 1981, is named Thomasin Davis Franken.

Tom jokingly refers to himself as the Garfunkel of Franken and Davis, but it might surprise folks that there were times that I harbored self doubts and thought Tom was the funny one. See? Codependent.

And, as you will see, Tom is hilarious. There are laughs big and small in here. In fact, the partnership worked because Tom had comedic talents and skills that I don't. You see, while I was wasting my time at Harvard, Tom was trained in the improvisational method of Second City at a place called Dudley Riggs's Brave New Workshop. John Belushi, Dan Aykroyd, Bill Murray, John Candy, Chris Farley, and many before and after have been trained in that technique.

For a writer (and Tom and I were mainly writers on *SNL*), the technique is invaluable. If we were stuck in a sketch, Tom would get us unstuck by finding an object to play with. Take the *Julia Child Bleeding to Death* sketch. If you've seen it, you probably remember it —and yet another brilliant performance by Aykroyd.

Julia's doing her show and demonstrates how to cut up a raw chicken with a very sharp knife. The knife slips and she cuts herself. Badly. The rest of the sketch is an orgy of spurting blood as Danny's Julia attempts—against her panic—to calmly show the audience what to do in such an emergency. Nothing works, including a dish towel tourniquet, and the chicken liver she's told the audience to save fails as a natural coagulant. Tom and I are looking for one last thing, one last thing for Julia to lurch for, before she passes out. Tom "finds" the phone. Of course! The wall phone on her kitchen set. Julia grabs it—"The phone! Simply call 9-1-1 . . . " And pulling it to her ear, she realizes "It's a prop!" and drops it, staggering woozily, somehow never losing her Julia Child cheeriness, and passing out, reminding the audience one last time to "Save the liver!"

I'm often asked to name my favorite moment at *SNL*. There isn't one. Not a "moment." But what I answer is Tuesday nights, or usually very early Wednesday mornings, when we were writing sketches for read-thru on the seventeenth floor of 30 Rock. My prototypical memory is of me and Tom rolling on the floor laughing at something that had come from one of us or Danny or Jim Downey or any number of the hilarious people we worked with. A job really doesn't get any better than that.

Tom had me laughing in high school. In tenth grade I transferred from public school to the Blake School, a prestigious private school in Minneapolis that had been chartered at the turn of the twentieth century as a school for Protestant boys. They started letting Jews in in the middle 1950s to get the SAT scores up.

When I got to Blake, I was surprised to learn that every school day started with chapel. Chapel began with the singing of a Protestant hymn, followed by a speech by a faculty member or student, another Protestant hymn, and then announcements. Announcements for the chess club, for a United Way drive, for any school organization with anything to announce. One morning Tom and I did an announcement for the drama society and everyone loved it. Soon, if you wanted students to pay attention to your announcement, you got me and Tom to do it. We were parodying movies of the day, like *Cool Hand Luke.* "If you don't go to see the glee club perform after school, you spend a night in the box."

So Tom and I got our start in show biz in chapel, making funny announcements.

During high school, Tom spent a lot of time at my house.

Tom's father, Don Davis, was the son of an alcoholic. In fact, Don's father drank himself to death. Don was rigid, judgmental, and had a giant chip on his shoulder.

As you'll see, what Don Davis was most afraid of was that his son, Tom, would drink, take drugs, have pre-marital sex, and drop out of college. Don Davis couldn't have done a more perfect job of guaranteeing that precise outcome.

I don't mean to be harsh about Don. I always had a soft spot for him because, well, he was Tom's dad. But the soft spot existed only in theory. It could never survive more than a few seconds of an actual interaction with Don, who resented me for getting his son involved in show business.

It's been years since I've seen Don, which is why I talk about him in the past tense. You see, Don is still with us. Sort of. He lives in Arizona in an Alzheimer's unit. He actually doesn't have Alzheimer's, but some other form of dementia. He's also psychotic. Tom tells me that the doctors believe that the psychosis kicked in while Don was in his twenties.

I bring this up only because Tom is taking care of Don. Tom's brother Bob, the straight-laced one, the hockey captain who went to Middlebury, the good son, has refused to speak to his father for years. And for good reason, Tom tells me.

So Tom's taken it upon himself to take care of his father. Tom goes back and forth to Arizona and keeps in touch with the doctors by phone. Oh, and Don's still difficult. Actually, more so. Quite a bit more so. A couple months ago Tom was in Minneapolis and came over and we laughed and laughed about Don and Tom's situation.

Something I love about Tom, something that comes through loud and clear in this book, is that his take on almost everything is so refreshingly unsentimental. And then, he lets it slip through. Oh, he doesn't go overboard. Never any danger of treacle. His last sentence in the chapter about our breakup: "I love Al as I do my brother, whom I also don't see very often."

I love Tom as I do my brother, whom I also don't see very often.

—Al Franken
2008

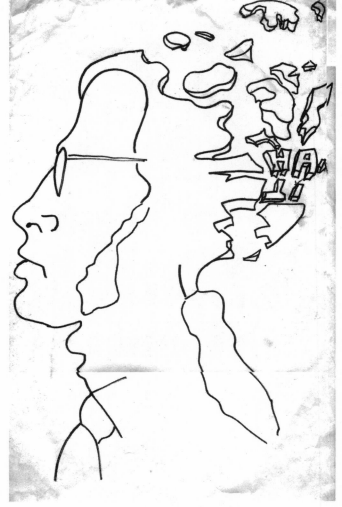

FELT TIP ON PLACEMAT, AL FRANKEN, 1974

NICE WORKING WITH YOU

THIRTY-NINE YEARS
OF
SHORT-TERM
MEMORY
LOSS

1

DAN AYKROYD

Dan Aykroyd had just signed autographs and posed for pictures for strangers on a New York City sidewalk. I complimented him on his graciousness.
Danny: "Every time I do that, those people are someday going to go out and buy tickets to one of my shows—that's what I do, Davis. I sell tickets."

I was sitting with Danny in his *SNL* dressing room waiting for the next scene to be camera blocked. It was late November 1976.

> Danny: "Davis—let's go somewhere for the break. Where would you like to be for Christmas?"
>
> I: "Easter Island—and San Francisco for New Year's!"
>
> Danny: "All right—you research it, make sure your passport hasn't expired—we're going."

Sunday the thirteenth, after the Candice Bergen Christmas show, Dan and I flew LAN Chile from JFK to Santiago. There was one flight a week to Easter Island, the most remote point on the planet in terms of distance and landmass. We had a few days to kill, so we wandered around the European-style metropolis, which impressed us with its wine and beautiful women. There were many

soldiers with Uzis standing on street corners and loitering in front of banks and government buildings. Riot-control personnel carriers with water cannons were parked on the median of the boulevard in front of the university.

The snowcapped Andes beckoned us from our hotel window, so Danny rented a Fiat. Looking at a map, we found a destination high in the mountains, called Baños Caliente. Hot baths in the Andes—let's go!

As we went higher up into these mountains, civilization and other cars became less and less frequent. Finally there was a restaurant that looked like a house in Bavaria. Sure enough, it was German, our host was wearing lederhosen, and we dined on Wiener schnitzel and Spaten draft beer. Danny picked up the tab and left a generous tip, as is his custom, and we resumed our quest. Two miles up the road, the pavement disappeared. Twenty miles farther up, the road ended at some kind of mining operation with huge, yellow ore trucks that had tires taller than me, rumbling past each other like titanic bees. But there was a guy with a signal flag and red vest in the middle of the dust-clouded chaos. Danny jumped out of the car and strode up to him, trying to communicate by using the map. He came back and jumped in the car; he was laughing. "Davis—if there's hot baths here, it's probably for the ore. Hot, sulfuric acid ore baths!"

So, we turned around and began speedily retracing our route. When we reached the point where the pavement started, a soldier—an officer with an Uzi—stepped out of a small guardhouse and stood in the middle of the road, signaling us to halt. We complied, and he stuck his head in the window and blathered something in Spanish, to which we could only stammer, "No habla Español." He was more frustrated than we were in our inability to understand, and he opened the door and motioned for Dan to get out. Uh oh—we're in the middle of nowhere near a strategic mine, and the junta wants to talk to us. We had told no one where we were going; we'd "disappear" and they'd never find us. Dan got out, and the soldier jumped in the backseat—he wanted a ride! No problemo.

As we circled the island in the LAN Chile DC-8, we could see that Isla de Pascua, or Easter Island, was almost an equilateral triangle with a dormant volcano in each corner. Only a handful of us got off at Rapa Nui Airport, which had only one rusty fire truck parked alongside the single runway. Everyone else stayed onboard for Tahiti and points west.

The owner of the only hotel was a gregarious middle-aged German, named Gerhard, who threw our duffel bags in the back of his pickup truck and drove us to his single story hotel atop a bluff overlooking the shimmering Pacific. The first thing we did was run to the famous, restored monolithic figures that stand in a row, facing west, above the beach. We exulted in their majesty as the sun set.

© 1976 DAN AYKROYD

We ate Pacific lobster tails and drank white wine in the dining room, which, aside from ourselves, was populated only by an older couple from Belgium. Our host, sensing we were game, invited us to go to the "disco."

Our pickup truck pulled up to a Quonset hut, where two or three other smaller vehicles and several bicycles had gathered. Inside were some young Rapanuians wearing T-shirts and flip-flops that glowed beneath two black lights. There was an old record player playing contemporary music, and a folding table where Pisco was served. Pisco is a tequila-like drink distilled from Quebranta grapes common in Central and South America. As we mixed company and drinks, it was clear that there had been a unique civilization that was rapidly evolving—linguistically, culturally, and genetically. Almost everyone was Catholic, Spanish speaking, and of Polynesian/Spanish descent.

The Pisco had a nice stone to it. Danny is a social drinker, but he was most social on this occasion. On the way back to the hotel, he and I were standing in the back of the pickup, holding on to the outside roof of the cabin, but in a rough section of road, Gerhard told us to get off as he traversed some huge potholes. Danny hung on to the back of the truck and let it drag him a hundred feet.

COURTESY OF TOM DAVIS

Back in the hotel room, our host produced his stash and a guitar. Danny played his harmonica, and I the guitar, as Gerhard danced enthusiastically while flashing a hunting knife. We wound up in the small swimming pool. I remember Dan took a running dive, clearing the edge by an inch or two. No problem.

The next few days were spent exploring. As we crossed an overgrown field, I stumbled over the nose on a giant stone face. There was a quarry where some of the huge statues (Moai) were unfinished and had yet to be removed from their volcanic beds. There were two small sandy beaches. As far as I could tell, aside from the fishing village that sold to Australian clean-and-freeze fishing trawlers, the only industry was tourism.

I had brought along a paperback copy of Arthur C. Clarke's *Childhood's End,* a wonderful science-fiction novel in which alien

spacecraft eclipse the sun, hover over major cities, and save mankind from itself. Because they resemble devils, and know what the reaction will be, they do not allow humans to see them for a hundred years. I finished it and handed it to Dan, who read it in one sitting.

I had some acid, and we wandered into the most remote place on the island, got lost, and sat down in the shade. A native girl came up to us. Her name was Merina, a sloe-eyed beauty. She guided us to some remarkable spots, and got us back to the town before sunset. Danny was cracking me up all day by grabbing his head and loudly moaning, "The Heads! The Heads!" We would write the *Coneheads* on the first show back.

As the DC-8 lifted off of Easter Island, I glanced at the in-flight magazine with a feature article about Easter Island's Cave of Skulls. Fuck. I should read about these places *before* I go to them.

We arrived in Tahiti, Papeete Airport, renting the only vehicle available—a surrey/golf cart thing with what seemed like a lawn mower engine. Danny always drove. We checked into a gorgeous hotel, put on swim trunks, and headed for the beach. I brought a Frisbee. Dan is many things—an actor, writer, musician, master of ceremonies, wielder of chain saws, businessman, rider of motorcycles—but he can't throw a Frisbee to save his life.

As I realized that, two beautiful girls in bikinis came walking up the beach. Honest to God, it was Jodie Foster and a friend. She had just hosted *SNL* a month before. Jodie could really throw the Frisbee. The four of us washed the sand off in a hot tub, nothing happened, and the girls disappeared.

Dan drove that poor surrey all over the island, with me hanging on. Black sand beaches suck during the day, because they're literally too hot to walk on. Papeete was filled with French sailors, but we had lunch with a French couple who invited us onto their yacht where we smoked their pot. As the sun set, we were sputtering through a funky village on the precipitous side of the volcano. We left the next morning, but as we approached the airport, the transmission froze up—the surrey died.

I: "What do we do now?"

Dan jumped out and hung his leather travel bag over his

shoulder. "Get on the plane."

It was a six-seater seaplane that flew us to Rangiroa, a coral atoll 150 miles away. We got a cabana on the beach; there were only a few other wealthy tourists. The bar was on a dock over the azure water. There I met the pro who took people fishing and scuba diving, etcetera. I dubbed him Captain Largo and negotiated a water-skiing session to start and end right there at the bar. "Can I zigzag, or should I stay behind the boat?" Captain Largo: "Do whatever you want." So I got up on a slalom ski and made some nice cuts back and forth, jumping over the wake. This took strong arms, something I've never had. By the time I released the rope and glided to the bar, my whole body was shaking from the effort (I had been showing off). The next day, we tripped while snorkeling in the same area in which I had skied. There were immense coral heads that reached just two feet below the surface. Could've scraped my 'nads off. Captain Fuckhead Largo.

There was this old couple, he dressed in Indian white cotton carrying an expensive walking stick like Gandhi with bling. The bartender said the old guy was considering buying the whole island and operation. Apparently, he was the founder/owner of Club Med—got his start during World War II when the government paid him to create places where concentration camp survivors could recover. Good for him.

On our last day, we were the only ones drinking in the bar in the morning, except for one guy who could really knock 'em back. He had a boat with twin outboards, tied right there at the bar. It turned out he grew up in a suburb of Toronto. "Hi. I'm E. Buzz Miller. How you doin'?" He invited us to his place for lunch, so we hopped in the boat and sped to a nearby atoll, inhabited by natives, dogs, chickens, and pigs— no tourists. We entered his cinder-block house with a corrugated metal roof and met his pretty, native wife who smiled and fetched us each a cool one from the vintage refrigerator. They had a baby and a dog; she didn't speak much English, so the three of us chatted as she made sandwiches.

Dan: "E. Buzz . . . how did you make it here from Toronto, eh?"

E. Buzz: "It's a funny thing . . . I had just graduated from high school, and a couple friends and I were under this

bridge, drinking the last bottles of beer from two cases. As I drain it, I says, 'Christ, I'd sell my soul to the devil for a case of IPA [India Pale Ale],' and as soon as I said that, this guy pulls up in a '65 Chrysler, and pulls a case of IPA out of his trunk. After that, everything went to hell so bad, I had to flee the country for good."

E. Buzz now made money by taking pictures of topless native girls for advertising in an interisland tourist newsletter.

We took E. Buzz's name and inspiration to write the first in a series of popular sketches for Danny's character:

Announcer: "And now, Public Access Cable Television Channel D presents . . . *E. Buzz Miller's Art Classics*."

[dissolve to E. Buzz Miller and Christie Christina (Laraine Newman) sitting on a couch in a darkened room]

E. Buzz Miller: "Good evening, welcome to Public Access Cable Channel D, this is *Art Classics*. I'm your host, E. Buzz Miller. And my lovely guest to my left here is Miss Christie Christina, and she's opening at the Coach & Pole Bar tomorrow night. But enough talk, let's get right to tonight's art classics."

[E. Buzz holds up classic painting of a nude reclining on a bed]

E. Buzz Miller: "Now, the first one here is called Venus of Irbino, and it was painted in 1538 by a guy in Venice. And, this is for real, his name is spelled T-I-T-I-A-N. Titian! Honest to God!"

Christie Christina: (giggles profusely)

We flew to San Francisco for New Year's Eve with the Grateful Dead at the Cow Palace. I remember Danny dancing with this beautiful, smiling girl whose face was disfigured—probably went through the windshield once. Two years later, the Blues Brothers would open for the same event.

2

BEGINNINGS

August 7, 1994, a jungle-steamy afternoon on the Rolling Stones' stage in RFK Stadium. Danny is doing a promo for the *Voodoo Lounge* tour, which would begin the next night. We're all standing around, and Ron Wood and I are discussing the recently released movie, *The Mask.*
I: "Wow—Jim Carrey . . . where did *he* come from?"
Ronnie: "Well . . . we all come from somewhere."

Both sets of my maternal great-grandparents were Swedish immigrants named Johnson. The family joke is that when Swann and Anna came over, they were Larsen, but they thought there were too many Larsens, so they changed it. Good Minnesota joke, but it has the ring of truth.

In 1945, dad was twenty years old and in the navy when he served at Okinawa. On the way in, a kamikaze flew over the bow and hit the troop carrier across the way; he heard the screams. He remembers hitting the beach and eating an egg salad sandwich. I don't believe him. He lies all the time. He's always claimed he never saw combat, or shot any Japanese, but he and his buddy were checking out the perimeter in back of the beach and shot a goat by mistake. I probably never would have existed if they hadn't dropped the bomb on Japan twice.

My mother is a twin. As children, she and her sister Jo each had a doll; Jean's was named Tom, and Jo's was Nancy. Jo's firstborn was named Nancy. Mom had married "the businessman" and Jo had married "the cowboy."

In 1951, "the businessman," Don Davis, drove a '49 Studebaker

Minneapolis
Minnesota

Champion on his rounds as regional Scotch Tape salesman in half of Montana out of Great Falls. But he had just been promoted by 3M, and reassigned to Minneapolis, his hometown. Jean Jacqueline Johnson was a waitress in the Skyroom restaurant on the top floor of Dayton's department store, which is ten stories high. As Miss Dayton, she became Queen of the Lakes, to reign for a year for the Aquatennial, a summer celebration in Minneapolis.

When they married, she was twenty and very passive, he was twenty-five and a controlling adult child of an alcoholic. I came a year later. As a tot, I grew up before a television. For *The Mickey Mouse Club*, I wore the mouse-ears cap while I watched.

My father started me skiing at age two. Before that, I rode in a rucksack on his back with my arms around his neck as he swooped down a snow-covered hill, something that would be frowned upon today. I still love him for it.

I have an early recollection—maybe age four or five. My mother, being a recent Aquatennial Queen, was going to be on a float in the Aquatennial Parade, and my dad was going to be a clown. Someone had given him a clown-makeup kit and he showed it to me—a laminate box with a handle and luggage snaps that opened like a fishing tackle box. He pointed out the sweet-smelling grease paints, brushes, face cloths, cold cream, and the mirror attached to the inside of the opened top cover. I remember sitting in the bleachers of Parade Stadium with my grandmother, watching fat Shriners on pimped Harleys followed by some clowns. My grandmother pointed.

> Grandma: "Look, Tommy—there's your dad. See that clown?"
> I: "No."
> Grandma: "There—that one with the bald cap and orange smile."
> I: "No!"
> Grandma: "And there's your mom—see?"

I could see Mom fine, but I could not recognize my fa-**DAD** ther. To this day, I dislike clowns, circuses, makeup, and sweet-smelling soaps and cologne.

Dad also taught me how to swim enough to take lessons (provided free for children by the Minnesota School System summer program). Dad taught me to play baseball, football, and tennis. He gave me a boxing lesson because some day I would come up against a bully, "and the first thing you do is punch him in the nose" (my father is a lifelong knee-jerk Republican). When I was afraid of being hit in the boxing lesson, my dad, who was kneeling (I was five), dropped his gloved hands to his side.

> Dad: "Go ahead, Tommy, hit me in the face as hard as you can."
> I (shyly): "No."
> Dad: "Go ahead. You can't hurt me."
> I: "I don't want to."
> Dad: "I'm not going to hit you back. Go ahead—hit me!"

I was an athletic five-year-old, and I hauled off and clocked him with a right hook to the nose. He fell forward onto his hands and shook his head, then went back to his knees as he checked to see if his nose was bleeding.

> Dad: "Wow! I didn't know you could hit like that."
> I: "I'm sorry, but you told me to hit you."
> Dad: "I know. It's okay." But that was the end of the boxing lesson.

At that time, we moved into a new house, and the next day my mother was bathing me when the phone rang. When she left to answer it, I thought it would be funny to play dead, so when she returned, I was motionless and floating facedown in the tub. She did not think it was funny at all.

My dad bought me a bicycle and a briefcase for schoolbooks. He helped me with my homework. He insisted on Heine haircuts for me and my younger brother, Bob, usually administered by my mother with the pet clippers. We had a schnauzer named Hans.

Dad paid me fifty cents a week allowance, for which I mowed the lawn, raked the lawn, fertilized the lawn, watered the lawn, or shoveled snow off the drive-way, steps, roof, and sidewalk. I helped him paint the house and stain the cedar-shake shingle roof, then wash and take on or off the storm windows or screens as the season dictated. We barbecued T-bone steaks every Saturday, even in the winter, unless he and Mom went out to a party. On those occasions, I heated up frozen Swanson's chicken

ME

pot pies or TV dinners for my brother and me to eat while watching professional wrestling, and then a Johnny Weissmuller *Tarzan* movie.

I still laugh at the memory of my brother's face when he entered our bedroom and I shot a rubber suction-cup dart gun so the dart stuck to the middle of his startled forehead. Being my little brother, Bob was dominated by me. We had much love and happiness between us, but three and a half years is almost a generational difference when you're eight. When I entered my teenage years and struggled at private prep school and fought with my father, Bob determined he would not go through that. He stayed in public school, lifted weights, and became a very successful student and hockey player. He went on to graduate from Middlebury, and lives quietly in a suburb of Detroit with his wife and daughter. Bob and I exchange brief e-mails and speak on the phone once or twice a year. He has not spoken to our parents in ten years. Now he won't speak to me either. I miss my brother. There is great irony in the fact that I am now the dutiful son who visits our parents.

My parents laughed as I crooned along with Robert Goulet on "If Ever I Would Leave You" on *The Ed Sullivan Show.* They also took me to an art theater in Minneapolis—the Westgate—to see Jacques Tati's *Mon Oncle.* We laughed as a family. It was a revelation to me. I totally related to the little nephew. Then we saw *Les Vacances de M. Hulot (Mr. Hulot's Holiday),* which is still one of my favorites. The first Pink Panther we watched in a drive-in movie (the 7-Hi, on Highway 7 in Minnetonka) in Mom's 1960 Hillman convertible. Peter Sellers trying to get in bed with Claudia Cardinale made my mom laugh until tears rolled down her cheeks.

Once, as a preteen, I accidentally tucked the restaurant tablecloth into my belt along with my napkin. When we rose to leave, I showered the next table with dirty dishes and the check. Everyone laughed. They had to—I was a kid.

The Blake School glee club attracted me, not because I could sing, which I can't, but because they did a spring road trip, and I would do anything to get out of the house. The final performance was at Wake Forest Academy in Chicago. Our showstopper was "Captain Hook." We stood on risers, center stage, and our captain, standing in the back row, descended through the rest of us while singing the opening refrain. I went right and the captain went left; I lost my footing and sprawled onto the piano, knocking the keyboard cover onto the accompanist's fingers and scattering the sheet music. The auditorium howled with laughter as I picked up the music and tried to put it back like Stan Laurel.

Throughout my life, Mom has always laughed at my stuff, though she can't distinguish between my singing in my Dr. Denton's along with Robert Goulet, and crafting an inspired sketch on *SNL*. Dad never liked the Franken and Davis act, which he found "raunchy." He did like the Emmy I gifted them, and which they displayed in the lit crystal and china cabinet in their pristine house beside a golf course in Arizona. That's what Emmys are for. But, so far as he's concerned, I was a lot more fun as a child, and he regrets sacrificing to pay my tuition to go to a prep school, where I was supposed to make lifelong friendships with old money, get into a good college, and become a lawyer. Instead, he got a hippie with attitude. God grant him the serenity.

For Christmas in 1969, I gave my parents tickets to *Oedipus Rex* at the Guthrie Theater. When they returned from the performance, I asked them how they liked it.

Dad: "It was good!"

Mom: "I liked it." After all, it *was* the Guthrie.

I actually wrote two different *SNL* sketches about "Don, Jean, and Tommy" that made it to air. My parents saw them but did not make the connections. The first had Tommy (I played myself) announcing at the breakfast table that he didn't feel like going to school today. Don (Bill Murray) says sarcastically, "Oh, great . . . fine. Maybe we should ALL stay at home and see what happens, because we just don't give a damn! Jean—call up my office and tell them everybody should go home in a handcart, because Tommy doesn't feel like going to school!"

Jean (Jane Curtin): "Oh, Don, I don't know."

Don: "Give me the phone!"

Cut to spinning newspaper headlines: "Everyone stays home," "Tommy Stays Home—Country Likewise," "Pentagon Shuts Down."

Cut to: stock footage of Soviet missiles and jet transports, Soviet soldiers charging.

Cut to: Don, Jean, and Tommy at the kitchen breakfast table, Soviet soldiers kick the door in and drag them away as Tommy pleads, "I'm sorry, I'm so sorry!"

The second featured John Lithgow as Don, who is very cranky and disparaging at the kitchen breakfast table. Then he reveals he is not feeling well, it's probably cancer, and he's going to die.

> Jean (Jane): "Don—I'm going to call your doctor and make an appointment for this afternoon."
> Cut to: Don and the doctor, who is examining an X-ray.
> Doctor: "Oh my God. Don—you're going to surgery."
> Don: "What is it?"
> Cut to: Don discreetly covered for what must be rectal surgery, under local anesthesia. Using large forceps, the doctor removes a huge wriggling bug.
> Cut to the next day: Don at the breakfast table—loving, supportive, sunny disposition.

The only *SNL* they attended was when O. J. Simpson hosted in 1978. They were thrilled to meet him.

Back in 1968, my Blake School classmate Mark Luther called me on the phone. "Ho, Tom. Say, I've got two tickets to see this guy they say is as good as the Beatles—Jimi Hendrix. Wanna go? Dutch treat."

As I walked into my first rock concert, I wanted to be a marine in Vietnam. Three hours later, I walked out wanting to grow my hair long, smoke pot, and make love to girls. Hendrix at the Minneapolis Armory, and it was all over.

MY SECOND CONCERT, 1968

© 1968 JEFF CORAN

BEGINNINGS

The polarization of the '60s was no less powerful than in my own high school. My Hendrix epiphany now slotted me among the radicals, and while I still had friends who were jocks, the headmaster, the dean of students, and my father observed that I wasn't "the same Tommy" anymore, and they didn't like my attitude. Dad sent me to a psychiatrist when I didn't want my hair cut. After a series of tests, including the Rorschach, the doctor told me I was going through a period of adolescent disillusionment, which he said was normal. I said that if there is something wrong, and I am normal, why doesn't he examine my father? Shrink: "Because he's paying the bill."

I came home on a Saturday afternoon to find the dean of students in my living room, talking with my father. This display of power was supposed to scare some sense into me, but it just hardened the polarity. Then I got called into the headmaster's office, where he quizzed me on my politics and my plans for the future. In survival mode, I turned on the charm and tried to put spin on everything. Then he revealed that he had listened to a surveillance tape of a meeting of students from several schools in a private home, where David Pence, a wire-rimmed-glasses-wearing local member of the SDS (the notorious Students for a Democratic Society) spoke and answered questions. Apparently, I had asked too many questions.

At the beginning of August 1969, Al Franken, as a new Harvard freshman, was invited to a party of Harvard alumni at a mansion on a shore of Lake Minnetonka. In the spirit of the Marx Brothers, he decided to make an entrance. Mark Luther's wealthy grandmother also lived on Minnetonka and we were free to use her old Chris-Craft launch to go water-skiing. On this occasion, using red electrical tape, I put a big red "H" on Al's chest—he was wearing only a bathing suit. When he got up on the skis, Mark, who was driving the boat, twice buzzed the party on the shoreline, honking the horn, before Al let go of the rope and glided onto the lawn. Al would flourish at Harvard, but he would never truly become a "Harvard Man" per se.

In the middle of August 1969, the week of Woodstock, my dad took me to look at colleges in California. I knew I wanted to go to

California. We looked at Claremont, Pomona, and USC while he did some 3M business. We flew to San Francisco, rented a car, and visited Stanford. We stayed in the Jack Tarr cylindrical hotel on the top of one of those hills. I loved San Francisco. Because of

my interest in the Brave New Workshop in Minneapolis, a comedy troupe started by Dudley Riggs, Dad was cool enough to take me to see the Committee, a comedy group affiliated with Second City. I was impressed. I believe I saw Howard Hesseman, Del Close, and Garry Goodrow perform in the cast. Then Dad made a big mistake. To show me firsthand how disgusting and revolting hippies were, he took me to lunch across the Golden Gate at the Trident Restaurant on a dock over the bay in Sausalito. The waitresses were gorgeous hippie chicks and the patrons were musicians, artists, and drug dealers. Dad started giving the evil eye to a long-haired pirate at the next table, who snarled at him, "What are *you* looking at?" Dad turned away and didn't say a word. I was surely coming back to this place.

As soon as Dad and I returned, Al and I wrote and produced a show for the Blake School, using the Dramatics Association and girls from our sister school, Northrop Collegiate School for Girls. It was a series of comedy sketches we titled *Son of True Grit,* after the then-current John Wayne movie inspired by the book. John Wayne was an object of ridicule because of his pro–Vietnam War activism. The sketches included a parody of *On the Town—Seamen on Broadway.* We also did an over-the-top Soupy Sales silly soap opera, a gay version of *The Lone Ranger,* and we ended the show by projecting a film we found in the Minneapolis Public Library, titled *Camera Thrills*

AMY WARNER, REED HARDIBURG, AL, AND ME.
COURTESY CALL 'O PAN YEARBOOK

of World War II, to which we played Barbra Streisand singing "People (Who Need People)." Al had just graduated in the spring (it was my senior year) and we had to put on the show before he left for Cambridge at the end of September. The Blake School administration refused to be associated with our production, so we found a stage in a gymnasium at Holy Angels Academy, who allowed us in for a pittance. Because of the controversy, the whole school showed up to sell out the show, which was enthusiastically received, to the dismay of the school authorities. It was a sweet victory that made us confident we had a career in show business.

To my own credit, knowing that my grades weren't good enough to get me into Stanford, I applied to Callison, a small college at the University of the Pacific, in Stockton (within striking distance of San Francisco). They sent all their sophomores to a campus in Bangalore, India. From them, I got an early acceptance in late October. Everybody at Blake School knew all I had to do was pass, and it would be good riddance. Nice to have people cheering for you.

Dad, in one of his searches of my room, found a half-written letter to a friend, in which I described my experience making out with a girl, where I succeeded in getting her shirt off. The subjects of sex and love made my father most uncomfortable. When I was fifteen, he took me down into the basement and told me a dirty joke, to see if I knew about the birds and bees. This time, he hustled me out into the crisp autumn air and, with his face red with fury, he demanded, "Do you want to make some girl pregnant?!," which was rhetorical. Then, the anthem of uptight parenthood: "If you want to become an alcoholic bum by the time you're nineteen, fine. But while you live under *my* roof, you'll live by *my* rules!" And finally, frustrated by my monosyllabic, passive-aggressive answers, "Go ahead—hit me! Hit me as hard as you can!" Of course I didn't, but he open-handedly struck me in the chest and knocked me down, then stormed into the house. He couldn't hang on, and he couldn't let go. That was his problem. I was already gone.

A few years later, postcoitus, the same girl asked me, "Remember that time in high school when you got my shirt off? Why didn't you fuck me?"

3

AL FRANKEN

Famous epistemological conundrum concerning sense
data and the nature of truth: "If a tree fell in a forest,
and no one was there to hear it, would it make a
sound?"
Al Franken: "If Helen Keller were alone in a forest, and
she fell down, would she make a sound?"

From: Tom Davis
Date: Wednesday, 22 March 2006 5:31 PM
To: Al Franken
Subject: My Memoir

Quick question: what do you think was the best F&D Show, either theater, college . . . whatever?

From: Al Franken
Date: Wednesday, 22 March 2006 6:58 PM
To: Tom Davis
Subject: Re: My Memoir

Hmmm. Some of the college gigs, I'd say. Remember St. Anselm? It's a Jesuit school in N.H. We rehearsed doing the slides for the bit about [what was it like working with] Gilda, Laraine, and Jane—fucked her, fucked her, blew me. And the head Jesuit expressed concern. But we told him all the profanity in the show was necessary. He didn't censor us and after the show, he said that he agreed that every profanity was chosen for a reason.

From: Tom Davis
Date: Thursday, 23 March 2006 10:01 AM
To: Al Franken
Subject: Re: Re: My Memoir

Thank you for this. Do you remember Kansas State (Uncle Lionel) or Kentucky State—you smashed your shin on a folding guardrail [it was outdoors in the stadium] as Mick Jagger, our closing number [with a local band and me on guitar as Keith]? There was also Gustavus Adolfus (?) in St. Paul, when I doused the heckler with the drink/microphone thing, interviewing the audience. I should probably do a generic amalgam of the college gig experience. I don't know. I thought this would be easy. Fuk. Tom

From: Al Franken
Date: Thursday, 23 March 2006 12:12 PM
To: Tom Davis
Subject: Re: Re: Re: My Memoir

Kansas was a different school—a private college—near Kansas City. I can figure it out at some point. I think the Kentucky show was Western Kentucky. The worst injury on the Jagger bit was when I jumped into the orchestra pit at a school in Louisiana—in Lake Charles. Between rehearsal and the show, they had lowered the hydraulic pit another entire floor, and I jumped in and broke my heel. You came to the medical clinic with me. The St. Paul gig was St. Thomas I believe.
Then there was the disastrous gig in Cincinnati brought to us by a fraternity at Xavier College. It was one mishap after another, starting with their putting the wrong time on the Ticketron tix.
We should talk these through. Al

Al and I met in 1967. He was in the class above me at the exclusive, all-male, prep Blake School in a suburb of Minneapolis. He was one of those faces I passed in the hallways each day, but what a face—buckteeth, Coke-bottle glasses, and that mouth. On demand, he would demonstrate by slowly and dramatically opening his maw to its fullest extent, then inserting his pudgy fist completely inside. He had a cherubic build, but, incredibly, his body was literally denser than anyone's I've ever seen. He could lie on the bottom of the deep end of the pool, his head supported by one bent elbow. He could sink like a stone. Of course, he had almost no body fat as a young man.

Soccer VI; Wrestling V, VI; Class Vice-President VI; Union V, VI; Science Club IV, V, VI; Blakely Barb V, VI — Assistant Editor; Chess Club V, VI; Literary Club VI; Winner Fourth Form Declamation Contest; National Merit Semi-Finalist.

ALAN STUART FRANKEN

Al, Alphonse . . . "Well, Sir" . . . subtle humor . . . golf caddy . . . physics genius . . . 800's on his boards . . . absent minded . . . Pep Fest M.C. . . . draws cartoons for the Barb . . . Fig Newton . . . has an affection for words . . . The Claw . . . "WENN-delll" . . . school spirit leader . . . "And there I was, taking the oath of office for President of the United States" . . . gets down to earth on the soccer field . . . biggest grin . . . studious aspects . . . the true Blake cohort . . . "Looks are deceiving" . . . mathematically inclined . . . good debater.

He was one of those Jewish guys who dominated scholastics—perfect SATs and such. Franken was equally competitive on the athletic field. He was a good wrestler, and as a soccer player, his lack of finesse got him the position of "enforcer." And when he broke his wrist, the plaster cast made him even more effective, earning him the title of "The Claw."

Some Franken family lore: supposedly, when Al's mother Phoebe gave birth to him, he came out jaundiced, pointy-headed, and cross-eyed. The doctor said, "Now *that's* a baby!"

When Al was a precocious four-year-old, there was a city worker digging a ditch in front of the house who became annoyed as young Franken counted aloud the successive number of each shovelful.

Phoebe was a real estate agent. As an eleven-year-old home alone, Al answered the telephone. Apparently she was selling a house to the actor Clayton Moore, who was famous in the midfifties for his leading role in the popular television show *The Lone Ranger*. Now he was retiring to Minneapolis:

Al: "Hello?"

Mr. Moore: "Hello . . . is Mrs. Franken there?"

Al: "No. Who is this?"

Mr. Moore: "How old are you, young man?"

Al: "Eleven."

Mr. Moore: "You know what? This is the Lone Ranger calling . . ."

Al: "Yeah. And I'm Tonto."

© OWEN FRANKEN, CIRCA 1959

As a fourteen-year-old, he was going out on his first date, and his father, Joe, realized he had never explained the birds and the bees to his son. Beginning with a gentle inquiry, Joe discovered that Al didn't appear to have a grasp of the facts. After carefully explaining the differences between the sexes, Al was confused and upset. "You mean women don't have penises?" Joe tried a different approach, but his son became even more upset. Joe had to start all over again before Al finally told him he was joking. Poor Joe.

We took a canoe trip into Canada in '73 with pals Jeff Frederick and Paul Flum. We had a wonderful time fishing, tripping, and swimming, but coming back through U.S. Customs at International Falls (this is where Bullwinkle went to high school) was always an ordeal. We were easy to identify as young hippie freaks. We were told to get out of the car. Naturally, I was holding a quarter gram of hash and a hash pipe. I swallowed the hash and threw the pipe into the river, right in front of the officers. Now they were pissed off. Inside, we were being processed beneath a picture of President Nixon, and, when asked his profession, Al said, "Comedian." They didn't like that. Jeff leaned over the counter to get a glimpse at the Interpol report spewing out of a teletype. He said my name came out highlighted as a suspected drug dealer, and he begged Al and me to stop making Nixon jokes as his car was being torn apart. We each got strip-searched individually. Paul said next time he was going to put a note up his butt. Al was last to reappear. They let us go with a $100

fine. Once in the car, Al explained that they had started his interrogation with, "All right . . . your buddies told us everything," and Al blurted out, "We didn't mean to kill that Indian—it was an accident!"

BRAVE NEW WORKSHOP

founded by
Dudley Riggs
in 1958

4

DUDLEY RIGGS

COURTESY BRAVE NEW WORKSHOP

My descendents will ride swift ponies, know supple
women, wear cloth of gold, and they will not know to
whom they owe all these things.   —Genghis Khan

Al Franken thought that December 8, 2006, might be his last broadcast for Air America Radio, which was bankrupt again. The next day
he was to leave for another three-week USO tour of Iraq and
Afghanistan. He decided to do the show with a live audience from
the Brave New Workshop, the small Second City–type theater
where Franken and Davis got their start on a public stage while still
in high school. It was Dudley Riggs's Brave New Workshop from its
inception in 1958 until he sold the place in 1997. So Al flew me to
Minneapolis. We would do something old, something new, and talk
to Dudley. It hadn't changed a bit. Before the broadcast started, I
stood backstage. I knew every squeaky floorboard with my eyes
closed. The show started, and then Al introduced Dudley and me,
and we had the following exchange on the air:

Al: "We couldn't afford to buy tickets, but we started coming to watch the improv sessions because they were free, then I think it was me who approached Dudley to let us perform."
I: "Probably."
Dudley: "Actually, the first time I saw you two, Al, was one afternoon when you came in here with your mother, who told me 'You should put these boys on your stage.'"

COURTESY OF TOM DAVIS

Dudley Riggs had always been a colorful figure about town, clad in a sport coat and bow tie. He told me he grew up in the circus. As he put it, "I ran away from the circus to my family," but he actually left after a trapeze accident. I didn't believe him until one day I saw him talking to some freaky old geezer covered with tattoos and sprouting a gray ZZ Top beard. On my inquiry, Dudley answered, "That's my dad."

In the fall of '71, Al returned to Harvard and I began the first year of my life without school since kindergarten. I was sharing a ramshackle apartment in a turn-of-the-century tenement building in Minneapolis with my musician friend, Paul Flum. I was walking distance from Dudley's Brave New Workshop and I started taking improvisation workshops, where I trained in the Second City technique, first with Paul Menzel, who was in the cast, and then with Del Close, whom Dudley imported from Chicago's Second City to direct a new show.

This is the improvisation technique as I understand it: When you walk out onto the stage and begin improvising with other actors, you have to figure out who, what, when, where, and why. And to physicalize—are you in a kitchen? There are all sorts of things to do there (pantomiming refrigerator, sink, light fixture, string, knives, etcetera). This became invaluable to me as a sketch writer: when you get stuck, go to the physical and play with it. Also, never pun. Then there were trust exercises—never deny anything another actor creates. Go with it. Never break character.

Paul Menzel and Del Close didn't like each other—kind of a turf thing, because Paul was the resident director, and Del was a big, greasy, pockmarked, scary guy who enjoyed his status as a founding member of this school of acting.

Del was out front by the big brass espresso machine hitting on an actress in the cast. I approached him just to socialize—stupidly, because it was not a good time. Somehow my effort at a conversation went to "Haven't you ever observed that everything has an opposite—dead/living, up/down, day/night . . ."

Del: "What's the opposite of green?"

He and the actress laughed at me so derisively that I got up and left. As soon as I was outside, I realized that red is the opposite of green.

I was participating in a special New Year's Eve Improv Night at Dudley's when Menzel and Close were onstage acting out their hostilities. Menzel pantomimed the preparation of massive quantities of drugs with a giant syringe, and then Del pantomimed tying off his arm and offering it for Paul to inject him. Everyone else was too intimidated to go out and change the scene—except me, of course. I entered from offstage, but before I could open my mouth, Del picked me up and carried me backstage where he dropped me and rushed back out to continue his battle *royale*. He broke all his major improv rules in that single act.

Ten years later I ran into Del on a street in the West Village and he was glad to see me. We went to my apartment on West Twelfth and spent the afternoon drinking, snorting, smoking, laughing, and talking about everything but work.

But back to the fall of '71—I got a job at the Rainbow Café, a Deco eatery in Minneapolis since the '20s. It was run by the Lagaris brothers, second-generation Greeks. In the basement they had their own

RAINBOW CAFE

HENNEPIN AT LAKE
SINCE 1919

vegetable, bakery, and butcher departments. A middle-aged gay couple did the dishes. I started out at the soda counter making malteds and desserts. The short-order cook was temperamental and argued with the two younger waitresses (all the others were old and fat and had worked there forever). An old guy, Mike, worked the broiler and handled the top-end items like steaks, chops, ribs, and rainbow trout. Nobody messed with Mike.

Then they had the temperamental cook train me in his art: how to crack eggs quickly, make cheese omelets, cook freshly ground hamburgers to order on homemade buns, and prepare sandwiches—grilled cheese, pastrami, liverwurst, even peanut butter and jelly from the kiddie menu. They were always packed at lunchtime. I once had thirty burgers going at the same time. One day I looked out at the lunch counter, and there was Dudley Riggs in his bow tie, having a liverwurst sandwich and bowl of vegetable soup. He saw me see him and motioned me over. "How much do they pay you here?"

Dudley was opening a restaurant/dinner theater at Seven Corners—near the West Bank and the University of Minnesota. His establishment was adjacent to Del's Tire Mart, next to a water-bed store and across from a couple of bars, where bums would mix with students and hippies. Dudley told me he had just raided a young chef from the Black Forest (good German restaurant—still exists), and he wanted me also to cook for him, paying a dollar more per hour than the Rainbow. What clinched it for me was the fact that Dudley's stove was not far from the stage.

When I gave notice to the Rainbow, they were pissed.

> **George Lagaris: "Christ—we finally get you trained and then you take off! I don't understand."**

Old Mike wouldn't even say good-bye. Several years later, this wonderful restaurant went out of business when a McDonald's was built across the street. George died shortly after that. I read in the paper that during his funeral, burglars robbed his house.

To get to work on my first day, I was hitchhiking and a blue '64 VW stopped and I jumped in. The driver was a big guy with a mustache, smoking Kools.

> **Big guy: "Where ya' goin'?"**
> **I: "Seven Corners."**
> **Big Guy: "So am I."**
> **I: "I just got a job at the new Dudley's."**
> **Big Guy: "No shit, me too."**

BIG JEFF CORAN CIRCA '71 COURTESY OF TOM DAVIS

Jeff Coran and I were friends before we arrived. When we got there he introduced me to his pal, Ralph Brown. They were both going to be waiters.

There are two kinds of people in this world—those who have worked in restaurants, and those who have not. You can tell just by the way they order food. I witnessed some guy with his date complain to Ralph about the prices as he got the check. Dudley heard this and strode over to the table. He deftly plucked the check out of the man's hand and tore it up. "Tonight, the dinner is on me—just don't ever come back to my restaurant."

Dudley showed me how to make a ham sandwich: start with

the best ham, slice it paper thin, and pile it in ruffles and folds to allow air and flavor—people don't want a slab of meat on bread. He carefully instructed me in the making of soups from scratch—vegetable, chicken, lentil, and pea. First, sauté lots of onions and garlic in the bottom of the soup kettle, then add water or broth. Use some Tabasco and a little salt. Always stir so it doesn't burn, and if it does burn, don't stir it.

The house music was exclusively baroque and Dudley made his displeasure known when we were busted playing FM rock before closing time. I was remonstrated for feeding hot soup to freezing bums—this was a restaurant—"throw yesterday's soup away, damnit." The ceiling was Victorian pressed tin. Dudley paid a hippie named Jacques to lie on a scaffold and meticulously paint its intricate design in black, gold, silver, red, and green.

There was a cute girl who worked in the water bed store and lived above it. If the restaurant was slow, I would run over to her place and we'd fool around. If Dudley suddenly showed up, Big Jeff would call me on her phone. I'd do the fireman's exit and reenter the restaurant from the bitter cold, out of breath.

Dudley: "Where were you?"

I: "I was smoking a cigarette. Any customers yet?"

There was a doorway from the kitchen to the basement stairs, and to the back of the theater the walls and ceiling were painted black to shrink the space of the old brick warehouse. The stage was wide and rectangular, with a stairway, stage right, to the basement green room. Dudley booked lots of independent acts, including Penn and Teller, Louie Anderson, and Bill Foster, a serious actor who did a one-man show called *An Evening with Mark Twain!* In the two weeks of his engagement we became friends. He and his wife lived in a new apartment complex on the spot where my mother used to buy fresh eggs and chicken from a farmer (and right near the Mann France Avenue Drive-In Theater).

Bill wasn't yet thirty, so it would take him two hours to apply his makeup to look like the seventy-year-old Samuel Clemens. One night there was an ice storm and only three couples arrived for the show. Unlike Dudley's rep company, who were paid on a weekly basis and therefore would have gone on with the show, Bill's take was a percentage of the house. He and Dudley decided to cancel the show, so Dudley came out onstage to explain that he was giving them tickets to any other show for a year, except Fridays and Saturdays, to make up for the postponement. However, America's greatest author would be pleased to come out and say a few words and entertain any questions the audience may wish to ask—please welcome Mr. Samuel "Mark Twain" Clemens!

With that, the gray-maned and mustached patriarch of American literature shuffled out onto the stage, puffing away on a big cigar. He spoke in a craggy voice for several minutes, offering wry observations on American life and self-governance.

> Twain: "Now since you folks were dern fool enough to come out on a night like this, it would please me to answer any questions you may wish to ask."
>
> There was an awkward pause before one of the six raised his hand.
>
> Idiot at table #1: "Yeah—how long have you been doing this show?"
>
> Twain: "Well . . . I suppose the answer would be about sixty years or more. When I was a boy I listened to what the Big River had to say. It taught me all I ever needed to know . . . and, of course, Becky was a real person."
>
> Another awkward pause. I knew his act by now and I decided to step in and give him a lob.
>
> I: "Ah, Mr. Twain—I mean Mr. Clemens . . ."
>
> Twain: "I respond to either, but Mr. Twain is usually more entertaining. What is your question?"
>
> I: "Why do you think the French seem so dismissive of American culture?"
>
> Twain: "Well, the average American might not know who his grandfather was. But I think the American has a leg up on the average Frenchman, who is usually in considerable doubt as to who his father is."
>
> That got some tepid laughter, then another awkward silence until a hand tentatively pawed the air over its head.
>
> Idiot at table #2: "Yeah—how long does it take you to put on that makeup?"
>
> Mr. Twain straightened up and spat, "Oh fuck it!" and stormed off the stage.

When I would get home from work, it became my habit to play a record of Chopin and take a hot bath (there was no shower). I'd step into the antique claw-foot bathtub, with a glass of wine in one hand and a book by Sir Arthur Conan Doyle in the other. I read his complete works. I loved the Victorians—H. G. Wells, Jules Verne, George Sand, Bertrand Russell. They had a free love movement in the 1890s.

Big Jeff and Ralph were moving into a house with a couple of other guys. I took one of the upstairs bedrooms and left Paul the tiny tenement space to himself. The other guys were Pat and Larry Hayes of the Lamont Cranston Band. It became an archetypical animal house. Girlfriends would clean up the kitchen, whose sink would be refilled with dirty dishes the next day. Ashtrays overflowed; dead soldier beer bottles were only gathered up when it was time for another liquor store run, when every nickel counted. Food was a secondary concern. I don't think I drank any water that year. My ex-classmates from the Callison campus in Bangalore, India, were sending me letters filled with hash and opium, with return addresses to Captain Carma at 711 Cloudthrone Lane.

It was a bitterly cold winter. Frost was on the inside of my bedroom window. Waterbed Girl gave me a leaky waterbed and the clap. At the Teenage Medical Clinic I was treated by a doctor who was the mother of Paul Flum's girlfriend, Heidi. She had just accompanied us on a canoe trip during the summer. Small world.

Each morning when I awoke, there was a puddle beside my furcovered waterbed. Finally one night, we were all drunk and we rolled it down the stairs and out onto the arctic front lawn, where it burst and created an instant ice rink.

I had a thirty-gallon plastic garbage can in which I was fermenting homemade beer. It was covered with cheesecloth and sat in the hallway beside the telephone stand. Somehow, the rotary device fell into the frothy malt-yeast-and-molasses work-in-progress. After that, the sticky thing would no longer makes calls out, but it could still receive them, though the ring was more of a buzzing sound. The beer turned out fine.

On New Year's Eve, Ralph Brown and I took acid and went to the Silver Dollar bar on Lake Street (the site is now another

McDonald's). The Cranstons opened for Muddy Waters. He invited Pat to come out and jam with him. When the music was over, we walked out into the subzero night, I with a full pitcher of beer in my hand. Ralph's black '62 Corvair started right up, but the wheels had frozen so there were flat spots that made the car wobble. We laughed and made it back to Lagoon and Irving safely.

I thought I was finally going to sleep when the sounds of a reveler broke the silence of the newborn morn. I went downstairs to find Pat in a rare state of inebriation. I recognized he'd been dosed, as he was laughing demonically, dancing on the sofa, and throwing fistfuls of twenty-dollar bills around the living room. I picked up the money and went back to bed. At noon I was awakened by angry voices and roused myself to go downstairs to see what the commotion was all about. Two of Pat's bandmates had him by the collar of his shirt and were pressing him to remember where the money went. Pat could not remember. I laughed.

PAT HAYES 1972, COURTESY OF TOM DAVIS

TOM AND PAT © 2008 LINDSAY BRICE

One night before closing time at Dudley's Seven Corners, a drug-dealing friend of Ralph's sold the three of us a several-gram-weight lump of black hash. We locked the place up and hurried home to have one of these conversations:

"Okay—let's see that hash."
"Don't you have it?"
"You're joking."
"Fuck."
"We gave the money to your friend who handed it to you in the aluminum foil."
"Yeah, but we opened it up to look at it again and then you

wrapped it back up and put it next to the stove . . ."

". . . for Dudley to find tomorrow morning."

"Okay. Let's go back to Dudley's."

"The three fucking stooges."

"Shut up, Curly."

We got there, unlocked and lit up the place—no dope. We went out in the subfreezing temperature to search the trash bin that was barely lit by the closest streetlight. We opened the heavy steel cover so it banged against the building. We tore open trash bags and pawed around. Then Ralph spotted it, there in the mess.

Big Jeff and I quit at the end of March and went to India.

I returned to Minneapolis in June 1972 to work on a Franken and Davis Show for Dudley Riggs. I wore Indian whites and sandals around town for about a week and then got over it. We had two weeks between regular shows at the old Dudley Riggs's Brave New Workshop on Twenty-sixth and Hennepin. This meant a show on Tuesday, Wednesday, Thursday, two shows on Friday, three on Saturday (a midnight show), and a matinee and evening show on Sunday. Monday was dark. Friday and Saturday, Dudley set up folding chairs in the aisles and sold standing-room tickets to the first shows. Matinees had a rough reputation, but as we peeked from backstage before our first matinee we could see a decent crowd. Huh. Maybe word's gotten out about how great our show is. We're gonna be stars in Hollywood soon. Make our own movies. Do Vegas and Carson.

So we took the stage with renewed energy. But the crowd seemed to be talking among themselves, and even making comments on the show. In the middle of our weakest piece about two guys driving across the country—we pantomimed the car stuff—some guy said something too loudly and Al broke character. "Hey what is it with you—are you drunk or retarded?" No laughs. Fuck them. We finished the piece and launched into Brain Tumor Comedian, where Al goes backstage to get our next guest.

> I: "Before we bring him out, I have to explain that he's not a professional comedian, although it has always been his wish to perform comedy in front of an audience. Recently he was diagnosed with an inoperable brain tumor . . . and he's starting to fade, so this is really the optimum time to do it, and if

you could just give him a break and help his dream come true . . . Al, is he back there yet?"

Al from backstage: "Yes, he's here—introduce him!"

Tom: "Ladies and gentlemen, Franken and Davis Productions are proud tonight to present the comedy stylings of Mr. Lenny Binkey. C'mon!—put your hands together!"

Al emerges as Lenny Binkey, his head wrapped in bandages with a marked swelling of his left frontal lobe. There is a yellow stain there. I step behind him and motion for the crowd to cheer louder. Al grins with joy, turns to me, and points to the audience, like "do you hear that?" When he turns to the audience I wince behind his back, then rush forward to adjust his microphone stand, and in the process, accidentally hit the tumor with an amplified "bump!" Al grimaces in pain and recovers. He holds a glass of water and a sponge.

Tom: "What's this?"

Al: "If I start to pass out—just dab my face with some water."

Tom: "Got it. Okay—have fun out there!"

Al: "Did you hear the one about the rabbi . . . (Tom overdoes some cracking up) . . . about the mohel who never charged for circumcisions—he . . . he only took . . . t . . . give me some water . . ." (Tom wipes his Al's face with the wet sponge).

Tom: "You're doing great. Keep going."

(Al regains consciousness but forgets to give the punch line. Tom is horrified.)

Al: "A guy walks into a bar and orders a gimlet with a hazelnut . . . (grins at Tom who tries to crack up). Then a kangaroo walks to the bar and orders a gimlet—NO hazelnut! . . . and the bartenders says . . . (Al starts passing out. Tom has to douse him. He regains consciousness.)

Al: "He only took tips!"

Tom: "Let's hear it for Lenny Binkey!"

After the show we found out that Dudley had sold a block of tickets to a local institution, and the audience was a busload of mentally challenged teens.

As a young man, Al occasionally suffered from migraine headaches that were painful and sickening (and, I thought, stress induced). One night Al was stricken. Dudley comforted him before the show and spoke proudly of the show business ethic: the show must go on. And he meant it. "Also, do not vomit onstage. They will leave." We put a bucket backstage into which Al vomited at random times during the show. If it was in the middle of a bit, I stayed in character and vamped until Al reappeared. Al's distress was audible to the audience. After the finale they gave us rousing applause.

During this run, we would end the show with a demonstration of why some things are funny and some things are not, using the time-honored convention of a pie in the face. I would hold the pie and give the rap while Al would watch the pie, with a Milton Berlesque look of reluctant anticipation (mugging), and remove his glasses. One night in the intermission I discovered that we didn't have enough shaving cream to fill the aluminum-foil pie tin. I rushed back to Dudley's office and asked him to run next door to the corner grocery and remedy the situation. When I hit Al in the face with the pie and said "Good night," Al stood there for a two count and then screamed in agony, clawing at his eyes, "It's menthol! It's menthol!" I led him back to the green room where he doused his eyes and wiped them with a clean towel. Boy, were they bloodshot.

Al returned to Harvard in September. I was now living in a house in a suburb of south Minneapolis with Paul Flum again. Paul listened frequently to John McLaughlin's Mahavishnu Orchestra, *The Inner Mounting Flame*. Miles Davis's *In a Silent Way* was still my favorite album (except, of course, for any Grateful Dead). We were hippie freaks who didn't mow the lawn. We installed a bedroom in the basement for me, but before we got the window in, the neighbor kids stole our tools and my record collection. Paul would jam with Bill Buchen on drums and Dave Olausen on guitar, during the day, and the neighbors would call the police. The house was in rough shape. (It was condemned after we moved out, though I still used it to tryst with my girlfriend, the gas heater still not having been disconnected.) On the first night Paul and I moved in, we discovered that it was rat infested. The second night I opened the oven door, saw a rat in it, and lit the gas. The rat ran out the back of the stove

and jumped into the toilet in the bathroom. I flushed him away.

A cast member of Dudley's rep company left suddenly and I was hired to replace him. I had two days to learn his part and didn't entirely succeed. The first night I struggled and stammered, but fortunately, Dudley veteran Paul Menzel made some jokes about my performance. After the show he told me I was going to be fine, and after that, I was.

Most sketches in Dudley's shows came from successful improv sessions, and thus I helped to create a show that Dudley still remembers fondly, *The Day the Muzak Stopped*. We went on to do a record-setting run—something like 180 shows—that played at both of Dudley's theaters.

I was desperately attracted to an actress in our cast. I shared my confidence with fellow cast member and told him (another Jeff) of my desire to seduce her. He suggested I get her alone and tell her I think I might be gay. This would never have occurred to me, but I thought I'd give it a try. Sure enough, after the show one night, I walked her back to her apartment. I had a bottle of wine. I used the "might be gay" line. I don't think I needed to do that because nature probably would have taken its course anyway, but I did. A few weeks later I was onstage with her before an audience, when the improvisational situation lent itself to me trying to seduce her. I used the "I think I might be gay" line. I saw her eyes widen and her nostrils flare. When the scene was over, she came up to me backstage and raised her hand to slap my face. Then she burst out laughing. She was beautiful and of fiery Swedish stock. So was I.

There was some graffiti on the green room wall at that time: "Let him who is without sin stone the cast first." But Dudley forbade the use of drugs. It was grounds for immediate dismissal. I was doing lots of drugs (but never used a needle—ever). I knew Dudley liked me, and he liked to drink at that time, so I wasn't fazed when he tried to shake me down. He called me into his office to do it. He had an antique rolltop desk stacked high with mail and notes from 1959 (just like W. C. Fields in *Man on the Flying Trapeze*). Some creative people, myself included, have their brains wired so we can remember spatially where everything is, thus leading to clutter. If we cleaned everything up, we'd never find it again. When I saw Dudley at Franken's 2007 radio broadcast, I asked him about the rolltop desk and what it was like when he moved out. He laughed and said he found a lot of uncashed checks.

After we won our first Emmys in May 1977, we returned in triumph to Minneapolis to do one more show for Dudley at Seven Corners. We wanted to stage some rejected *SNL* sketches starring us and tape them with the audience eating it up, then show it to Lorne. This required a supporting cast. We got five guy friends to participate, and we costarred with Mary McCusker, a talented, funny, and attractive actress we knew from our days with the Pitschel Players in L.A. At that time she was married to Joe Roth, before he became chairman of Walt Disney Studios. People would tell her she looked like a young Ida Lupino, because she did.

We did a parody of the Miss America Pageant—*The Mr. USA*

Pageant—with Al and me as the finalists. Mary was the host/emcee. She interviewed Al after his promenade in the bathing suit competition (we wore Speedos, black socks, and Oxfords. Al wore a ribbon

that said MR. ARKANSAS, I, MR. CALIFORNIA).

> Mary: "Okay, Brad, that was very nice. Now I want to ask you a question to test your poise and ability to think on your feet . . ."
>
> Tom (nervous but confident): "All right."
>
> Mary: "If, as you were promenading just now, one of the heels of your shoe broke off—what would you have done?"
>
> Tom: "I would have removed both shoes and continued promenading."
>
> Mary: "Now, Brad. I'm told you're a student of UC Palm Desert. What do you do with your summers?"
>
> Tom: "I have a job at Boraxo where I teach handicapped children how to drive the twenty-mule team. My watchwords are from the last four letters of American—I can."

Then, in the talent competition, Al, still in his swimsuit, came out wearing a football helmet and pads. Two other contestants in tuxedos, wearing their state banner ribbons, held up a tackling dummy, to which Al launched a series of blocking drills. Starting from a three-point stance, he would then violently shoulder-block the dummy, to the tune of Frank Sinatra's "High Hopes." Whoops, there goes another rubber tree plant—wham!

Mr. USA made it to air on September 24, 1977, as a Franken and Davis *SNL* spot with Jane, Bill Murray, Danny, Belushi, and the host that night, Steve Martin, backing us up. I got called into Lorne's office the following Monday to meet Mike Nichols, who was sprawled on the couch, still laughing at my talent competition. I had performed an interpretive dance to Stockhausen's *Zeitmasse for Five Woodwinds*.

At Dudley's we took our *Final Days* sketch and expanded it, Mary playing Pat to Al's Nixon. I played Kissinger. At the end, where Nixon is alone before the portrait of Lincoln, shouting, "Why *me*? Why *me*?" Lincoln's mouth moved while it said, "Because you're such an asshole." When Danny had done it on *SNL,* the censor finally agreed to the portrait saying, "Because you're such a dip."

We had submitted that script at *SNL* with "schmuck" as Lincoln's word choice. But there was an objection even to "schmuck," which, our censor at the time, Bill Clotworthy, said was a Yiddish word for "penis." Al recalled to him the Lenny Bruce explanation, "Like a schmuck I drove all the way to Brooklyn," which, Al pointed out, did not mean, "Like a penis I drove all the way to Brooklyn." Lorne, who didn't feel like going to the wall for this one, sent Al a memo: "You can't say 'schmuck,' schmuck."

I wrote a sketch for Dudley's in ten minutes while sitting at the Frankens' dining room table. It was for Al to bring out his real parents, Joe and Phoebe, introduce them to the audience, and sing to them this Vegas-type song:

> *Hey Mom and Dad,*
> *This song is for you.*
> *It was your hard-earned money,*
> *That saw us through.*
> *And no matter how far I go,*
> *I will never forget you.*
> *I hope this is your fondest dream come true,*
> *Hey Mom and Dad.*

Iiiiieeee . . . loove . . . yoooou.

Al: "Thanks, Mom and Dad. I meant every word of that song."

Phoebe: "It was very nice, Alan."

Al: "How are you enjoying the show?"

Phoebe: "Most of it is very funny, but I think some of the things you say are of questionable taste."

Al: "That's just great, Mom. I bring you out here and you trash the show!"

Joe: "Alan—all your mother is trying to say is you don't have to use foul language to be funny."

Al: "Yeah? Well fuck you, Dad!"

Phoebe: "Alan! I can't believe you said that."

She starts weeping.

Joe: "It's all right, Phoebe—it's just that his head has swelled ever since he got on *Saturday Night Live*."

Al: "Okay—that's it. Get off the stage—both of you! Get out! Get out!!"

He shoved them offstage and kicked his dad in the ass as Phoebe wailed. This piece also made it to *SNL* air, and was the first in a series we called Parent Pieces, always with Al's real parents. Of course, we cut out the "fuck you, Dad" part when it was broadcast on *SNL* and added Phoebe recalling

© 1977 OWEN FRANKEN

Al wetting his pants at school.

This F&D Dudley show of July 1977 sold out every performance in a matter of hours after tickets went on sale. There were actually members of the public with picket signs outside the restaurant,
protesting "unfair ticket-selling practices." This was our kind of
problem. It really did swell our heads, and now we were probably a
bit too demanding for such a shoestring production. Dudley didn't
like that. Al and I always bitched, and we could whip up each other's
frustration. We had a conversation in the green room about how
perverse Dudley was to be happy on nights when six people showed
up, and to be crabby when the place sold out. Later that day, I had
the occasion for the first time to enter Dudley's office in the Seven
Corners basement. I was dismayed to discover that he could hear
every word that was said in the green room.

There was one other sketch in this Dudley show that made it to
air. Alan Zweibel had an idea that he didn't know how to write up:
in the sense that there was a guy named Argyle who became epony-
mous with a pattern on socks, so there could have been someone
named Douchebag. We thought it was hilarious, and Zweibel
granted us permission to take a stab at it. We got our fellow writer
Jim Downey to lend his wit, and mounted this sketch in our Dudley show with great confidence, fully aware that we were not com-
peting with Ibsen. Cut to seventeenth-century England, powdered
wigs, Rococo decor, etcetera.

> Major Domo: "Announcing Lord and Lady Argyle!"
> Enter a dandified couple. Cut to a conversation attended by
> a servant with an hors d'oeuvre tray.
> "These steaks are delicious, Lord Salisbury."
> "Thank you. What is it you're doing with those pieces of
> bread, Lord Sandwich?"
> Another elegant couple enters the ballroom.
> Major Domo: "Announcing Lord and Lady Douchebag!"
> Sandwich: "The Douchebags appear to be in top form this
> evening—though I shouldn't be surprised. Quite a tradition,
> there."
> Argyle: "I can't remember a time when there wasn't a
> Douchebag in the parliament."

Salisbury: "By God—give me a Sandwich and a Douchebag and there is nothing I cannot do!"

This sketch from Dudley's '76 was broadcast as the first sketch in our "final *SNL* show" with Buck Henry (May 24, 1980).

The Guthrie Theater was built in 1963 and immediately became the Carnegie Hall of the Twin Cities. Famous actors and directors came from all over the world to perform Shakespeare and Brecht. The Who performed there on the first *Tommy* tour. In early September 1982, Franken and Davis were booked for a single Saturday evening performance. Our act was hot from many college gigs. We came to Minneapolis a month early and immediately went to the venerable venue to meet the faces and familiarize ourselves with the backstage area.

We were shown the stage, the backstage, the green room, and the hallways adorned with mounted color photographs of famous actors in full performance. Our guide, the Events Lady, said, "Why don't you come to the show tonight? Robin Williams is doing his final of three sold-out performances. Here's the last two tickets."

Now, we had never cared for *Mork and Mindy*; Robin's act was not our style—it made me nervous. It seemed kind of desperate. We were probably a bit jealous of his success. We had met him once in Hollywood at a house in the hills after we won at the Emmys. He seemed like a decent fellow, and he was quite open about his desire to host the show, which would snub him for years.

So we went to the Guthrie to see his show—and he *killed*. The audience cheered for another encore and gave him a standing ovation. We went backstage and he saw us and embraced us, inviting us into his dressing room. Before we could congratulate him, he told us how much he respected us and that he loved our stuff. We invited him to take a midnight tour of Minneapolis. He was delighted, and brought a couple of pretty girls along. We smoked a joint beside Lake of the Isles, and later he thanked us as we dropped him off at his hotel. Robin Williams was a class act and we were humbled.

A week later, we got a worried phone call from the Events Lady. The Guthrie box office was freaking out because tickets weren't selling for our show. There was still enough time to cancel. No! The show goes on! We promised to do an all-out media blitz. Fuck us gently, this was not Dudley Riggs's, and that was clear. What's the term—a prophet in his hometown? Then we learned that Eric Clapton was playing in the Sports Complex on the same night. Apparently, a few months before, the Rock God had collapsed in Minneapolis while on tour, and he began his recovery there. A sponsor had gotten him to go fishing. Most Minnesotan musicians fish (except Prince), and now Eric was enamored with the lifestyle, and grateful enough to make up for his canceled show with this first performance since his paradigm shift. Great. I would like to have seen that show.

We immediately made a radio spot claiming that Eric had not completed his recovery, and listen to this—(a botched solo of his J. J. Cale cover, "Cocaine"—courtesy of Larry Hayes. The ad was funny and we bought time on the right radio stations. Tickets started to sell. We did every television and radio interview show, and got write-ups and articles in the newspapers, but we were nervous wrecks. When no stone had been unturned, I suggested we take a canoe trip with Jeff Frederick and Big Jeff Coran into the Northern Minnesota wilderness to mellow out and think about something else. We'd come back three days before the gig to rehearse. We got way back in the woods on a pristine lake, and all we could do was kvetch about ticket sales. When we crawled out of the wilderness, Al went to the first telephone we could find and called his mother. He came running back to the car with his arms up in jubilation, "Yes! Sold out! Seventy comps. We got it." It was a relief when the show finally started. Everything clicked and we ended with our Rolling Stones parody—backed by the Lamont Cranston Band. The crowd was appreciative, and both sets of our parents were in the audience—and right next to them was Dudley Riggs, applauding and beaming with pride.

5
INDIA

Fools rush in where angels fear to tread.
—Alexander Pope

When the Dudley Riggs show, *The Day the Muzak Stopped,* finally ended its run in February 1972, I decided to go to India, as I had promised myself. Big Jeff Coran said he wanted to go, too, so he quit waiting on tables. He had the gift of understatement and a laconic sense of humor. Once, he and Dave Olausen were buying a half pound of pot from two black guys who were in a soul band with Dave on guitar. They produced guns and pistol-whipped Jeff and Dave who bled profusely as they left. They looked at each other and broke into laughter. Dave still has a scar on his upper lip. Another time, Jeff sold a gram of hash to a white guy with shoulder-length hair who had just shot up speed in front of him. The guy was a narc, and Jeff did almost a year in a penitentiary in Northern Minnesota. When he first got there, some huge inmate tried to push him around. When that guy fell asleep, Jeff put a bar of soap in his sock and hit the giant in the head. When he finally came to, Jeff was there to tell him that the next time he wouldn't wake up. I was glad to have Jeff as my travel wingman.

We started west in his '62 blue VW Bug that had to be parked on a hill so it could be started by popping the clutch. Once we started, we didn't turn off the engine until we got to San Francisco. We were smoking a joint when we came around a curve of Interstate 80 and there was an Agriculture Inspection Station stretching across the border of California like a toll station. We pulled the car over and pretended to be searching for forbidden fruit in our luggage as the smoke cleared. Fortunately, we found an apple to submit and Jeff managed to fart in the car for extra cover as we pulled up to the uniformed Agriculture cop.

We finally turned off the engine on a hill in San Francisco, near Winterland, where we saw the Grateful Dead. Jeff said Jerry Garcia was the only talented guy in the Grateful Dead. I disagreed. Jeff's favorite music was Cleanhead Vinson and the J. Geils Band. We left the car at his mother's place in Anaheim and flew to Honolulu, where we rented a car to explore the island and to sleep in. The next stop was Tokyo. There I was impressed with the sidewalk beer-vending machines and the Japanese hippies who didn't seem to know what pot was. We walked around Ginza and gave up on Japan. We flew to Hong Kong and checked into a modest hotel. Our bellhop asked us if we wanted a "fuck-fuck girlfriend." Walking through the crowded city, we seemed to be a foot and a half taller than everyone else. I went to a tailor and had a sport coat made with button-down breast pockets. We took the train all the way to the Red Chinese border, where it divested itself of everyone who couldn't go beyond and then continued across the border. We took a cab to a lookout point. It drove so fast through the bustling peasants that one headlight knocked a dangling bunch of scallions off a guy's bicycle handlebars.

We flew over Vietnam at night. I could see fires burning in the black jungles below as I sipped a Bombay gin. Stepping out of the plane in Bangkok was like walking into a steam bath. The lobby walls of our hotel held dozens of plaques bearing the insignias of various American army and marine divisions that came there for R & R. On the streets, hookers would grab us by the arm and try to pull us into bars. I could sense the violence and fear from neighboring Cambodia.

Bangkok is known as the Venice of Asia because half the city is intersected by canals populated by a whole civilization of boat people who fish, drink, swim, and shit into the swirling delta waters of the Chao Phraya River. We paid a native to give us the tour, which included a ride in one of those longboats with a small outboard motor on the end of the tiller. They can go surprisingly fast. We went to a small island with a lavish shrine where believers and visitors buy one-inch squares of the thinnest gold leaf on a piece of tissue paper, and then rub it onto the big gold Buddha for good luck. I always respect religious good-luck practices.

Calcutta was a graphic introduction to India's timelessness. The antique cab took us from the airport through the dusty suburbs. The driver honked the hoarse horn constantly as we maneuvered through half-clad masses of humanity who shielded their eyes from the sun to see who was in the car. White cows wandered the buzzing streets; their big, unblinking, impassive brown eyes could see it all and accept it. It is good to be a cow in India. Donkeys pulled worn wooden carts that had two car tires.

In a letter, one of my Callison buddies had recommended we stay at the Carleton Hotel. The place was run by an old British lady. It was a marvelous throwback to the Empire: big heavy telephones from World War II sat behind the great wooden registration desk and there were keys and messages in pigeonhole boxes on the wall. Ceiling fans churned slowly but effectively, and English breakfast was served precisely at 7:00 a.m., ready or not, by an old brown man in a spotless white uniform.

I was out exploring, and behind a tall wrought-iron fence I saw tennis courts and a cricket field on a beautifully manicured expanse of gardens with huge, ancient trees. I walked into the perfectly preserved clubhouse as if I knew what I was doing. The bar was gorgeous. I sipped gin and tonics and looked at the yellowing framed photos of happy, overdressed Anglo-Saxons.

We boarded a DC-3 that was perhaps refurbished in 1950. Our pilot wore a turban and mirrored aviator glasses. As we taxied into takeoff position, the sari-clad stewardess offered us rock candy from a small basket. I saw a really big cockroach scuttle for his seat inside the wall of the fuselage. The pilot called our attention to the peak of Mount Everest shortly before we landed. When I exited the aircraft, my eyes beheld what looked like a Salvador Dalí painting of a hobbit city on a plateau surrounded by a wall of sugar-frosted peaks. The taxi was relatively new, made in China, and one of the few cars to be seen. The driver took us to a "modern" hotel owned by his family, a steel and concrete affair on the outskirts, with plumbing and electricity. We threw our bags on the beds and walked out into the Himalayan afternoon.

Kathmandu is an ancient city of temples, prayer wheels, incense, and holy men. Electricity was just being introduced. Many structures had ornately carved teakwood balconies, and windows framed with heavy shutters. The low doorways had unforgiving stone lintels. Most denizens got around on Chinese bicycles with thumb-activated traffic bells that tinkled constantly during business hours.

Then we found the hippie holy grail, a government-sponsored dope store that served tea and snacks. The sign said THE CABIN RESTAURANT and had the image of a smoking chillum. We entered the indirectly lit, low-ceilinged confines of wooden tables and chairs populated by an international collection of hippies and upper-class young Nepalese. There was a glass counter containing displays of three kinds of hashish—black, green, and gold. We sat at a large table with some American hippies who initiated us. A chillum is the way most of the world smokes hashish. It is a conical pipe that is held vertically. A small stone or ceramic stopper fits imperfectly inside, holding the burning substances in while allowing the smoke to be inhaled through the bottom. The hash would be "softened" by holding a match flame to the hard lump. This would cause it to crumble into a powder. The tobacco would be "toasted," usually by holding a match flame up and down the length of a cigarette until the paper burned off. The tobacco would be mixed with the hash and packed into the chillum. A wet rag (*safi*) is wrapped around the bottom to catch sparks and embers, which occur once the chillum is properly cupped with the hands to allow an aperture through which inhalations are made, as fire is applied to the top of the pipe. Then it is passed around the circle, a very social event. When Jeff and I took our first hits, the tobacco caused us to cough uncontrollably, to everyone's amusement. Greenhorns. For some chemical reason, tobacco multiplies the speed and effectiveness of the active ingredient, THC, in accessing the bloodstream. Jeff grinned back at me. Now I figured I would purchase a round. I went to the glass counter.

I: "Yeah . . . gimme a gram of that and a gram of that . . . and . . ." I spotted a jar of greenish chocolate chip cookies. "Jeff— do you want a cookie?"

Jeff: "Sure."

Outside, the sun passed under the rim of the world. Another hour elapsed.

I: "I don't feel anything from that cookie, do you?"

Jeff: "Nope. Tasted good, though."

I: "You want another?"

Jeff: "Sure."

As I swallowed the last bite of the second cookie, the first cookie checked in like a velvet freight train.

I: "Whoa. I'm fucked up."

Jeff: "Me, too. Let's find the fucking hotel."

We staggered out into the dark, crisp Himalayan air and all the stars were moving. Eating dope has more of a physical effect on motor function, vision, and balance centers. Retracing our steps in a strange city was a real challenge in our condition, which was not lessening. Dogs barked at us but kept their distance—we were the scary ones. Finally we could see the hotel—it had an electric light out front. The last twenty yards I was on my hands and knees. I woke up in the morning, lying on the cement floor beside my bed.

We rose at noon and went back to the Cabin. There I saw my friend from Callison, Jack Young. He was delighted to see me, and I was delighted to see his animated face, wild blue eyes, and blond mane and mustache. He always had such energy and a delightful sense of humor that started with disparagement and ended in self-deprecation and laughter. He asked where we were staying, and then went with us to check out of the tourist place and move into some real hippie digs. Jack led us through the winding streets down to the river and past a place where at sunrise they would slaughter a couple of yaks or Asian water buffaloes. A hundred yards farther on there was an old building with a couple of big trees in front. There was no sign. Jack led us through the front door and introduced us to the proprietor of the Matchbox. He showed us to the second floor where there were two available cots. We would share this space with several other male and female hippies. There were candles for after dark, and there was a standard shitter out back with the two footsteps over the hole, a roll of toilet paper on the window sill, and a large can of water and an empty coffee can for "flushing." This is the way most of the world does it, and will probably be the way of the future.

The Matchbox was a perfect name. Everybody smoked and used these ubiquitous small wooden matchboxes with a myriad of brand names and symbols.

Jack then took us to anther hippie hangout, where my Callison buddy Mike Payne joined us—the Chai and Pie Palace, chai being tea, and traditional American pies featuring the best lemon meringue I've ever tasted. It was a chillum sanctuary and they sold lots of chai and pie. There was a really cool couple from Canada. They dressed in impeccable Oriental clothes and were independently well off. He played polo. They spent their winters in Asia consuming opium, and then summered outside of Toronto, drinking booze. It sounded like a plausible lifestyle to me. He was the Chai and Pie chess king—unbeaten.

Opium was not advertised, but was available upstairs at the Cabin, as I discovered when struck by traveler's intestinal distress. A ball of opium the size of a peppercorn cleared me right up. Beat the hell out of Kaopectate for my money.

Jack was staying with his girlfriend and another couple in a house up on the hill, rented from a Nepalese family who were glad to move in with relatives for a month's fee. As we arrived, Jack was on a tirade—his wallet had fallen in the shitter. We laughed. That night we sat on the porch and watched the moon rise over the twinkling city lights. Dogs would start barking on the outskirts to the east and a wave reaction from the doggie population traveled west through the city to the opposite outskirt. The natives said the dogs were reacting to Shiva as he walked through the city at night. There was a salute when chillums were lit: "Shiva Bombulay!"

There was another establishment that catered to hippies—Highway 61, named after the Bob Dylan song (Highway 61 was on the way from Hibbing to Minneapolis). This place specialized in a potent beverage made from ganja (pot) and some kind of fermented milk—I didn't ask. They called it bhang (pronounced "bong"). We drank some of that and stepped out into the afternoon sun. From this vantage point, Jeff and I could look up the valley and see what looked to us like pot plants growing all the way to the horizon. This was as close as we got to leaving the city, even though we had trekking permits. We heard some weird music coming out of Swambu, the Monkey Temple. The circular, pointed structure had the Tibetan Eye at the top and colorful banners fluttering in the wind. We stooped to enter. As my eyes adjusted to the dim interior, I saw twenty priests sitting in a circle doing the basso profundo throat chant thing. They tried to ignore us, so we ducked right back out. We were in the way. We walked over to sit on a wall under some shade trees, but the monkeys started to fuck with us. When they began to throw small stones, I decided it was time to leave Kathmandu.

We flew over the wall of mountains and landed in the first place on the other side, Patna. They exchanged some freight and refueled, and a few hours later we landed in Madras, where we had to change planes to get to Bangalore. With some time to kill, we walked around the gardens in the front of the airport. I had a Marlboro hard pack half filled with joints, a couple grams of hash, and a half-dollar-size flattened lump of opium. We smoked a joint and congratulated ourselves on the decision to carry dope into India—there had been no customs at all. Of course, it was like bringing grapes to a vineyard. We walked back inside and joined the other passengers who were forming a line. When everyone was assembled, four Gurkha soldiers

with M-1 rifles entered and began taking each passenger behind one of three curtains to be searched. It was too late for me to walk out or run to the lavatory. A soldier only a year or two older than myself took me behind curtain #2, patted me down, took my cigarette pack, looked at my dope, closed the pack, and put it back in my breast pocket. He was looking for something else.

The avenues of Bangalore were rife with small, three-wheeled, gaily painted sputtering taxis with retractable roofs that were more like umbrellas than convertibles. We found a funky motel-type place with a shower and toilet. As we stepped out of the room to explore the capital of the state of Karnataka, an old man with a huge mustache was waiting for us with a large basketlike container and a small, reeded horn. He motioned for us to behold. He sat down, opened the container, and began tooting the horn. A big hooded cobra stood up out of the top and "danced" for its weather-worn master. We understood by now that just making eye contact with these people obligated you to reward them with "baksheesh," or alms, or, in this case, a tip. When we did that, we were then accosted by a woman with an infant who held out her empty hand and beseeched us with, "Pleese, sarh—my baby!" and when we gave her some coins, a group of street children came after us. I threw down a handful of coins and we ran for two blocks and ducked into a restaurant. We learned not to give away money on the streets of India.

In that restaurant we each ordered a Kingfisher beer and looked at a menu, which was completely unfamiliar to me. I chose "Sikhabob." An Indian gentleman at the neighboring table tried to engage us in conversation to exercise his English.

>Gentleman: "So—you are American?"
>Jeff and Tom: "Yes. Hi."
>Gentleman: "New York?"
>Jeff: "Always a good guess."
>I: "Not exactly, but close enough."
>Gentleman: "You are wealthy, no?"
>I: "No."
>Gentleman: "Everyone in America is wealthy. Rockefeller—he is from New York."
>I: "Yes."
>Gentleman: "He is most wealthy."
>I: "Yes."

My Sikhabob arrived. I took a bite of the sausagelike object of my hunger. It was the spiciest thing I'd ever tasted and the heat kept coming on despite prodigious quantities of the native pilsner.

My Callison ex-classmates greeted us warmly. We were invited to crash at a residence in the "campus" area of the nicest part of Bangalore. Then they took us out for dinner at a favorite restaurant where they had been tipping for several months, so we openly smoked chillums. Two of the guys got up and played guitars, mostly Grateful Dead tunes. The weather was gorgeous and that night we slept on the rooftop of the adobe-like house.

The next day I almost literally bumped into the dean of students for the Bangalore campus. She recognized me and asked, with some concern, how long I'd be staying. It did me good to be in India, standing there in front of her and seeing the displeasure on her countenance. She bore a resemblance to Eleanor Roosevelt. I told her I was in the neighborhood and decided to drop in to say hello.

I had not been a good student. After being prepped my whole life to go to college, it was no small thing when I dropped out of Callison at University of the Pacific. It had become clear that I was never going to be a lawyer, doctor, or scientist. Textbooks bored me because I loved to read, and I didn't need teachers to choose books for me. If I had to go to India, I could go on my own (besides, I was going into show business and would make a million bucks). That was the real capper for me—the expense. Dad (wisely) was going to pay for half my tuition and I would have to bust my ass for the other half. I got a student loan from the government, painted houses in the summer, and worked in the university cafeteria washing dishes, none of which was going to do the trick. The dishwashing money went for booze, drugs, gas, fast food, and rock 'n' roll tickets.

One day I made the mistake of taking Windowpane LSD in the morning so when I punched in at the cafeteria, I still had fish-eye-lens vision. I felt ridiculous putting on my apron, hairnet, and rubber gloves to take my place at the stainless steel, water-flushed trough into which we scraped the mountains of uneaten institutional food from the endless line of used trays that came through an aperture on a conveyor belt. Plates and silverware were loaded into racks that we fed into the huge, steam-breathing Hobart dishwasher. It was spaghetti night, I was orange up to my elbows, and I was tripping my ass off. The guy next to me was my friend Larry, a big gay lineman for the football team.

> Larry: "What's the matter, Tom?"
> I: "Fuck . . . I don't know if I can do it. My motto is 'function' but I don't know . . ."
> Larry: "Are you sick?"
> I: "No, Larry . . . I took a shitload of acid . . . I got to get out of here."
> Larry: "Oh. Gosh—you can't go until you tell Eduardo first."

Eduardo was senior dishwash captain. He was from a "wealthy" family in Guatemala. I'm sure his father was a member of the junta. The hint of cruelty in his smile meant he "didn't need no stinking badges." He saw my dilated eyes and the stricken look on my face as I told him I was feeling poorly. He put his arm around my shoulders and smiled, "Tom, in Guatemala we have a saying: if assholes could fly, we would have no sunlight. If you got to go, go. Next time you're fired."

On April Fools' Day, 1971, I walked into the office of the dean of Callison in Stockton. I heard the words come out of my mouth.

Without hesitation he rose, walked around his desk, and shook my hand. "Not everybody belongs in college, Tom, and I respect your decision." They sent me a bill for the cost of painting over a mural that I had painted on my dormitory wall: a winged dragon in flight, and a wolf in sunglasses and a suit, saying in his cartoon bubble, "If it doesn't work, force it." I never paid that bill, but the government got its student loan money back in 1978.

In May '72, while still in Bangalore, Jeff somehow got news from Ralph Brown in Minneapolis. I had sent a letter to myself at Lagoon and Irving; it contained hash and opium. Those boneheads opened it immediately and sampled the contents. Twenty minutes later police kicked open the door. A new resident—an acquaintance of mine named Randy—was upstairs filling up a water bed, and stuffed the opened envelope underneath it. When everyone was being shaken down, he asked if he could go back upstairs to turn off the garden hose. The cops went up and found the prize. Randy did time.

My Callison College friends took Jeff and me to the funky part of Bangalore where they frequented an old opium den on Slaughter-house Road. It was late evening and we had to walk the last block stepping over people sleeping on cardboard on the sidewalk; rats were as big as schnauzers. We entered the dark, single-story establishment that had been run by the same family for a hundred years. There was a skinny old man in the corner spitting into a coffee can. Our host was about ten years older than we were; he was gracious and charming, fluent in multiple languages. We were arranged on mats and pillows by fours, head to foot in a square around the flame of the oil lamp. Our host positioned himself in the center where he could administer the real stuff of which dreams are made. Over the course of the evening, we ordered a series of servings called "trays," which appeared to be an impervious leaf with edges folded up to contain the dark brown syrup. Then a wire was heated over the flame and its tip twirled in the tray causing the "hafeem" to gum up on its end so it could be stuffed in the small hole in the gourd at the end of the long pipe. The smoker remained prone on the pillow while inhaling as the host held the hole over the flame. After such a session, many people can become faint or nauseous if they rise too fast. I found I had a remarkable capacity for the sweet fruit of the poppy. I could get loaded and then go have a big meal. Such is my constitution. When we were ready to go, our host walked us back to where he could load us into taxis.

A couple of weeks later, I was finishing an evening at Slaughter-house Road when I accepted another hippie's offer to crash at his place. His place apparently was beside a swamp. In the late morning I awoke on a bed that was nice enough, but there was a four-inch-square rent in my mosquito netting. That's when I noticed about fifty of the engorged insects clinging to the inside of the breeched barrier. Angrily, I swiped my hand to crush them against the netting, and then found my palm and fingers covered in my own blood. Time to leave Bangalore.

We rode on one of those Mercedes buses in the evening so we could traverse the hot and arid Mysore plateau at night. The moon was nearly full, so we could see the landscape. By morning we were descending a lush mountainside; a winding road deposited us in Goa, which was Portuguese until 1961. Consequently, everyone there is Catholic, but the cultural effect is a pleasant combination of East and West. Hippies were attracted to the plentiful white sand beaches, pleasant climbs, and tepid but clean waters of the Indian Ocean. We checked into a modest beachfront hotel, took some Or-ange Sunshine LSD, put on our swimsuits, and hit the beach. We saw people sitting motionless under shade trees, but we walked for miles and the only others we saw out in the sun were a stunningly beautiful surfer couple plying the waves on their boards. They were bronzed and athletic, naked except for loin cloths. We turned around and went back. What's that thing about mad dogs and Englishmen? After we had some beers, I went to the room and saw myself in the mirror. I thought I looked sunburned orange. I went back to the bar.

That night was a full-moon festival. Christmas lights and torches lit the decks and beaches; a band was playing outside a fancy hotel.

There were men on the moon at that time—*Apollo 16*. Not one Indian I'd spoken to believed it. I found myself alone among the dunes and I sat down to meditate on the brilliant orb. When I was sure I could see the mountains on the moon, I took off my clothes and swam out from the beach. It was easy to float on my back in the super salty water, watch the twinkling lights, and hear music and people's voices waft out over the waves. I swam back and put on my pants and walked to my hotel, dripping wet and carrying the rest of my clothes in a bundle. As I walked into the lobby, the guy behind the desk got all upset.

Desk guy: "You did not just go swimming, did you?!"

I: "Ah . . . yeah, I did."

He pointed to a framed photograph on the wall. It was a young Indian man with a mustache.

Desk guy: "That was my brother—Olympic swimmer for India. He drowned swimming at night in the rip currents!"

I: "Oh."

Animals in third world countries are looked upon differently than in the West. In Goa, pigs would be snuffling around under the outhouses as you were above. No wonder most of the world abhors pork. In India, dogs are not household pets, but wretched, diseased scavengers to be avoided. I was told of a house on the beach where a dog entered and fell asleep on someone's bed pillow. He took the dog out and beat it to death with a chair leg. Time to leave Goa.

We took a crowded ferry boat to Bombay. I have recently come to understand that the eighteen million citizens want us all to call the place Mumbai (Mumbailiwood?).

We slept on the deck like everyone else. A Sikh and his family were my neighbors when I first bedded down, but he didn't want me in the vicinity. Sikhs tie up their long hair and beards into their turbans, they wear a silver bracelet on their left wrist, and they always carry a knife. In Bombay they carried curved bladed knives in scabbards on their belts. So I complied and slept at the bottom of a stairway.

Entering the harbor, Jeff and I beheld the Gate of India, a monument like the Arc de Triomphe, but bigger, built to please King George V when he visited in 1911. We were very pleased. Nearby was the Taj Mahal Hotel, which we could not afford, but we walked into their luncheon room and treated ourselves to turkey club sandwiches and gin and tonics.

We found lodging at a hippie hotel six blocks away—the King Hotel. Jeff and I got a room with two cots, clean sheets, a toilet, sink, shower, and ceiling fan.

It was starting to get hot. On the ferry I had developed wicked prickly heat on my thighs and ankles. I immediately bought native white cotton pajama-like pants, a long-cut shirt, and sandals. The jeans and boots were not working for me anymore. May was approaching and we were about to run out of money. I was scheduled to do a Franken and Davis Show for Dudley in July; Jeff wanted to go to Afghanistan and Europe. I lent him $400, figuring I could live on $100 until I could get Dad to wire me enough to fly back home. Jeff left for Afghanistan.

I found a new roommate—Gurt Krueger, a hippie from Germany. He was an experienced traveler and very funny, in a German sort of way. Then I got feverish; my piss turned orange, my shit was white, and my face and eyes were jaundiced—I had hepatitis A. I probably got it in Kathmandu, judging by the incubation period. Gurt instructed me to stop drinking alcohol, eat vegetarian, and stay out of Indian hospitals—that's where hippies died.

So my parents got that collect phone call from Bombay. It took hours just to do that. First I found a bank to which money could be safely wired, and made arrangements. Then I had to go to the telephone office and wait in a long line. My turn came, looking through a bank teller's barred window at an operator with antiquated gear. She had to talk to a relay of Indian, European, and American operators before I finally got through. When my mother asked me if I was sick, we both choked up. Dad came through when it counted most, but it would take weeks to work through the bureaucratic systems to get money from an Indian bank. I anticipated this, and resolved to heal myself in the meantime and try to enjoy the ride. At first I was bedridden sick, and it was hot. Thank God for the ceiling fan and Solzhenitsyn's *One Day in the Life of Ivan Denisovich,* about a guy freezing to death in a prison camp in Siberia. That helped.

In my delirium, I thought I was destined to meet up with an old Indian guru–vina player, P. D. Shah, whom I'd met and befriended a year earlier at Callison. I knew he lived in Bombay. However, finding someone named Shah in Bombay is twenty times more difficult than finding a Johnson in Stockholm, which is very difficult. Really stupid. But I opened up the directory and found a listing that glowed before my jaundiced eyes—a sign from God. I took it upon myself to simply find this address as an act of faith. With my map, I traveled on mass transit (steam engines) into the outer reaches of Bombay's urban sprawl, and located the address in a nice neighborhood of row houses. I climbed the steps and knocked on the door. A middle-aged Indian woman in scarf and sari opened the door, and seemed very annoyed. Neither of us spoke the other's language. By repeating "P. D. Shah" and "Callison College," and pointing at her house, I got her repeated answer of "No, no." Then she shut the door in my face. God appeared to have nothing to do with this situation that I now recognized as a delusion. I retraced my steps to the train station and looked around me on the platform as I waited for another steam engine from the '30s to take me back into Bombay proper.

It was strange to realize that I was surrounded by literally millions of people who didn't speak English. There were several skinny brown guys wearing curly toed Persian slippers and sandwich boards covered with dozens of choices of lottery tickets. I got the flash that lotteries exploited poor people.

I managed to catch the train back to downtown Bombay, but then I got lost. I stumbled upon the notorious red-light district ("Fuck Street"), where women were supposedly on display in cages. I didn't have the guts to go see for myself. To avoid it, I found myself in a winding back alley where I came upon a man with a cow, who was selling milk from a stainless steel canister with a ladle and a glass. What idiot would drink from a glass of unpasteurized, unrefrigerated milk in a smelly back alley in Bombay? But something told me to do exactly that, and that's what I did. I drank down the entire glass with gusto. It was delicious. The cow proprietor smiled proudly, and the cow swished her tail. I paid him a few pennies. Immediately I felt better. From that moment on, I steadily regained my health. God made up for the P. D. Shah thing, and I thanked Him.

Gurt and I would start almost every day with a visit across the street to the Fruit Palace. It was a café that would squeeze the juice from any of an amazing array of fruits—how about a glass of watermelon or mango juice? No problem. That, an international selection of newspapers, and an espresso machine made it a popular hippie hangout.

On Friday mornings, a shunned population of transvestites in saris and full makeup would come into our neighborhood and clap their hands and chant before the various businesses, whose owners would come out and pay them to keep moving and go back to their own part of town. That was the Indian way of dealing with things. Very practical.

Gurt had crystal LSD and I had hash and opium. Two guys can have a lot of fun in Bombay with stashes like that. The Bombay museum took up several days with their massive collections of art, fashion, weaponry, and opium pipes, some of which were thousands of years old. A nearby theater had a Looney Tunes Festival. Before the cartoons there was a two-minute commercial for tea bags whose aroma and flavor were so wonderful that when a woman sitting in her front garden pours herself a cup, the mailman smells it and jumps over the hedge to join her. If this commercial had been American, I would have found it annoying, but because it was Indian I found it comically innocent. Looking back at it, I think there was something racist in my reaction. Similarly, in a newsreel short that followed, *Wounds of Glory,* an Indian general inspects a military hospital to visit soldiers wounded in the war with Pakistan. The casualties showed the camera their amputated limbs, etcetera, and again my humanity was affected by racial condescension. But another time, when a hash dealer offered to sell me pornography, I had to laugh. The Indian man and woman having sex in the 8 x 10 glossies had very uncomfortable looks on their faces and were looking into the camera. I should have bought those fucking pictures.

Our favorite restaurant was the Bagdadi. It had a long S-shaped

CABLE ADD: "BRAJI" BOMBAY, OR "NAREN" CALANGUTE, GOA.

TRAVEL NOW PAY LATER
BARGAIN DAILY JET FLIGHTS

INDIA — LONDON
LONDON — NEW YORK
EUROPE — U.S.A. CANADA.

IMMEDIATE CONNECTIONS TO:
TORONTO, MONTREAL, VANCOUVER, EDMONTON, LOS ANGELS
SAN FRANCISCO, WASHINGTON AND ALL OTHER DESTINATIONS
IN NORTH AND SOUTH AMERICA

STUDENTS — NON STUDENTS COME AND GET
YOUR STUDENT DISCOUNTS ON ALL TRAVELS

DUE TO HEAVY DEMAND NOW WE HAVE PLEASURE
TO ANNOUNCE TWO EXTRA CHARTER FLIGHTS A MONTH
BOM/DELHI / MOSCOW / LUXUMBURG / LONDON / AUSTAND / AMSTERDAM.
ALSO.

FROM APRIL 72.
KATMANDU / CALCUTTA / BANGKOK / BALI / HONGKONG / SINGAPORE / TOKYO.
SINGAPORE / DJAKARTA. BOAT. (PENLI LINES.)
EVERYDAY.
CALANGUTE / PANJIM. / BOMBAY SPECIAL DISCOUNTS
FLIGHTS LEAVING 30th MARCH, 1st, 7th, APRIL EVERY WEEK THRICE FROM APRIL 72.
OFFICIAL APPROVED AGENTS FOR: AIR INDIA, B. O. A. C. CHARTER CO'S'

GOLDFINGER TRAVELS INT. U.S.A.
720, S. CROUSE AVE,
SYRACUSE, N. Y. 13210
U.S.A.

FOR ALL TRAVEL BOOKINGS

NANABHAY MANSION
B... P. M. Rd.
Tel: 262409
364951

IN COA

DEVIL'S BOUTIQUE
Calangute Beach,
Goa.

AND FROM SEPT 72.
CALANGUTE GOA / KATHMANDU NEPAL TO
LONDON. BUS SERVICES.
PEOPLE LEAVING BY VAN - BUS - CAR WANTING,
RIDERS, CONTACT US, FOR PASSANGERS,
TO RENT HOUSES IN GOA AND ALL TRAVEL PROBLEMS

FREE CUNSULTATION ON TRAVEL PROBLEMS FOR ANY PLACE

WHILE IN GOA VISIT DEVIL'S BOUTIQUE CALANGUTE BEACH

counter where businessmen sat next to beggars; it was clean, cheap, and exquisite. Two domed clay ovens baked bread (roti or puri) to order. Fresh seafood and vegetable dishes abounded. (In 2005, I was riding with the Aykroyd family in a limousine and their driver was from Mumbai. He said the Bagdadi was one of his favorite restaurants and he assured me it still exists today, exactly as I remember.)

After weeks of making daily pilgrimages to the bank, Dad's $400 arrived. With a brochure I picked up at the Fruit Palace, I found the address of a travel agent who catered to hippies with chartered flights. I walked up six stories of a once-grand building that now reeked of urine. A middle-aged man in Nehru-like clothing sized me up in thirty seconds. "You're sick, aren't you?" I suddenly felt very vulnerable. If his ticket turned out to be bogus, I resolved I would come back and kill him. Six days later I boarded an Air India 707 to London. The first drops of the monsoon season fell on the outside of the window by my seat.

When I arrived at Heathrow, British customs were all over me and my metal Nepalese trunk. Of course I was wise enough to have given my stash to Gurt. But these guys were disgusted with me. One picked up my copies of Gandhi's *My Philosophy of Life* and Gurd-jieff's *Meetings with Remarkable Men*. He sneered, "Looks like you've been reading too many philosophy books," to which I retorted, "Probably not enough." He then informed me that the London–New York leg of my ticket was bogus. I only had fifty-five American dollars. They talked about putting me back on a flight to Bombay to try to shake me up, and then they said I would have to be confined. They kept my passport and handed me over to a Heathrow jailer who was very kind. As we entered the detention center, he said, "Don't let them worry you—you'll get home. You'll just be staying with us for a few days before things can be sorted out. Not so bad—three squares a day." From my studies of the American Revolution, I knew that the phrase, "three squares a day" came from the eighteenth-century British army, which issued to each soldier a square piece of wood off of which he would eat his doled-out pro-vision.

I stayed in the detention center overnight, dining off a plastic tray, and the next day I agreed to give TWA fifty of my remaining dollars. I signed a promissory note for $180 dollars (which I paid two months later, after first remunerating Dad). Then they put me on a nearly empty TWA 720 and a stewardess (that's what they used to call them) gave me a couple of gins for free. I passed through cus-toms at Kennedy and sent my trunk COD to Minneapolis. Then I hitchhiked and walked to Manhattan. Making my way to Grand Central Station, I gawked at Radio City and looked up at the tow-ering 30 Rockefeller Plaza—the RCA Building—and thought,

"What a magnificent structure for people to work in." After purchasing a ticket to Poughkeepsie, I had two dimes and a nickel in my pocket. My old Blake classmate Mark Luther, was at Vassar, and I stayed with him for a few days before borrowing some loose cash and hitchhiking back to Minneapolis. Mark told me he didn't do psychedelics anymore because the last time he got on a crying jag. LSD is not for everyone.

When I arrived home I'd proven to myself that the world was round. Then I remembered that Indian gentleman in Bangalore, talking to me about Rockefeller and how all Americans were rich. He was right.

Since my birth in 1952, the population of the United States has doubled to three hundred million. Since 1972, India's population has doubled, to one billion.

winterland ballroom
grateful dead
yogi bhajan
sufi dancing & choir
march 24 wed.
9pm to 2am
$3.00

Tickets available at: San Francisco: Fox Plaza Box Office 9th & Market, City Lights 261 Columbus,
The Town Squire 1118 Polk, Outside in 2544 Mission, New Age Natural Foods
Berkley: Shakespeare & Co., Wholly Foods, Sausalito: Tides, Rock Island Line
San Anselmo: Everybody's, San Raphael: Record King, San Mateo: Town & Country Records,
San Jose: Discount Records, Menlo Park: Discount Records.

6

FIRST LOVE AND SEX

Sigmund Freud: "The answer to all mankind's problems is not simply bigger and more frequent orgasms."
I: "Maybe not, but it's worth a try."

So I passed like a tomato seed through my noble high school, which gave me a good education, in spite of myself. It was the end of April 1970, and in a week I would receive my diploma. Naturally, I was in a celebratory mood. I was seated at the family dinner table on the screened-in porch, as the season allowed, when my friends pulled up in a '57 two-tone Pontiac and honked the horn.

After I jumped into the empty backseat, the driver, Paul Flum, turned around with something in his hand: "Here—take this." It was an orange capsule and I swallowed it.

I: "What was that?"
Jeff Frederick, riding shotgun, turned around.
Jeff: "It's LSD. We already took ours—we want to get off before the movie starts."

I: "No shit?"

Paul: "No shit. When I was in Florida visiting my grandparents, I bought a little bag of it from a musician. I emptied
these Contac capsules and stuffed them myself."

I had seen *2001: A Space Odyssey* in its original release. But the
Mann France Avenue Drive-In Theater was touted as the largest in
the world. Now we were standing right under the screen. The sound
from hundreds of small speakers, designed to hang on the interior
of partially rolled down car windows, bounced off the curved surface of the world's largest projection screen. After the show, wandering around the edge of the empty parking lot, I could see the
grass grow. A city street sweeper passed with its yellow warning lights
flashing, and it looked like a spaceship. We were all so delighted that
we returned the next night, tripping, and for Sunday night as well.
Now we knew many of the speeches by heart. "Open the pod-bay
door, Hal . . . Hal?" By God, that was fun.

I graduated from high school on May 4, 1970. It was stifling hot
inside the ancient Blake School gymnasium, basketball hoops retracted like landing gear over the yellowing lacquered parquet where
the assembled sat in old wooden folding chairs. My parents didn't
come. My own alienation had taken all the fun out of it for Dad. In
fact, I think I embarrassed him. I heard the headmaster intone my
name. I approached him as in a dream. With a cursory handshake and
an impassive "Congratulations," he handed me the damn diploma.
At the same time, the Ohio National Guard was shooting students
at Kent State.

I drove home in my mother's '67 VW Bug, parked it in the
garage, went up to my bedroom, and threw some clothes in a bag.
Dad had left a small newspaper clipping on my pillow. The caption
read: TEEN TAKES LSD, CUTS OFF PENIS.

I kissed my tearful mother good-bye and walked out from under
my father's roof. In August, after my eighteenth birthday, I was at
orientation at Callison College of the University of the Pacific in
Stockton, where I fell for a gorgeous Jewish girl from San Francisco.
She had her own new, yellow VW Bug, and she drove me to her
mother's empty apartment on the top of one of those hills that
looks down on the Golden Gate Bridge. We went to Chinatown

for dinner with a few of her friends, one of whom leeringly inquired, "And what are the sleeping arrangements tonight?" She took me home and unburdened me of my ridiculous virginity. Referring to my awkwardness, she asked if it was my first time. I said that it was my second time. She knew better.

Ignorant, I thought I was in love. Certainly I was infatuated. We went with a dozen other classmates to a levee on a sunny afternoon. We all took our clothes off, went swimming, sunbathed, and chased each other through an endless vineyard, throwing grapes at each other.

She suggested we break into the stadium at night and make love on the fifty-yard line. In my naive sexuality, I immediately dismissed it, not realizing what an excellent idea that was.

She dropped me for a hunky blond senior who had been around the block a couple of times. I was crushed, of course, feeling the pangs of love lost for the first time. A week later, heavily under the influence of LSD and malt liquor, I found myself in a beautiful girl's room a few dormitory doors down from my ex. This girl let me do my thing just to get me out of there. The next day, my ex read me the riot act: "You can't go around forcing yourself on women." Remorseful at what I had done, I asked the beautiful girl for forgiveness, which she graciously granted me. Big lesson.

On March 24, 1971, I attended a Grateful Dead concert in San Francisco. I still have the poster. Its artwork is unremarkable, but here's the billing:

> WINTERLAND BALLROOM
> GRATEFUL DEAD
> YOGI BAJAN
> SUFI DANCING & CHOIR
> MARCH 24 WED.
> 9PM TO 2AM
> $3.OO

By five in the afternoon we were sitting on the sidewalk in a line that started at the entrance and wound around the corner of Post and Steiner, all along the white stucco exterior. We had taken Windowpane acid in the car. It was called Windowpane because it came in small, golden, translucent gelatinous squares. We carried joints, cocaine, balloons of nitrous oxide, and half-pints of booze in our boots. It had become a sport to see who could consume the most drugs and still function. The winner usually drove back. But that wouldn't happen for another eleven hours. As the cool shadows from the building across the street crept across us, the doors opened. We passed through the big security guys in Graham Productions T-shirts by smiling and looking them in the eye. If you were an asshole they shook you down to your boots and divested you of any liquor.

We ran to the front row balcony, directly across from the stage, and claimed our seats. The hall only held about five thousand. It had been built in 1928 for prizefights. It became Winterland in the '30s when recreational ice-skating was a popular thing to do. There was a large wooden dance floor surrounded on three sides by graduated wooden platforms with old wooden folding chairs. The balcony rose to the Deco plaster ceiling (which, in its last year, was literally falling down in chunks). Of course, there was a large mirror ball. Bill Graham projected Looney Tunes onto a movie screen for those of us, the faithful, who came early.

There was a green-eyed girl, whose boyfriend was too cool to endure this kind of Deadication. We were short one seat, so she sat on my lap. As the acid kicked in, we washed down some reds (barbiturates) with tequila. She wore a cotton India print dress that showed off her body—long legs, ample bosom, aeroflo ass, and her imperfect smile could make your balls tingle from across the street. We got onto a sex-vibe trip that amused us both. We decided to get up and walk around. She took my arm like the new Miss America, and the crowd parted before us. It was as if we were some kind of conduit for a collective mind-trip energy. Without a conscious thought, we breezed through backstage security and walked right up onto the stage behind Jerry's amps. The crew recognized how dusted we were and let us stay.

Looking back at the stage-area entrance, I saw Pigpen (the original GD keyboard player–R&B biker vocalist) pose for a picture with two girls, whom he goosed for the flash. Then he assisted some other guys in pulling two thirty-gallon plastic garbage cans of fluid out into the house.

Phil Lesh (the bassist) showed up apologizing for being late. As he opened his guitar case and extracted his psychedelically painted SG bass, he looked at Green Eyes and me and asked Ramrod, the roadie, "Who are those people?" Ramrod said: "They're okay."

Between the songs, Jerry smoked what I thought was a joint, until I took a big hit and saw it was a Pall Mall cigarette. Tasted good.

There was a cowboy/biker guy named Boots, who was absolutely adept at igniting magic flash-paper squares and tossing them over the heads of the band and the audience standing in front. He'd time it for crescendo moments, like the thunderous E chord coming out of the drum solo, to begin their signature "That's It for the Other One." Suddenly the show was over and the band had disappeared. I asked high-profile roadie Big Steve Parish if there was an extra beer and he said, "Why don't you leave?" I bowed, clicked my heels, and said, "Thank you, and good night." Green Eyes and I stumbled back into the auditorium where the house lights were up. It looked like a battlefield. Apparently those garbage cans contained electric Kool-Aid, and hundreds of people had unwittingly gulped down what should have been sipped, so they were lying on the floor and crawling around. We made it back to the car and our friends. I drove. We hit that heavy San Joaquin Valley fog on the way back. I had to open my door and look down to follow the outside line of the left lane.

Several nights later, I was getting into bed in my dormitory room when there was a gentle knock on the door. It was Green Eyes. She slipped into the room, closed the door behind her, and instructed me to be quiet because her boyfriend was in the building. In a single movement she removed her dress, revealing that she wore nothing but her zippered boots. Thank you, God. We made love in the candlelight; she rode me like a horse. At one point we heard her boyfriend calling. When she left, she peeked out into the hallway to see if the coast was clear, kissed me, and disappeared into the night. It was a gift. I knew that this was a one-time-only thing, and I was grateful. Also, her boyfriend was a good guy. I liked him.

Three months later, I visited my parents at home for lunch. Dad asked if I had seen the Grateful Dead in San Francisco in March. I said, "Yeah." He put a small newspaper clipping beside my plate. The caption read, "6,000 Dosed on LSD." He was ashamed. I felt like it was the greatest thing that ever happened to me. That was his problem.

In 1972 I fell in love with Jo. We met under the pool table in the Triangle Bar on the "West Bank" in Minneapolis, near the University of Minnesota. My friends, the Lamont Cranston Band, were playing their funky blues on a frozen night in February. She was plain looking, in a very sexy way. Jeans and a sweater, no bra, no makeup, no jewelry, brown shaggy hair. She liked to get fucked up, and then fuck. So did I. Also we were both broke, and didn't give a fuck.

I was rooming with Paul Flum again in the small house that would be condemned after we left. I lived in the makeshift bedroom in the basement. The first night I brought Jo home, we broke my antique bed. She was also breaking up with some guy from the Lake Street Stink Band who came to the back door and poked his finger in my chest while telling me what an asshole I was. I pointed out that it was up to her. She stayed. His problem was with her, not me, as I would learn. But what did I care, so long as we were having so much fun?

When I was moving to new digs, I stayed for a couple days with my parents, and when Dad opened my bedroom door in the morning, he was treated to the sight of Jo and me in bed. It was a big deal for Don and Jean. Jo and I giggled. What were they going to do?

What were *we* going to do?

After not hearing from her one week, I phoned her dad. She was in the psych ward in Golden Valley, a suburb of Minneapolis. When I visited her, she seemed fine to me, still with a sense of humor, but kind of shaky. She said she had to get out of there. Her doctor had a worried look on his face when he told me she was undergoing electroshock treatments. I knew nothing about psychiatric problems, and after all, wasn't love the answer? I was in love.

Somehow, and I literally cannot remember, we found ourselves in San Francisco. We stayed with her Minnesota friend, Kathy

LaBerge, who let us crash at her place for weeks while I looked for a job and pilfered food from supermarkets. I got turned down as a dishwasher, for lack of experience—and I had experience. We looked at apartments we could never afford. Jo found a ride back to Minneapolis and I crashed with other San Francisco friends.

Six months later, I returned to Minneapolis via Boston. I immediately went to the small house she shared with a friend. When I knocked on the door, she yelled, "Come in!" Jo was naked in a hot bath, laughing and chatting on a telephone she held tenuously above the water. She smiled "hello" at me and continued her conversation. I thought she could be electrocuted (I didn't know that's impossible with a phone). I insisted she hang up and hand me the thing.

Four months later, when Al and I were living in L.A. and barely scraping together a living, I flew her out to live with me. Hollywood is a desperate place for even the most reinforced personality. After some extraordinary lovemaking, she once said, "Ahh . . . that's why I don't have to become a prostitute," and that made *no* sense. A friend of hers was driving through. Jo returned with her to Minnesota, and fell off the end of the earth. I finally got it. She made me cry.

FRANNI © 1970 BY CARLA BRYSON

Al Franken fell in love with Franni Bryson in Cambridge, in their freshman year, at a Harvard/Simmons mixer in 1969. In their senior year, 1973, they planned to be married, sometime around commencement, going so far as to print up invitations. Al called it off. He said, "I told her I got cold feet, and maybe I should have sex with a few other girls first." I was aghast. "You didn't actually tell her with those very words, did you?" Al: "Ah, yeah. It was the truth." But they continued on as a couple, as if nothing had happened. Franni obviously got past it.

We drove to Los Angeles and moved into an apartment on some money Al's parents lent us. Franken and Davis started playing the clubs, especially Sammy Shore's Comedy Store, a small place with a tiny stage in front of a picture window that looked out on the Sunset Strip. But we performed for free. Only the headliner got paid. Franni got a job there, as a cocktail waitress, and she sometimes babysat for the infant Pauly Shore. Then Franni announced she was moving into her own place with her sister, Carla, who had just arrived from Maine and had accepted the same job cocktail waitressing. They wore lots of makeup, Afro wigs, and listened to Steely Dan.

I was behind the wheel of our '63 Buick LeSabre convertible with the engine idling, in front of her apartment building, as Franni had it out with Al in the backseat. He was crying. A couple of weeks later she started dating the Comedy Store bartender. Ouch. After most of a year, they got back together, and have been inseparable ever since.

LUCY AND ME IN L.A. © 1975 BY MIKE LAWLER

In 1974, while doing a few weeks of a Franken and Davis show at Dudley Riggs in Minneapolis, I fell in love with Lucy. Pat Hayes from the Lamont Cranston Band introduced us. They had dated once.

Lucy was cute, bright, feminist, sexy, and sweet, with Bettie Page bangs. She loved the Jefferson Airplane, and still lived with her parents in St. Paul. They had an orange family cat named Pieface.

Lucy came to live with me in L.A., and brought some balance and stability in the close living quarters we shared with Al and Franni. Then the call came in July 1975 for Al and me to travel to New York City, where an as yet unnamed live comedy show had hired us as writers, with a six-week contract. The girls stayed in L.A. until we were sure the thing was going to happen. In September, they sold off the furniture and drove across the country to join us in Al's grandmother's apartment (she was in a rest home). This two-bedroom, two-bathroom affair had been under rent control since 1926. That was a break.

As Al and I struggled at the show, Lucy looked for a job but could only find temp work. One day she leafleted every office door in the Empire State Building. At *SNL*, Herb Sargent dubbed the girls "the runaways."

Lucy inspired one of the first sketches I got on the air, and she loved it. It was Chevy and Jane as a couple at the breakfast table, in their pajamas. Jane asks, "What are you thinking about?"

> **Chevy: "Oh, I don't know. I guess I was thinking about how much I love it that you wear those fluffy slippers, and like to eat Grape-Nuts for breakfast every morning. What are you thinking about?"**
>
> **Cut to: close-up of Jane's eyes.**
>
> **Cut to: weird stock footage of warthogs jumping around in the African bush.**
>
> **Music: Wild John Coltrane solo.**

Lucy and I came home one day to find that Al and Franni had impulsively gone to City Hall and gotten married. Something stuck in my twenty-three-year-old heart. Lucy was fine with everything. But I knew I was still a child who did not want children, and Al and Franni were unabashed about their intentions. That summer, on a camping trip somewhere in Minnesota, I broke it off with Lucy. The Frankens, in their tent, could hear Lucy weeping in ours.

Several months later, I fell in love with Emily Prager, one of the *Lampoon* crowd. She was moving me out of the Frankens' apartment into her third-floor walk-up in the West Village, and I said, "Wait a minute. Suppose we break up?" Emily: "Then it'll be a big, messy disaster."

7

SAN FRANCISCO TO CAMBRIDGE, EARLY '73

When the going gets weird, the weird get going.
—Bob Marks

In mid-January of '73 Jo left me in San Francisco. Somebody she knew from Minneapolis was in town and driving back. I can't remember why I didn't go with her. Maybe I sensed that I was just a wild, dreamy distraction for her, and she would never live anyplace else. Maybe returning to Minneapolis seemed like failure to me.

I was going to meet up with Al at Harvard in February. He was in his senior year, and we had agreed to pursue our future in show business as the comedy team of Franken and Davis. He wanted to perform in New York City and get on The Dick Cavett Show before graduation.

Jo's friend Kathy LeBerge had been more than hospitable in the two weeks or so that we crashed there, and when Jo left I betook myself elsewhere. I called up my Callison College and Kathmandu friend, Jack Young. He was rooming on the first floor of a co-opted old mansion near the corner of Scott and McAllister, atop that park. Jack had a mattress for the express purpose of being a place for friends to crash. The next day I asked him if I could stay for two weeks. Jack wisely said it was fine with him, but to stay that long in the house, I should talk to the other tenants: in the room next to Jack's there was a hippie woman with a day job. She was fine with it. The artist on the second floor drew my likeness with charcoal and paper. "There's some sadness in your eyes." Two hippie brothers who did odd jobs lived on the third floor, and they liked me. A German man, a former Nazi with a troubled past, didn't care. Then there were the super and his old lady. They were a hippie couple who lived in the basement suite with a door to the back courtyard where there was a cage for their pet orangutan on nice days. The super had lived in that house the longest.

On the first floor there was a large kitchen with an adjacent bathroom and a cement shower stall. This I would use when everyone was asleep or out of the house. I washed dishes, swept the floor, and took out the garbage. Late at night I would pilfer a handful of garbanzo beans from a large sack in the pantry, and fry them with a shoplifted onion.

There was a kitchenette at the top of the house. It had a view looking down on the rooftops to the west. I often sat up there with the hippie brothers, listening to the jazz station on a transistor radio, sipping their Postum and smoking their pot. I was curious about the padlocked door with a small, barred peep window. Inside I could see there was a skylight, an easel with an indistinguishable oil and canvas work in progress, an altar with candles, and a set of small books.

Hippie Brother #1: "That's the super's room—he always keeps it locked."
I: "What are those books?"
Hippie Brother #2: "He's an Aleister Crowley freak—that's a leather-bound set of Crowley's complete works."
Hippie Brother #1: "Kinda creepy Crowley."

We laughed. Then I took their advice and listened to the public-service message listings on KSAN, and heard that some guy wanted someone to drive with him to Boston and share expenses. I called the telephone number and talked to the guy. Yes, I had a valid driver's license. I was booked—he would pick me up at 7:00 a.m. Sunday. I had a couple of days left.

I went walking through the Haight and met a young black hippie who claimed to have been in Jimi Hendrix's entourage. He took me to an apartment where a party of young people were inhaling nitrous oxide from a hissing blue tank through an octopus-like inhaler distributor such as I'd never seen before, or since. We sat down and got high and talked about rock and roll. My host dismissed the recently released *Europe '72* Grateful Dead double album, saying, "The only good song on it is 'Jack Straw.'" Of course I begged to differ.

As I emerged from this party, I was making my way to a Ticketron outlet to use my last couple of dollars to buy a ticket to see the GD at Stanford on Saturday, the night before my departure. A fierce young black man was sitting on the steps of a funky residence with his fierce girlfriend. He stood up and blocked my way on the sidewalk.

Fierce Black Guy: "Gimme your money!"
I: "No."
I walked around him.
Fierce Girlfriend: "Kill 'im, Jimmah!"

Jimmy let me go. It was obvious that I had no real money, and he would have to kill me to get it. I didn't care, having so little to lose. It may have been idiotic, but I was a very free idiot, and a wild one, too. Jimmy was waiting for something better and I knew it.

The winter was cold, even in San Francisco, so I was wearing my winter coat as I hitchhiked to Stanford. The band was set up on one of the sidelines of a basketball court, which was packed to the rafters. A lot of us piled our coats up against the far wall because these shows always got steamy hot. Palo Alto was the place where the Grateful Dead was born as a band, and they seemed to play like it was a homecoming. As the audience danced to the soaring music, we discovered that the basketball parquet was on some sort of spring system, so that if we jumped rhythmically, the floor would bounce. This encouraged the sweating crowd to dance harder, which, in turn, caused the band to play harder, until the floor was rolling like an earthquake. The roadies were desperately struggling to keep stacks of amplifiers from tumbling down. I found it impossible to light a joint, but I kept my feet. Everyone seemed to be laughing except the roadies.

The music ended and the houselights went up. I pushed through the milling crowd to find my coat. After a futile half-hour search, I was forced to accept the fact that one of these goddamn hippies had stolen my coat. Great. In a few hours I would begin driving across the continent in the dead of winter without winter clothing.

I got back to Jack's pad as the sun was coming up. Everyone was sound asleep. The few objects and articles of clothing I called my own fit into a paper grocery bag with room to spare. Jack's closet was open, and there, shining like a jewel, was his white fluffy yak-skin coat from Nepal. At 7:00 a.m. I looked out the front window and saw my ride pull up: a '65 VW Bug with a guy behind the wheel. I scribbled a note thanking Jack for everything and promised to return his coat. I took it from its hanger and put it on. Fit like a glove (which I didn't have). I closed the door quietly behind me.

Though my memory is uneven on this, the fact that I cannot recall this guy's name or what he looked like says more about him than me. By the time we passed Berkeley I knew that he was no better a conversationalist than he was a driver. I took over in Sacramento. He immediately fell asleep. I reached into the breast pocket of my flannel shirt and pinched one of the purple microdot pills and swallowed it. LSD takes all the boredom out of long-distance driving and keeps one wide awake. This was going to be a long haul.

Of course, it was snowing heavily at the Truckee Pass. Mobile blinking highway warning signs advised the use of chains on rear wheels. I didn't even slow down. VW Bugs are great in the snow. The front bumper could rise up on the snow while the rear-mounted air-cooled engine put weight on the rear wheels. My host slept through Nevada and then the salt flats, but when we climbed up the mountains outside of Salt Lake City, he was wide awake. It was *really* snowing. Again I drove past the blinking yellow CHAINS ADVISED warning signs. The flapjack-size snowflakes were falling out of the darkness and stacking up fast. Soon I was driving around other stranded motorists who waved for me to stop but I couldn't or we'd get stuck, too. I finally turned around and headed back to the chains station. Passenger Man plunked down the deposit and the fee, professionals put on the chains, and we retraced our route. On the other side of the pass we stopped at the chains recovery station and he recovered his deposit. I drove into the Wyoming morning and pulled over to a rest area to catnap. My host couldn't drive in the snow and we were now in a blizzard.

I woke up freezing, forty minutes later, and like Popeye eating his spinach, I downed another microdot. Nebraska and Iowa drifted past like one of my passenger's dreams. The gravitational pull of Chicago slingshot us toward Cleveland and that section of Highway 80 that is perpetually under construction. I ate the last of my pills. Outside Cleveland, I steered east by northeast onto Highway 90. It was just me and the road now, and she was singing. We entered the outskirts of Boston and looked across the Charles River at the gold cupolas of the redbrick dormitories of Harvard and took the next bridge. Franken had told me to find him at Dunster House. The first person I asked pointed to the dormitory right in front of us. "That's Dunsta House." As I stepped out of the car onto a dirty, icy snowbank, the faceless one walked around and got behind the wheel. He handed me my bag. I looked at him. "Do you want me to find my friend and get some expense money for you?" He shook his head. "Forget it. 'Bye." He sped away and disappeared around the corner. I walked into Harvard wearing boots, jeans, a yak-skin coat, shoulder-length hair, and dark wire-rimmed glasses. I would not get laid for the next three and a half months.

Harvard is everything it's cracked up to be. It is an oasis of intellectual freedom that is very difficult to get into, but once there, the pursuit of excellence is largely up to the student and his own sense of shame, which is powerful when surrounded by so many brilliant minds focused on the future. Dunster House had a reputation for being the least serious about being a house. It was an atmosphere of tolerance, freedom, and liberalism within a 1930 Georgian-style redbrick dormitory, topped with a white cupola with a red and gold clock and spire (a smaller version of Tom Tower of Christ Church, Oxford). The house was named after Harvard's first president, Henry Dunster, inaugurated in 1640. I immediately got copies of the keys to the security gate and the library. There was a nice recreation room in the basement with pool tables, pinball machines, and a munchies concession. Frisbee and football play in the spacious inner yard was a daily pursuit. The dining hall was spacious and the food was good. It was staffed mostly by townies, but there were a couple of Dunster students as well. One, Bob Briggs, became my friend. Everybody knew I was crashing in Al's room. Nobody cared—except the dining-hall supervisor and his immediate staff. They knew I was eating Dunster food, and they wanted to catch me in the act and have me thrown out. Up until then, people would bring me some fried chicken rolled up in a napkin. But now that the gauntlet was thrown down, it became sport to bait the Evil Supervisor. For several days in succession I spent time in the dining room, not eating but only chatting with my friends. Then our man on the inside said that a bust was being planned. The next evening I sat next to Al and his friend Bob O'Neal, with two more in league across the oaken table, each with his dinner on a tray. Al got up and returned to the steam tables to get seconds on the Salisbury steak and mashed potatoes. Then he carried the laden tray out of the dining hall, followed by the others. I stayed. They went into a smaller dining hall/study that was behind a door. Four minutes later I said good evening to someone with whom I was chatting, and sauntered out of the dining hall. Four minutes after that, Evil Supervisor burst into the dining hall/study room with his lieutenant. "Aha!" But no. Everyone was eating except me, and I was reading Boswell's *The Life of Samuel Johnson*. That was the last time they ever tried to bust me. They knew I'd be gone in May. Fuck it.

Roger Rosenblatt—later of *The NewsHour with Jim Lehrer*—was house master at the time, and he graciously invited me up to one of his regular "sherry evenings" at the top of Dunster House.

Bob O'Neal was a big guy from St. Louis who was a talented songwriter and musician who played with some guys in a bar in Harvard Square. We shared the same tastes and later became close friends in L.A. We loved that David Crosby album, *If I Could Only Remember My Name*.

I was doing anything to try to make some money. I posed nude at the Art School. I showed up at Manpower at 5:00 a.m. with all the other bums to find "day labor." A street person and I spent the day at the municipal bus garage, pouring fifty-five-gallon drums of changed oil and antifreeze down a sewer. When I took the subway back to Harvard Square at rush hour, no one would stand near me, I smelled so bad. When I got to Al's room, I removed my wallet and boots and walked into the shower with my clothes on.

I got a job at Tommy's Lunch—a little dump of a soda fountain with pinball machines—run by a big, burly Southie with a cigar in his mouth. I cooked short-order, swabbed the floor with a bucket and mop, and locked the place up. After a month, Tommy fired me. "I don't think you really want to work here," he said. I couldn't argue.

Tommy's Lunch was only a stone's throw from the *Harvard Lampoon,* which would have nothing to do with Franken, whom they snubbed. So in the previous three years, Al had taken over Dunster House Productions, which staged shows in the dining hall. They did *Nixon,* using some Franken and Davis stuff; he played Lenny in the Marvin Worth play; they did Chris Durang's *The Greatest Musical Ever Sung*—the life of Christ done to Broadway show tunes.

Al had a class, Social History of the United States (Soc Psy 134), taught by Daniel Bell, noted doctor of sociology. But Al was staying up late, staging *Lenny,* and the class was in the William James Building, which, according to Al, was always overheated. That caused him to sleep through almost every class for the semester. Al had to pass this one. It was important, and might affect his graduation. He approached Bell's teaching assistant and asked what he had to do to pass. "You better talk to Bell. He thinks you're a drug addict." So Al made an appointment with Dr. Bell at noon the next day. He arrived a few minutes early, and was instructed to wait in a room where there was a couch, on which he promptly fell asleep. Bell awakened him. "Do you want to sleep or talk to me?"

Al: "I want to talk."

Bell: "I always thought it was the job of the student to stay conscious during class."

Bell told him that the exam in three weeks would be based on the reading. Looking at the list for the first time, Al saw it was lengthy and rich. He read for three weeks and finished the last book the day before the exam. Two days after the test, Al went to pick up his blue book to find out the result. The teaching assistant handed it to Al. "Bell is really pissed—you got the highest score in the whole course." Al was then reminded he had selected a pass/fail grade.

Al's Uncle Erwin Franken lived in Cedarhurst, Long Island. He was going to sell his '63 Buick LeSabre two-door convertible, but Al's dad prevailed on him to give it to Al. So we went out there to pick it up and thank him. Al had once told me that in 1962, he and his brother, Owen, were supposed to meet their cousin Chuck, Erwin's son, in Queens, at the gate to the World's Fair. When they got there, they were dismayed at the sea of tens of thousands of people going in and out of the massive "gate." How could they find Chuck in such a crowd? Al went up to an ice-cream vender and asked, "Have you seen a kid who looks like Alfred E. Newman?" and the guy immediately said, "Yeah! He's right over there," and pointed. There he was.

Now that we had wheels, we drove down to New York City every weekend, either late Thursday night, or in the late morning on Friday, as the traffic on the I-95 corridor would allow. Left lane all the way. We drove too fast, as young people do. We were lucky never to have been in an accident. We had plenty of flats because we could only afford retreads and plugged flats ($10). We became proficient at changing tires in hideous urban settings beside that highway. But gas was cheap, and I did have skill as a driver. We'd park on the street near Eighty-sixth and Riverside where, on the fourth floor of the Clarendon Building, was Al's maternal grandparents' "lovely apaht-ment." Having been under rent control since 1926, the rent was $260 per month. There were Persian carpets, a Steinway piano, two bedrooms, two baths, a dining room, and a kitchen, all furnished but rapidly being cluttered up by Owen's stuff from all over the world. Al's older brother, Owen, was a very successful photojournalist who traveled everywhere except war zones and sold pictures to *Time* magazine and textbook publishers. Owen had graduated from MIT and escaped the draft by going underweight. To this day, he is too skinny. He was rarely in the country and I enjoyed some red hash he brought back in his lens cap from Morocco. We also helped our-selves to centimes, the French coin worth a fraction of an American penny, which fit perfectly in the New York City subway turnstiles.

We would sometimes be so exhausted that we'd go right to sleep. I remember I once heard Al wake up in the fully curtained master bedroom. He picked up the phone and dialed the operator.

> Operator: "This is the operator—how may I help you?"
> Al: "Ah, yeah . . . ah . . . what time is it?"
> Operator: "I can connect you to 'Correct Time.'"
> Al: "No. Just tell me what time it is, please."
> Operator: "Ten o'clock."
> Al: "A.m. or p.m.?"

The parking rules were not made for sleep-deprived comedians. We'd alternate the responsibility of rising at 7:45 a.m. to move the car. The street sweepers and morning traffic and deliveries are fa-vored. Usually this meant double-parking some place else and sitting in the car for an hour and a half before parking was permitted on the other side of the street again. Once, Al fell back to sleep after the alarm clock went off. The car was towed—a $65 ticket! We were devastated.

I would make soup, or we'd occasionally go to either the Four Brothers at Eighty-sixth and Broadway, or the Szechuan Chinese on Broadway and Eighty-first. Then around 10:00 p.m. on Fridays and Saturdays we'd go first to perform at Budd Friedman's Improv near Times Square. We were allowed two free drinks. We decided it would be funny to wear tuxedoes, so we'd carry them with us on the subway in plastic garment bags, and change right there in the crowded bar. We were popular right away; the audience was with us. We were frequently lined up with Freddie Prinze, Jimmie Walker, Andrew Johnson (the first "redneck" act . . . "If there's anything southerners like more than a good car—it's a good car wreck"). Andy Kaufman would bat cleanup after our act, with his mother double-parked outside in a Cadillac. He spent as little time in the club as possible. There were a couple of singing-comedy acts. Two guys from New Jersey, Weden and Finkle sang, one of them on the piano:

> *I love to drive to Trenton, New Jersey,*
> *Trenton, New Jersey is heaven on earth to me.*
> *Hey! Someone is calling me,*
> *Saying, "I long to be,"*
> *Where some cute Trentonian,*
> *Is calling to me . . . and saying,*
> *Please! Get me out of Trenton,*
> *On the banks of the blue Delaware!*

And then there were the Untouchables, three guys from Brooklyn—Marvin Braverman, Buddy Montoya, and Bobby Alto. They did Jewish-Italian and marriage jokes, broke into "O Sole Mio," and pantomimed oaring a gondola. They were the house favorites. Jay Leno was also really good. He made us laugh, especially when he talked about his mother.

On Sunday we'd drive back to Cambridge, where it was relatively easy to park on the street.

Spring arrived, so I had the yak-skin coat steam-cleaned and the torn sleeve repaired, and then I finally called up Jack Young back at Scott and McAllister. He admitted that he had been very upset that I had taken his coat. I told him it saved my life in Wyoming. He was relieved that I was sending it back. He hated to lose friends. He also had some news. The Aleister Crowley–freak super's orangutan had suddenly gone berserk and bit the man a hundred times before he could get his gun out of a drawer and shoot it. His old lady butchered the creature, baked it in the oven, and they ate it.

8

F & D IN L.A.

It is not surprising that every man has his price. What is surprising is how low it is. —Adolf Hitler

FELT TIP ON PLACEMAT © 1974 AL FRANKEN

Uncle Erwin's '63 Buick LeSabre surely could take abuse. We just kept putting gas in it. In 1973, Mark Luther was riding with Franni, Al, and me to L.A. and we had just stopped off in Denver, where Mark's older brother lived. Driving over the Rocky Mountains, I insisted on stopping at the Continental Divide so I could piss into the Mississippi and the Colorado rivers in the same whizz. Determining the headwaters of any river is an arbitrary affair, but doing so with the Colorado is much more so than with the Big Muddy.

Both Wyoming and Utah claim to possess the headwaters, but the state of Colorado seems to be winning the PR battle for its namesake river. This controversy promises to be an interstate pissing match of the near future. Arizona certainly has something to say about it; Las Vegas is America's fastest-growing city, the San Joaquin Valley is America's salad bowl, and L.A. greedily drinks up an enormous aqueduct from the beleaguered river.

In November 2006, I recalled to Mark Luther this journey of ours.

MARK LUTHER © 2006 BY TOM DAVIS

Mark: "You know, Tom, I still can't believe that night in San Francisco. We were visiting your friends, who had a nice house, but then you drove us to a redwood forest on Mount Tamalpais and we slept on the ground. That was so stupid."

After San Francisco, we decided to make a beeline to L.A. on Interstate 5, down that lunar valley of endless agribusiness conglomerates sustained by Mexican hand labor. Franni announced from the backseat that she wanted a hot fudge sundae. I knew there were no exits that had ice-cream venues.

I: "How about an Eskimo Pie or a Drumstick?"

Franni: "No. Why are we in such a hurry all of a sudden? I've been sitting back here for four days and I want a hot fudge sundae."

I: "Okay, we'll stop at the first ice-cream place we see."

I ignored her protest. I had a little cassette-tape player and I was recording this conversation. In 2006, I played the ancient cassette for Franni and Al. Then I finally took responsibility for what I had done.

I: "Franni . . . I apologize for ignoring your request for a hot fudge sundae. It would have been an adventure. I was wrong."

Franni: "That's funny, Tom—hot fudge sundae . . ."

She laughed.

Our first week in L.A. we crashed at our Dudley friends' apartment near Melrose and La Brea. Sid Strong and Tom Sherohman, Brave New Workshop veterans, had acquired the rented space from Pat Proft, who had originally helped Dudley physically build his stage. Pat would eventually coauthor the hit movie *Airplane,* and then the Naked Gun series with Leslie Nielsen. But on this, our first night in L.A., a funny, skinny comedian named Budge Threlkeld burst into the room.

> Budge: "Fuck, man—I just got robbed at gunpoint right next to Pink's! Fucking junkie."
>
> Sid: "How much did he get?"
>
> Budge: "My wallet, with three bucks and my driver's license. Took the fucking hot dog, too!"

We had enough money with us for a first month's rent. We took Budge back to Pink's and we all had a hot dog. We found a two-bedroom apartment a couple of blocks away on Sycamore, and started to define our life in L.A. There was a library on Melrose where I borrowed James Brown and Mozart LPs. There was a golf course whose ten-foot cyclone fence could not keep us out at night. The Mayfair twenty-four-hour grocery had cheap, abundant food, gas was inexpensive, and the parking was free and easy in those days.

Sammy Shore's Comedy Store seemed to be the best comedy stage, and it literally looked down onto Sunset Boulevard. There was an accompanist on a piano, and the tables had those red cocktail candles. Sammy got up every night to do his Jewish/Vegas-style act that ended with an ad parody of Southern California's biggest used-car dealer, Cal Worthington, singing, "For a nickel or a dime, I'll screw you every time. Come see Cal, come see Cal, come see Cal." He also did what was, even at the time, a politically incorrect impression of a Japanese pilot parachuting into cold ocean water. Richard Pryor would occasionally come in to polish his latest material before filming. He was the best I'd ever seen. But Franken and Davis became part of the coterie of regular performers: Pat Proft, Bo Kapral, Tim Thomerson, Franklyn Ajaye, Johnny Dark, Carol White, Ed Bluestone, Paul Mooney, Budge Threlkeld, George Miller, Jimmy Martinez, Andrew Johnson, Steve Lubetkin, Gabe Kaplan, occasionally Stanley Myron Handelman, Rudy DeLuca, Jimmie Walker,

Freddie Prinze, Bobby Herbeck, Rickey Jay, Steve Landesberg, and Don Novello. We became fast friends with Don. His Father Guido Sarducci delighted our comic sensibilities.

Only the headliner got paid. The rest of us got half off on drinks. Landesberg became headliner one week and then got on Carson. He had a joke in his act, "I saw this beautiful woman on the street who was a prostitute and I went up to her and said how can a girl like you do something like this, and she said, 'I can't type.'"

© 1973 DAVE SHERIDAN

Don Novello and Kathy, his wife, had a home in San Anselmo and we would sometimes trade apartments when we wanted to see the Grateful Dead in San Francisco and he wanted to do a gig at the Comedy Store. Once, when we did such an exchange, Al and I were seated in the front part of the balcony at Winterland when the Grateful Dead took the stage. I was coming on to about two hundred micrograms of LSD and melting into my seat. As the music began to transport me, Al grabbed my shoulder, his other hand grasping his Jewish afro. "Tom—I got a migraine headache and it's killing me."

I: "Huh?"

Al: "I got a *migraine*—take me to the hospital!"

Fucking bummerfuck. I tried to explain that even if I could drive, I wouldn't know where the hospital was. He got that hurt look on his face and staggered away. So I was listening to the music of the spheres when, a short while later, I saw a familiar silhouette gyrating in the nearby aisle.

I: "Hey, Al!"

You really can't tell how loud it is until you try to talk to someone.

Al: "God, I love this music!"

I: "What happened!?"

Al: "Oh, a cop drove me to the hospital, and they gave me a shot of Demerol." My kind of place.

One Saturday afternoon in L.A., Don Novello took Al and me over to the apartment of his friend Matt Neuman, a comedy writer. I brought a few joints and a six-pack of beer, and then Matt played a reel-to-reel tape of Bob and Ray doing comedy bits on their radio show out of Boston in the '50s and '60s. It was the funniest thing we'd ever heard. Matt had hours of the stuff. We listened to all of it. We rolled on the floor with laughter and delight. I made copies of Matt's tapes. The formulas became imprinted in the minds of Franken and Davis. To this day we owe no debt greater than to Bob and Ray.

> Bob: The story of this man's trial has been front-page news of most newspapers across the country for the past several weeks. He is the corrupt mayor of Skunk Haven, New Jersey, Mayor Ralph "Moody" Thayer. Mayor Thayer . . . ?
>
> Ray: Thank you.
>
> Bob: Is the jury still out?
>
> Ray: Yes, but my lawyer is negotiating with the fore-man of that august group now, and we feel we have nothing to fear. We believe we can attract more flies with honey than you can with vinegar.
>
> Bob: Now to go back over your checkered career, you were a petty forger, a master swindler, a convicted embezzler . . .
>
> Ray: Convicted of perjury *several* times.
>
> Bob: How does one start on a life of corruptness such as you've built for yourself, Mr. Mayor?
>
> Ray: Oh, I guess it all started when I was a kid. I used to cheat on exams in grade school. And I used to tell malicious lies about my fellow students to the teacher. You see, I always believed that I could build myself up by tearing others down.
>
> Bob: And then after you completed your formal education, I believe you developed an interest in financial matters? Lending money?
>
> Ray: Loan sharking. Yes, I did that for several years, until the criminal element in town asked me to run for public office. I took that as a mandate.

Bob: I remember that first election. It still stands as the crookedest in Skunk Haven history.

Ray: Thank you.

Bob: That was the beginning, and now, down through the years, through your various administrations, you've managed to riddle each and every department with corruption, from the top right on through even to the visiting-nurse association. I'd like to ask you a question, and don't answer right away. Give it a little bit of thought. Would you say it's easier to be corrupt now than it was, oh, ten or fifteen years ago?

Ray: Oh, my, yes! Here, ten or fifteen years ago it was a disgrace to be corrupt. No, no, it's a rich, fertile field. I would recommend it to anyone with a devious mind who is willing to put in long, long hours without working hard. And he will find it terribly enriching, fully rewarding.

Bob: Thank you, Mr. Mayor. I'm sure we've all been able to draw something from your words, and we'll all be anxious to see what the jury finds when it comes back in.

Ray: Don't give it a thought. I'm not (hearty chuckle).

Bob: Mayor Ralph "Moody" Thayer.

Franni had her job cocktail waitressing at the Comedy Store, and when her sister Carla joined her, they inherited Sid and Tom's apartment. Al and I were both officially single again. Al's parents floated us the next month's rent, but we had to try making money any way we could—except waiting on tables, because when I had asked my dad for a loan, he said, "Why don't you become a waiter?"

One day Franni's landlady asked us if we wanted to earn twenty dollars. All we had to do was empty an apartment that someone had abandoned a couple months before so she could rent it out again. She led us to a third-floor apartment on the corner and unlocked the door. "Just throw everything into the garbage bin." She pointed to the industrial-size flatbed steel Dumpster in the alleyway below.

The apartment's interior was sparsely but tastefully furnished. There were pictures framed on the wall, and ceramic vases and kiln-treated objects on tables and shelves. We carried a couple of Deco cane chairs down the stairs, threw them in the bin, and climbed back up the stairs for the next load.

BOB AND RAY, AL, JANE, TOM, LARAINE, AND GILDA 1980. COURTESY OF TOM DAVIS

I: "Gee—I wonder what happened to the person who lived here?"

Al: "I don't know—some of this stuff is pretty nice."

He picked up a vase with peacock feathers in it. I grabbed a ceramic mask off the wall and led the way out the door.

I: "You know—we don't have to carry this stuff down the stairs—we can just toss it in the bin from here."

I dropped the piece of art. Al threw in a vase, which broke with the sound of a lightbulb popping. We walked back into the apartment. I took a custom-framed watercolor of a horse off the wall.

I: "Too bad—this frame is really nice but I don't have any use for it."

Al: "Let's just get the job done."

As he picked up a wooden nightstand, a figure appeared in the open door.

Figure: "Oh my God! What are you doing!?"

It was a gay Native American middle-aged hippie.

"My things! My pictures! What have you done?"

He looked below into the bin. "My God—my ceramics!"

I: "Gosh . . . the landlady told—"

Figure: "You Nazis! You animals!"

We just walked away, totally bummed out. We didn't even ask for the money. We were like Stan and Ollie. How could we be so smart and so stupid at the same time? We were very young.

Matt Neuman's girlfriend was a successful comedy writer, too. Marilyn Miller saw that Al and I were broke, so she hired Al to give her tennis lessons, even though, aside from his athleticism, he was not qualified. Bless her heart.

One night Flip Wilson visited the Comedy Store. Of course, they got him up to the microphone, where he cracked everyone up, as was his gift. Then he improvised with a couple of us. Afterward, out in the parking lot, he complimented me and gave me a twenty-dollar bill because he knew I was broke. Then he disappeared into the night like the Lone Ranger. My fellow comedian, Charlie Fleischer, who eventually became the voice of Roger Rabbit, had participated in the improv. He saw what happened and came up to me, demanding half of the twenty dollars. He gave me a ten, which Al promptly took out of my hand; it would go toward the rent, which his parents were lending us. When Redd Foxx entertained one night, he talked to me in the parking lot afterward and gave me a one-on-one snort of cocaine. That was nice—I didn't have to share it. Another night, when Franken and Davis came out of the Troubadour, the famous nightclub at Santa Monica and Doheny, and walked past the Palm restaurant, I spotted a twenty-dollar bill on the sidewalk and held out my arm to stop Franken. I pointed to some people getting out of a Mercedes at the valet parking,

"Look—isn't that Danny Kaye?" I picked up the bill while Al was gawking. Later, I went to the Mayfair supermarket and bought a steak and some Jack Daniel's.

Meanwhile, we were hustling, trying to meet agents and managers. There was a manager, Todd Schiffman, whom we approached because he'd seen us at the Comedy Store. We went to his designer decor office on the second floor of a white building on Sunset near the Beverly Hills border. As we entered, he was on the phone and motioned for us to sit down. He had his leather zipper-up-the-side boots with platform heels up on his uncluttered desk. The three of us were an unlikely set: Al and I with the long hair, jeans, Dingo boots, T-shirts, and corduroy sport jackets; he with the comb-over

coif, the shirt collar over the satin jacket, and the cologne. He was most proud to have Kenny Loggins as one of his clients. I recalled to myself that "Your Momma Don't Dance" may have been the reason Paul Flum gave up music and went to law school. Then he took off his tinted glasses and looked Al in the eye.

TOM AND FLIP, 1973, COURTESY OF TOM DAVIS

Todd: "What is it that you boys want to do?"

Al: "We want to move our act into casinos and theaters, and we want to perform in movies and television."

Todd: "Uh huh . . ."

He took his feet off the desk and pointed to a bad oil-on-canvas hanging prominently on the wall. It was the image of an old man playing an upright piano.

Todd: "You see that picture?"

Al and Tom: "Yeah . . ."

Todd: "You see the way his hat is cocked?"

Al and Tom: "Yeah . . ."

Todd: "That is *it*. Anybody can tell at a glance that it's Jimmy Durante."

Al and Tom: "Yup. Yeah."

Todd: "When you guys got charisma like that—you come back and talk to me."

Al: "And what are we supposed to do in the meantime?"

Todd: "Starve."

A comedian at the Comedy Store, Michael Alaimo, told us he had quit driving cab because of another robbery attempt. He said he was making money being Santa Claus at the Sears in North Hollywood, and they needed more guys. Michael always had a cigar in his mouth and spent his afternoons at the track. But thanks to his tip, Al and I gained employment. There were two costume jobs—a Santa Claus suit and Winnie-the-Pooh. We would alternate. As Santa, I learned to recognize whether a child was poor and unlikely to get what he was asking for. "All right, Sasha, Santa's going to try to get you the Hot Wheels set, but if I don't, I'll leave something else and make up for it next year, and I'll always leave lots of love. Now go tell your mom what you told me, and here's some candy." Small children were sometimes frightened, but I did well with kids. When my employers found a bottle of wine in my locker in the boiler room, they didn't fire me. When school let out at 3:00, the older Latin kids would approach me in a group, and I just opened up the candy compartment in the arm of my throne and let them help themselves. They didn't want to bullshit.

The Winnie-the-Pooh gig involved a heavily padded bodysuit and big, round footwear. The headgear had a jar of honey on top, which was where my own head would go, looking out through the wire meshed letters that spelled HUNNY. Pooh would walk around the store saying hello to the kiddos and adding to the festive atmosphere, but there was something about the suit that caused every ten-year-old boy to slug you in the stomach. When Mommy wasn't watching, sometimes Pooh would kick the brat in the ass. Pooh didn't command the respect Santa had. Young women were amused if he asked them if they'd like to go out sometime, but they'd never give Pooh their phone number.

When Christmas was over, we were invited to come back the next year.

I had a one-night stand with a girl who was the piano player at the Comedy Store. A couple of days later, she came to pick me up on the night of my birthday to celebrate. I was sitting on the steps of my apartment building, talking to Budge Threlkeld, when she walked up the sidewalk. She sat down between us, and then invited him to come along, too. I'd never considered such a thing, and went along with it, until we got to her place and stuff started to happen, and I was turned off. I had to leave. No doubt about it, I like straight, one-on-one sex. When Jo lived with me in L.A., she once asked me in her most innocent voice, "Do you and Franken ever fuck each other in the butt?" I had to laugh, but it made me realize that some people wonder. In Hollywood that's probably always a good question.

Bob O'Neal from Harvard, and his musician friend from Cambridge, George Kincheloe, started a Byrds-like band called the Evening Stage. They all moved into a ranch-style house, which they called the Ranch. It was a few blocks from our apartment. There was lots of poker playing, joint smoking, and home cooking. We were all struggling artists and a bond formed among us. They were very talented musicians. Larry, George's older brother, lived there, too. He had a VW van that could hold us all. Once, Al was getting into the passenger seat and the sliding door closed on his hand. When the door was opened and his hand released, all the fingers were bent like Wile E. Coyote. He didn't cry, but jumped up and down the block with his hand in his mouth. He was young, and no bones were broken.

Once, somebody got a bag of peyote buttons and we all went to Skull Rock in Joshua Tree National Park where all those '50s sci-fi films were made. We ate the peyote in the afternoon—I was the only one who didn't puke. The sun set, the moon rose, and we started a campfire. I ran through the desert in the moonlight.

There was a recording studio, Hollywood Central, on Cahuenga between Sunset and Hollywood Boulevards, an area dotted with other such small, independent studios. A wonderful guy, John Rhys, took us under his wing and made comedy tapes with us. It was invaluable to understand the process of recording, splicing, and editing, which also related to filmmaking and screenplay writing. Two years later, when Al and I returned to Hollywood for our first Emmy

Awards in '76, we gave John a couple hundred bucks and our VW van in exchange for the master recordings. Thanks to us, these tapes never went anywhere, and John was saddened that we dropped him like a rock. The VW van we had acquired in a trade-in deal with the Buick that never quit.

Sammy Shore had a messy divorce and his ex-wife, Mitzi, took over the Comedy Store. She had more business sense. She allowed us to throw a publicity event where we invited everyone in Hollywood who might be interested, and filled the rest of the seats with friends. John Rhys recorded our performance. I don't know where that tape went.

There was grumbling among our Comedy Store peers. Suddenly the club was making lots of money, and those of us who had been performing there for years felt that the club needed us and should pay us something. There was talk about going on strike to make our point. Mitzi felt betrayed and blacklisted the outspoken from performing in her club. Our inscribed 8 x 10 glossy PR photo was removed from its place in the entrance, and, on the outer wall facing the parking lot where everybody's name was hand-painted, our names were painted over.

Sid Strong became the lighting director at a new music club, the Roxy, next door to the Rainbow Club and up the street from the Playboy Building, which had its entire ten-story side painted with a giant version of the promotional ad for *Young Frankenstein.* The Roxy's upstairs bar overlooking Sunset had yet to be rebuilt

JOHN RHYS

over what had been a Japanese restaurant. The place appeared to be run by a guy named Mario who wore a big, diamond-studded pinky ring. All the servers were gorgeous girls, and they fawned over him. Every once in a while, I would stand in for Sid. I did the

1974, COURTESY OF TOM DAVIS

lights for Genesis, and the mighty, mighty Chi-Lites.

When Lou Adler brought *The Rocky Horror Show* from the London stage, he opened it in America at the Roxy Theater. He brought along Tim Curry, as well as its creator, Richard O'Brien, who wisely wrote himself into the show as the character Riff Raff. Adler chose producer Brian Avnet to mount the show at the Roxy. Brian hired Chip Monck to do lighting design. Mr. Monck had done the lights for the Stones. Chip hired Dick Miller, an even-keeled, hands-on lighting director, to work with Sid Strong, and Sid brought me in as an apprentice. The club closed for a week to transform into a theater with the *Rocky Horror* set and stage. This meant long hours for the crew. I was fine with that. I needed the money. Mr. Monck's philosophy appeared to be: if lots of lights are great, lots and lots of lights are greater and greater. I was learning on the job about Leucos and Fresnels, spotlights, control boards, and miles and miles of cable.

During that week, I was exhausted but engrossed in my task when Dick came over to see how I was doing. He burst into laughter. "Sid—you got to come over and see this!" Sid came over and started laughing. Instead of using jute (twine) or gaffers tape (duct tape) to attach a cable to a steel support column that held up a balcony-turned-bandbox, I had wound the lengthy cable around the column in a serpentine fashion. Not only had I ended up with female-to-female plug ends, but if electricity had ever coursed through that cable, the magnetic field would have shot the column through the floor and into the basement, or it would have traveled up through the bandbox to the roof.

Chip Monck did not spend much time supervising the construction of his designs, but when he did, he recognized that I was at the bottom of the pecking order. I still was not completely hip to lighting design vernacular. He pointed to some lights on the ceiling and snapped an order that sounded like, "Take a fork and c-clamp the lead-in to the prong Fresnel!" When I went, "Huh?" he went, "Give me that ladder!" I struggled to unfold the fifteen-foot stepladder, Chip lost his patience shouting, "*I'll* get it!" He grabbed the ladder just as I got the supports to bend in the proper direction and the ladder collapsed on his finger. "YYAAH!" He left. Everyone came up and congratulated me.

That week when I got my check, it was about 60 percent of what was due. I called Brian Avnet's number and his receptionist answered the phone. When I explained to her the discrepancy, she put me on hold. A minute later she was back on, "Yes, Mr. Davis—I'm told it's impossible to work that number of hours, and that's all he's going to pay you."

I had clocked in and out, so I went and got a copy of the record, and then I got Al, who was only too delighted to be moral support. We both had long hair, jeans, T-shirts, and boots. As we entered the office, it was easy to find our way to the receptionist: she sat behind her desk before the door that she guarded like the three-headed dog at the gates of Hades.

> I: "Hi. I believe it was you I spoke to on the phone—I'm Tom Davis and I would like to talk to Mr. Avnet about this paycheck thing."
>
> I put the copy of my hours on her desk.
>
> Receptionist: "I'm sorry, Mr. Avnet's not in today, but I'll be sure to give this to him."
>
> Al: "That's okay—we'll wait."
>
> Al flopped onto the couch, put his boots up on the arm, and locked his hands behind his head.
>
> Receptionist: "Who's that?"
>
> I: "He's my friend."
>
> Receptionist: "But Mr. Avnet's not here today."
>
> Al: "He's in there and we're not leaving until Tom gets his check."
>
> Receptionist: "I'm calling the police."
>
> Al: "Call the fucking police."
>
> Five minutes later we walked out with the check and went immediately to the bank to cash the damn thing.

For the first two weeks of its run, I was on Follow Spot #2 for the American debut of *The Rocky Horror Show,* now including Susan Sarandon and Meat Loaf. On opening night, as we were two minutes away from curtain up, I heard Sid in my headphones, exclaiming to Following Spot #1, "Jesus Christ—there's John Lennon—do you see him?"

Follow Spot #1: "Yeah! There he is."
I held down the switch that allowed me to join in.
I: "Where? Where?"
Sid: "He's right underneath your platform, Tom."

I never saw my hero, John Lennon, though I was within six feet of him. Several years later, I was watching *Monday Night Football* at Bob Tischler's apartment on the West Side of Manhattan, two blocks from the Dakota, when Howard Cosell made the announcement. I was sure I had heard the gunshots ten minutes before. Gilda and her husband, G. E. Smith, lived in the Dakota. He once showed me a small shard of glass he pulled from the errant bullet's hole in the thick plate glass of the Dakota's security window. I expect G.E. still has it today.

As 1974 began, the antidote to the Comedy Store was the Pitschel Players, which reopened the venue on Melrose that was once the Ashgrove. The Pitschel Players was organized and subsidized by Roger and Ann Bowen, and Joe Roth. The Bowens were cofounders of Second City, along with Alan Arkin, Nichols and May, Severn Darden, Barbara Harris, Shelley Berman, John Brent, and Del Close. Roger played Lt. Colonel Blake in Altman's *M * A * S * H,* and his steady income working in commercials and television floated the rent, so a stage was provided for those of us who didn't seem to fit anywhere else. This included the Credibility Gap—Harry Shearer, Dave Lander, Mike McKean, and Richard Beebe. We were delighted to learn that Harry had been the annoying little boy in *The Jack Benny Program*. He was in "the Beavers' Club" (like the Boy Scouts). I would refer you to the dentist episode where Jack, to calm the preadolescent Harry, tells him there's nothing to fear in the dentist's chair—and Jack ends up getting a tooth pulled.

My favorite bit that the Credibility Gap did was *The Self-Righteous Brothers* in cardigan sweaters, singing, "Not the right face, not the right hair, but you'll do—until something good comes along." And this TV news editorial by Dave Lander: "Last night we made an editorial supporting the recent laws enacted to make our highways safer. Here with the opposing point of view is Mr. Karl Chalwithe. 'I say this is America!—let's put the 'free' back in 'freeway,' and the 'high' back in 'highway.'"

I improvised with Mary McCusker, Chris Pray, Gerrit Graham (who subsequently starred with Kurt Russell in the movie *Used Cars*), Edie and Doug McClurg, and several other contemporaries who had something to learn from Severn Darden, John Brent, and Roger and Ann. The place also showcased musical acts like Roy Buchanan, John Prine, Bob Weir's band Kingfish, and the Jerry Garcia Band. Al and I would help run these shows. When Deadheads were trying to break into the Garcia show through the roof, Al was under the trapdoor, which, when he heard the footsteps and tampering, he would strike with a club with such force that it could be heard all through the house, thus scaring away the would-be intruders. I locked the place up that night; Jerry was the last to leave.

> Garcia: "Hey, how ya' doin'?"
> I: "Great. Nice show, man."
> Garcia: "Thanks. Good night." I was thrilled.

It was one of those Hollywood nights when I hopped into cars and went from party to party. Somehow I found myself in Mickey Dolenz's house. Though he's best known as the drummer of the Monkees, I remembered him better as the child star of the late-'50s series *Circus Boy*. Then I saw a couple of pictures on his wall of Jimi Hendrix laughing with the other Monkees in an airplane. Wow.

Mickey: "Oh, yeah. He opened for us on our first tour. I took those pictures."

Mickey had his own studio there in his home, and he played for me a new mix of his own rendition of "Peggy Sue," which I've never heard since.

The comedy producers Don Rio and Al Katz had seen Franken and Davis somewhere, and they invited us to breakfast at the Old World restaurant across Sunset from Tower Records. It was a very good restaurant and I savored my Eggs Benedict and washed them down with a gin Bloody Mary. Al had the buckwheat waffles with sausages on the side and a fresh squeezed OJ. Rio and Katz were taping a stand-up comedy special in Las Vegas, and they wanted to mix young and old acts. They shook hands with us on the deal and picked up the tab. They'd see us at the gig the next week.

We were flown to Las Vegas early in the morning. The show would be taped all day and then we'd be flown back that evening. Don Novello traveled with us. It was a joy to see everybody's act. Professor Irwin Corey, with his Einstein hair, dingy tuxedo, and high-topped tennis shoes, stole the show before uttering his first word. He strode out to the microphone, acknowledging the crowd. He paused to collect his thoughts, then pointed his finger in the air and opened his mouth to speak, but then thought better of it, and paced the stage as if what he was going to say wasn't profound enough. He furrowed his brow, ran his hands through his hair, and then it came to him. He returned to the microphone, but then again he slapped his hand to his mouth in frustration. He milked the crowd like this for another minute and then finally proclaimed, ". . . furthermore . . ." Big laugh.

Henny Youngman told old jokes like Hendrix played guitar—without thinking. He was the greatest example of how timing is everything. As he said, "I don't tell jokes—I just refresh your memory." Then there was Father Guido Sarducci, Benny Boulder (Budge Threlkeld's new nom de guerre), and Franken and Davis. As soon as we were done we went back out into the audience to dig the old guys. Stanley Myron Handelman was in the middle of his act when someone in the back started heckling him, "Hey you stale limp-dick motherfucker—you stole my joke!" I turned around to see—it was Slappy White.

There was to be a ten-hour rock festival on the beach in Venice

Beach and Franken and Davis were the emcees. It was no money, but we didn't turn anything down. There'd be ten thousand people who would see us do our act during the set changes between the bands. It was a glorious sunny spring day with the fresh sea breeze keeping everything cool and fragrant. After the first band finished, we went back out on the ten-foot-high stage and performed our bit about the prevalent Virginia Slims cigarette commercial that targeted women with the slogan song, but we wonder what that song would be like targeting black people for Afrosheen.

> You've come a long way negro,
> To get where you've got to today.
> Yes, you've got your own hairspray now, negro,
> You've come a long, long way!

The stage manager came running out and pointed out to us that a black motorcycle gang was making its way through the crowd. They were visibly angry and coming for the stage. Apparently, the people up front were enjoying our comedy, but the primitive sound system was affected by the gusts of wind, so that in the back of the crowd, only snippets of what we said were audible—like "negro." We leaped off the back of that stage and hit the ground like paratroopers. We dashed into the Buick and sped off in a cloud of dust and never looked back.

That piece would be broadcast on *SNL* two years later when Julian Bond hosted, and it was well received. The original Virginia Slims ad campaign had been conceived three years before by Don Novello when he worked at a big ad agency in Chicago.

In May 1974, Al and I were living in a one-bedroom apartment (I had a mattress in the living room) on the second floor of a stucco building at 7711 Ardmore, near Western and Santa Monica, not far from the Burger King where the Alphabet Bomber would be apprehended the ensuing August. The super was an ex-marine named Will Dimmit. He wrote pornographic novelettes for a living, and lived directly below us. I was learning to play electric guitar in the afternoons and I drove him nuts.

One day I came home with two hits of purple microdot LSD

and convinced Al to join me. As we were getting off, I turned on the TV. Frederick Wiseman's documentary *Primate* was on PBS. We had never seen it before—second-rate scientists using government grants to shave orangutans and perform experimental surgeries, like probes in the brain to cause erections. The tortured humanoid animals groaned in pain. That program is difficult for anyone to watch, and in our state of psychedelic vulnerability, we became overcome with emotion. There was a knock at the door. I wiped the tears from my eyes and opened it to reveal a gentleman who had been approaching us with the intent to be our manager for 20 percent. But when he entered, all we could talk about was the horrible cruelty of primate research and how something had to be done. That guy bolted from the apartment and we never heard from him again.

We decided it was our turn to throw a party, so we invited all our friends to celebrate Al's birthday. At the same time, the infamous fiery shootout with the LAPD and the Symbionese Liberation Army (who had kidnapped Patty Hearst) was unfolding fast.

Everybody showed up, about thirty people, including the girl who had asked for the threesome with Budge. She had a new boyfriend who brought a handful of joints, which he quickly distributed. I took a hit off one of them and immediately recognized the unmistakable burning-rubber taste of angel dust—a powerful psychedelic and muscle tranquilizer. I shouted out a warning, but it-was too late. Some guests tried to leave and wound up lying in the hall and on the front lawn. The LAPD showed up with their guns drawn.

> Cop #1: "Whose place is this?!"
> Tom & Al: "Mine. Ours. We rent it."
> Cop #2: "What's going on here!?"

Al: "It's my birthday."

More cops entered and started searching the place. Everybody had their stashes in their underwear by now. Mine was in the refrigerator. When they opened the bedroom, a new acquaintance, a gynecologist, was getting it on with his girlfriend in a state of oblivion. Our prop trunk for our act was there. When they opened that, they found the stained brain tumor headpiece, wigs, lab coats, and, among other things, a rubber-toy baby doll with a butcher knife in it. We used that in our lame shock-rock parody, which ended with me making guitar feedback while humping the amp, and Al would put down his guitar, pick up the doll, and mock molest and stab it.

Cop #1: "What's this!?"

I: "We're a comedy team and that's a prop."

Cop #1: "Good God . . . All right—we're going. But if we have to come back here you're all going to jail."

And many happy returns of the day.

Al and I befriended a house of hippie guys in Nichols Canyon. Among them was Mike Lawler, a high-foreheaded, wispy-haired Yalie with wire-rimmed glasses who was a brilliant photographer. He was paying the rent by contracting for Bob Banner Productions (he could build a rink for an ice show anywhere). He could do anything, including finding us a gig. Apparently, BBP owned *The Boob Tube Revue,* a lounge show at Harrah's in Reno, and a team music act had left the show suddenly. A stand-up comedy team would work just fine for them. We'd appear three times in the show and participate in a full-ensemble song and dance at the beginning and the end, three shows a day, six days a week. No problem.

We met with the director of *The Boob Tube Revue,* Joe Danova, briefly in L.A. (he was in town for a day before he had to be back— he was also an actor and emcee in the show). He was very bright and funny. He looked like a tanned Freddie Mercury. We were off to Reno. It was mid-November 1974.

The so-called "Biggest Little City" was still a cowboy town, which gave it a charm Las Vegas could never know. We found accommodations in a ridiculous 1950s motel a few miles out of town. It had a natural hot springs pool at one end, the office and a small restaurant in the middle, and Franken and Davis by themselves at the far end. Our kitchenette window looked right out on the rushing Truckee River. We had brought a record player with Grateful Dead, Herbie Hancock, and Leo Kottke LPs, and some good pot. I was continuing to learn to play guitar using the *Grateful Dead Songbook,* which had fingering charts for the chords.

Working in a casino was an education in itself. People love to piss away their money. It's twenty-four hours, no clocks, "free" booze if you're gambling, and "free" suites if you've distinguished yourself before. Neither Al nor I gambled a dime in the six weeks we worked there. The craps table was supposed to have the best odds and the most colorful examples of the nature of luck, hot and cold. I stopped to watch an excited crowd at one table where some guy was on a winning roll. He became very animated, hooting and hollering with joy. Then he "lost the farm," as they say, in a single roll of the dice, and he became hysterical. Security guards had to wrestle him into an unmarked door nearby.

The lounge was a cool place. Rich and poor people mixed freely to drink and be entertained. The bars at either end of the stage, with their cash registers ka-chinging and the unsexy but sexily clad servers, were an odd distraction at first, but we quickly got used to it. Good business is good for everybody, and the audience was alive. The show was vaudevillian musical/comedy variety. The cast was tastefully diverse. The Hawaiian guy had a couple of jokes like "I come from Komonae Wanalaya." Of course, with a Boob in the title, we had to have a sexpot comedienne with a décolletage diploma. That was Cassandra Peters, who went on to become television's alluring vampiress, Elvira. She got her movie done, too. She and Joe Danova actually did a couple of "doctor" routines ("Oh nurse! . . . Ah—there you are?!").

Harrah's management couldn't have been nicer. Our cast was twice invited to see the headliner in the big room. We were all seated at the best table and plied with champagne and great food. I don't think we even had to leave the tip. A nice guy named Holmes Hendricksen ran the hotel. Today he works the Harrah's in Atlantic City. Robert Goulet's show started with a tight spotlight on his hair as he launched into "A Man Is a Man." John Davidson invited us all backstage, where Al said, as Mr. Davidson shook his hand, "People come up to me all the time and say I look like you."

But the producer of *The Boob Tube Revue* had a cantankerous personality and a reputation for nickel-and-diming. He was one of the original Mouseketeers. I had watched him on television while we were both wearing mouse-eared caps, and now he was the guy cutting my check. Not that I would have recognized him, but he was still "Dickey." He gloated when he won a small bet with Franken and Davis: in the NFC play-offs, the Los Angeles Rams stomped on the Minnesota Vikings.

Our run ended on New Year's Eve. Dickey told us our last week's wages would be sent to us in the mail. As a cast, we agreed that there would probably be no "check in the mail." We (Joe and Al) informed Dickey that "if we did not get paid first, the cast would not perform the last two shows." We were counterinformed, "Fuck you." The checks arrived five minutes before the curtain was to go up at Zero Hour. I did some acid, so Al figured he'd better do some, too. At midnight, when we sang and danced the opening number for the last time, Al and I pretended to get our feet entangled, causing us to tumble to the stage. Al feigned a broken leg and crawled about the stage in mock agony that fooled some people in the audience. The cast struggled to finish the number as they were cracking up.

From: Al Franken
Date: Saturday, 10 March 2007 12:33 PM
To: Tom Davis
Subject: Hi Tom.

We did Harrah's in '74. I don't remember when exactly, but I think I remember Jack Benny died when we were there and we both cried. So, if you look up when he died, that might pinpoint the time frame. I can't remember the Mouseketeer. I remember that the show was *The Boob Tube Revue.* And you remember that Cassandra Peters, who later became Elvira, was in the show. And we replaced the Adrissi Brothers (sp?) who wrote "Never My Love." And Rip Taylor came through and there was an impromptu party for him and he was very sweet.

In June of '75, Herb Karp, an agent we approached at William Morris, told us to write up some comedy bits for television. There was a producer who just got a deal with NBC and was looking for people. We put together fourteen pages in a binder. The first bit was our commercial parody of a feminine deodorant that comes in a roll-on. Then we did our local newscast on the night of the day of World War III:

> Anchor: "Tragedy, death, and catastrophe highlight tonight's news at eleven. I'm Ray Thompson, substituting for the deceased Chet Newhelm."
> Weatherman: "Well, don't grab those umbrellas just yet . . . temperatures up to six thousand degrees tonight . . . winds gusting at five hundred miles per hour with occasional firestorms . . ."

Then we offered a network promo for a sitcom, *Führer Knows Best*. (V.O.: "Romp through Nazi Germany with Sebastian Cabot as Hermann Goering, Goldie Hawn as Eva Braun, and Jerry Mathers as the Führer. Join this week's guest star, Don Rickles, in the fun as Eva invites a Jew to dinner by mistake.") Then a Bob and Ray–type interview piece with a bitter, no-talent, professional farm-club baseball player ("Pepper, you're thirty-eight years old, you've lost what little speed, strength, and reflexes you had even during your prime. There probably won't be another chance. Think you'll go into coaching?" Pepper: "Naw. I hate kids. Can't stand 'em.") Then another promo: "See *I, a Wizard*. Follow a young girl's journey with three men, each with his own special need." Next, a POV piece of a grocery store's rotating security camera that's always catching only the aftermath of some kind of chaos (not a great sketch, but experimental). Finally, a parody of a variety show "with host Nat Totino, the Johnny Ralston singers, and special guest Cher." It's a taping, and the director has difficulty with the talent reading from lame cue cards.

Tom Schiller saw this portfolio as he and Lorne Michaels were examining stacks of submissions beside the pool at the Chateau Marmont. We were wise to submit just a couple of pieces—less is more in show business. We paid 10 percent to Herb Karp during our first year at *SNL,* and 10 percent to Bob Coe, a manager with whom we were associated. We dropped them because we had never signed a deal. Herb said he was disappointed in us. But we needed that 20 percent. Al made the calls.

Before we left L.A., we threw a party for our friends, the band Evening Stage, at the Pitschel Players. I engineered and recorded the event, where they played their hearts out. As I made copies of the tapes for each of them, I wept. It was the end of an era. Today, Bob O'Neal is a successful lawyer in St. Louis; George Kincheloe is still a bandleader and songwriter in Northern California.

9
FUCK JOHNNY CARSON

Woe be to the vanquished.　　　　　—Vercingetorix

For a stand-up comedian in L.A. in late '73, getting on "The Carson Show," as we called it, was everyone's goal. It was a rite of passage for all the great ones, who still crawled over each other to appear on that stage. Craig Tennis was *The Tonight Show's* chief talent coordinator. He would periodically attend a Friday or Saturday 10:00 to 11:30 at Sammy Shore's Comedy Store, sitting in the booth in the back, like an emperor at the games. You'd find out what you were worth by your order in the lineup. Each act was allotted ten minutes, but almost everybody would go overtime, some worse than others.

> Other: "Hey man—you were out there twenty-five minutes."
> Worse: "Yeah—but I was killing! Did you hear them?"

So a few acts on the bottom of the list would miss the Emperor's audience. It was not fun.

However, Franken and Davis were chosen to audition at *The Tonight Show* studio at NBC Burbank, along with two other standups. A van picked us up at noon on a Saturday in front of the Hyatt on Sunset, next door to the Comedy Store and its empty parking lot. Why didn't they pick us up there? I don't know.

At our destination, we were shown into the cold, cavernous *Tonight Show* studio and seated in the center, a few rows up from the floor. Finally, Craig Tennis entered with a gaggle of production staffers and they sat above us several rows, just outside the general stage lighting.

Steve Lubetkin was up first. He was maybe a year or two older than Al and I. He had a good act—I remember something about insect actors auditioning for *The Hellstrom Chronicles* (a popular low-budget documentary feature about how insects will rule the world). Watching Steve caught in the stage lights made it seem kind of ironic.

Al and I did our local news on the day of World War III routine.

The biggest laugh came when Tennis Augustus called on this young comedienne in a home-knit sweater with a Valentine heart, to take her turn. He called her "the girl with the heart on" (Get it? Yesss!). The staffer geese cackled at that one. That's why Mr. Tennis was where *he* was, and why we were where *we* were.

After we had all endured this scrutiny, we watched them climb the stairs up to the executive offices and disappear. After half an hour, an imperial guard appeared and announced, "Sorry, but we don't have a place for you on our show now. Thank you and good luck."

In the van on the way back, Lubetkin was very upset. "I can't believe it! I got turned down by Carson!"

> Al: "It's okay, Steve. There'll be other things."
> Steve: "But that was my best stuff!"
> I: "Fuck Johnny Carson."
> Steve: "No—*I'm* fucked."

Ten days later he took a running leap off the Hyatt's roof and landed in the Comedy Store parking lot. He had a note in his pocket: "My name is Steve Lubetkin. I was a comedian."

Al: "Why did he do that?"

I: "I guess he lost his sense of humor."

Our friend from the Improv NYC, Gabe Kaplan, successfully survived his *Tonight Show* first audition, and when he went to the taping, he asked us to come along to give moral support. As he went in for makeup, we went outside to wait in line with the other members of the audience. An NBC page came up and addressed us. She wanted to know, "Who would like to 'Stump the Band'"?

Stump the Band was a longtime regular feature where Johnny took his microphone into the audience and chose goofy-looking people with their hands raised to stand up and challenge the band to play some obscure sort of song. When the band didn't know it (usually), they would get a laugh trying to make it up. Then the audience member would sing the song while Johnny stood there listening with a funny look on his face. A prize was awarded, dinner for two at the Magic Castle or perhaps Alan Hale's Lobster Barrel. We were seated on the aisle—a good sign.

Gabe did very well. So well that Johnny called him over to congratulate him—we all called that "kissing the ring." During one of the pauses in taping, Johnny descended down our aisle holding his mic. Three, two, and . . . taping resumed with a lead-in from the band; the cameras turned around to face the audience, who were clearly thrilled.

Adrenaline pumping, I watched Johnny ask, "Who wants to stump the band?" and he picked an old lady from Florida who had an Irish folk song. Then he's standing on the step just above Al's elbow.

Johnny: "Who else wants to take a shot?"

Al and I raise our hands. Johnny steps down and looks at us. We stand up.

Johnny: "So—have you guys got a song for us?"

Al: "Ah . . . yes, we do."

Johnny: "What's your name?"

Al: "I'm Al Franken."

I: "Tom Davis."

Johnny: "Okay—so what's the song?"

Al: "Richard Nixon's campaign song from 1952."

The audience laughs, and so does Johnny.

Johnny: "Doc—you guys want to take a stab at that one?"

Cut to: Doc and the band. They smile and shrug. They're stumped.

Johnny: "Okay, guys—let's hear it."

We belt out the song we learned during research:

> *Vote for Nixon,*
> *On Election Day.*
> *Vote for Nixon,*
> *And you'll keep your take-home pay.*
> *He's got the heart and the strength and youth,*
> *He's never been beat because he tells the truth.*
> *So vote for Nixon, vote for Nixon,*
> *Vote for Nixon on Election Day!*
> *Dick! Dick! We want Dick!*
> *Vote for Nixon on Election Day!*

Johnny cracks up and the crowd applauds.

Johnny: "Say, you guys are terrific. What do you do?"

Al: "We're a stand-up comedy team."

Johnny: "Really? Maybe you guys should do the show sometime?"

Al: "We'd love to . . . (he points off camera) . . . but your talent coordinator said there's no place for us here."

Johnny is as stunned as everyone else. He turns to camera.

Johnny: "All right then—we'll be right back with Joey Bishop. Stick around."

Johnny disappears; the lights come down, the audience buzzes softly, and our hopes to appear on *The Tonight Show* have vanished like a fart in a tornado.

I: "Why the fuck did you do that?"

Al: "I don't know. It just happened. Damn it!"

Whenever I made a stupid mistake, it was because I was an idiot. When Al made mistakes it was a funny mystery. But he wasn't laughing at this mystery.

In 1978, the Ayatollah Khomeini returned from exile in France to Tehran, and ignited the militant Islamic movement that took the American embassy hostage.

One of Johnny Carson's most enduring routines was *Carnac the Magnificent*. He wore an oversize turban and, with mock fanfare, would accept from Ed McMahon sealed envelopes containing questions to which he would divine the answers, then open the envelope to read them. The jokes were always very silly, but it was Carson at his best. Al and I took his convention and made it *Khomeini the Magnificent*; Al was Khomeini and I was Bani Sadr, his Ed McMahon. The jokes contained our satirical, political sensibilities.

From: Tom Davis
To: Al Franken
Date: Saturday, 16 June 2007 6:01 PM
Subject: Memoir

Hi Al,
Can you remember any of the jokes we did with Khomeini the Magnificent? I'm going to be in Mpls for the first week of July; I know you're incredibly busy but I'll give you a call.
Tom

From: Al Franken
To: Tom Davis
Date: Sunday, 17 June 2007 12:16 AM
Subject: Re: Memoir

Gotzbadeh. (sp?) What does an Iranian farmer do if his wife won't have sex by night?
I remember also "Day-O, Day-O," what comes before Day One of the Iranian Hostage Crisis? But that was very dependent on the familiarity with Nightline's (America Held Hostage at the time) counting up the days.
I think there was one joke that had the answer "Lefty," but I can't remember what the question was—but it was something like "What do you call a convicted shoplifter in Iran?"
I bet Ken Aymong could get you a copy of this.
Give me some exact dates in July. I think we're doing a lot of parades. Seriously. But I'd love to see you.
Al

Khomeini the Magnificent went over very well with audiences, so we sent a tape of a performance to *The Tonight Show*, hoping that they might find it both funny and flattering, and invite us to perform it on their show. The letter we received back was thinly veiled hostility that concluded, "Your comedy is not even close to what we do."

In the summer of 1992, Al and I were in the first-class section of a flight to L.A. (we weren't paying for it) when we spotted Jay Leno, who had only recently been anointed successor to Johnny Carson. We knew Jay in '73 when he was still living in Boston and I was living in Al's Harvard dormitory room. I borrowed his Miles Davis album, *Bitches Brew*, and I returned it. We liked Jay's act, and he was known for working more clubs than anyone else. We could've been doing the Mic and Stool in Wichita, and he would have been there ten days before. So Jay shakes our hands and says hello, and, what both Al and I were thinking, "You guys should do the show."

Compared to 8H, the *Tonight Show* studio is like an airplane hangar. A caricature of Jay's face was painted on the thirty-foot steel doors. Back in the dressing room, we changed from jeans and T-shirts into clean T-shirts and sport coats. We went out for a dress rehearsal of our bit—an NBC censor was there at our request. We knew a lot about Standards and Practices from fifteen solid years working for Lorne Michaels. Then we returned to our dressing room to watch the show on the television monitor until our slot came up.

The taping starts. Jay does his monologue, the taping stops. Five minutes later the lights come up on "the panel"—the couch annexed to the desk behind which Johnny used to sit. The funniest thing Andy Kaufman ever did was his Carson parody where the desk was four feet higher than the couch.

Anyway, first one guest comes out, then another. The taping stops. We're given the heads-up and take our place behind the curtains. We peek through at the audience. They rise up in tiers from that studio floor of highly polished linoleum on concrete, on which the cameras moved like Faraday's praying mantises. The taping rolls, Jay introduces us, and we emerge from the curtains and sit in our talk-show chairs.

We hadn't written a new piece for our act in the last couple of years, so we had gone through the trunk and dusted off an obscure

Bob and Ray–type talk-show piece where Al is an eccentric expert on bulimia. Al's Dr. Robert Lipsky is a brilliant, overscientific, callous, disgusting character with a thick Long Island accent, who uses science to explain the obvious. "Many bulimics hold the belief that in order to get a mate, they have to be attractive. In several independent studies we have found that, in fact, men prefer young, lithe female bodies over those covered with a thick layer of fat, especially in the posterior and leggy regions. Oddly enough, even morbidly obese men prefer young, lithe female bodies."

> Interviewer: "Where does the name bulimia come from?"
> Lipsky: "It comes from the latin root, *"bulim, bulem, bulare*— to blow lunch."
> Interviewer: "What are the dangers of this behavior?"
> Lipsky: "Excessive vomiting can damage the digestive lining of the stomach, and digestive fluids can be irritating to the throat and erode tooth enamel, and severe vomiting can even cause whiplash."
> Interviewer: "What are the warning signs of bulimia?"
> Lipsky: "Someone who eats enormous amounts of food and does not gain weight; and does this person, after eating, lock herself in the bathroom and do you subsequently hear sounds like, 'Blahrrr . . . glalck! Bular!'?"
> Interviewer: "Thank you very much."

The piece works, the audience loves it, we go over to the panel and Al talks momentarily to Jay. David Sanborn performs with his band and joins us on panel. During the final commercial, legendary Carson producer, then exec producer, Freddie De Cordova steps up to the desk and whispers into Leno's ear. Sanborn does the panel, Jay says good night, the *Tonight Show* band plays off, and as the credits start to roll Jay leans over and says, "They have some problem with your bit."

> Al: "What? What problem?"
> Jay: "Jeez, I don't know. Talk to Freddie."

Freddie De Cordova remounts the stage and tells us: "You guys—bulimia is a very serious disease, and we decided we had to edit your bit out—but we kept the panel in." With credits and cameras still rolling, Al jumps up off the couch and faces the old fuck.

> Al: "You can't do that! The audience loved it! It was fine with

the censors! If you had a problem, you could have told us a week ago when we submitted it and we would have done something else!"

Obviously the executive producer hadn't looked at it. De Cordova's veins bulge in his face.

De Cordova: "Nobody talks to me like that! Not in thirty years! And in front of the crew and audience!"

Jay's face turns ashen gray.

Jay: "I got two shows in Vegas tonight—I got a plane waiting." He gets up and almost runs for the door, leaving me and about half the audience who've come back to watch this clash of the titans. I listen to Franken take a year off the old man's life. He walked with him to the edit room, wherever that is. I just sit there on that couch as the lights go off and watch the audience drain out of there. By the way people are looking at me, you'd think I'd just backed my RV over somebody's child. Finally, Franken reappears.

Al: "Okay—I stood there with De Cordova while they edited our act back in. We're in."

It was a victory—but at what cost? I didn't care anymore.

10
SIGNIFICANT OTHER

We're all in love with someone we can't have.
—Jenni Muldaur

In the fall of 1977 I was single again, and I saw this girl talking to Tom Schiller at his desk in the *SNL* office. I walked over and Tom introduced us. Her name was Emily Prager. She smiled and flapped her Betty Boop eyes. In conversation she had a funny cigarette voice and a sardonic sense of humor. She was in that circle of *National Lampoon*ies. She had recently ended a brief relationship with Doug Kenney (soon to write *Animal House* and *Caddyshack*), and she and I started dating. I was still living in the Frankens' apartment on Eighty-sixth and Riverside. Emily and Al had a vehement argument about a movie, which says something silly about the both of them. After that, she moved me and my meager possessions into her tiny apartment at 288 West Twelfth. It was a beautiful old creaky brownstone with a fireplace. My *SNL* colleague Anne Beatts had the apartment upstairs (she spent much of her time at Michael O'Donoghue's at 23 West Sixteenth). Emily had been to only one rock concert in her life—the Beatles at Shea Stadium. In the kitchen she had oven mitts with swastikas on them.

Emily liked to say that she was half Catholic and half Jewish—the bottom half. Her father, Arthur, had been a navigator on a B-24 in World War II. "The Nazis made one mistake." "And what was that, Arthur?" "They made me mad." After the war he was assigned to several bases, but wound up in Taiwan with his bride and new-born daughter. Emily has fond memories of her Chinese nanny. Today Em lives in Shanghai with her adopted daughter.

She had three cats—a fuzzy gray named Basil; a Siamese, Peasblossom; and a black cat, Max. I had always thought of my-self as a "dog person." At first I was annoyed at a cat snuggling with the top of my head while I was sleeping, but soon I loved those cats. We adopted another half-Siamese kitten, Clea (named after the ex-girlfriend of Dr. Strange, from the Marvel comic books of the same name. The character's favorite haunt was a real bar on Thirteenth Street—Hell's Bells.). I bought the apartment next door, and we knocked down the wall between the kitchens. Arthur owned a saltbox house in Sag Harbor, Long Island. In the summer, the town was populated by a lot of writers and journal-ists and was the funky alternative to the nearby, wealthy Hamp-tons. Betty Friedan lived a couple of blocks away—I'd see her watering her flowers.

I took Emily to Minnesota for Christmas with my folks. Mom loved her and Dad didn't (six months before he had argued with her at their first meeting in the Spaghetti Factory on Ninth Avenue in midtown Manhattan. I can't remember what the argument was, but Dad had an attitude about attitudes, and Em didn't suffer fools lightly). Then we flew to San Francisco to see the series of Grateful Dead shows leading up to New Year's.

We were staying at the Berkeley Marina Marriott to be near some friends. Em couldn't drink but she was great on acid. Both of us tripped in the front-row balcony of Winterland to ring in the New Year. The show ended and as we were driving across the Bay

Bridge she turned to me: "How about that couple fucking on the floor in the crowd?"

I: "What?"

She: "You didn't see them? They were right in front of us."

I: "Really?"

She: "Yes, they took their clothes off, the crowd gave them space, and they really went at it. They seemed to go on for the longest time."

I: "Huh."

I had been riveted to the performance, as usual, watching Jerry's hands and trying to figure out how he made those sounds. Back at the hotel, nobody was going to sleep. Someone's suite became a party. As I stumbled into the room, somebody entered behind me. "Okay . . . who's got the drugs?" I turn around and it was Jerry Garcia. Far out.

Emily was a talented writer and actress. Before she worked at the *National Lampoon,* she played Laurie Ann Karr for the last four years of the soap opera, *The Edge of Night.* She wanted to be in the *SNL* cast, but it became clear that was not going to happen in the near future. She was working with Anne Beatts, Deanne Stillman, and Judy Belushi on a book of feminine humor called *Titters.* John Belushi hated this, and that was enough to put the kibosh on *SNL* for her (for the time being). Emily did not like rejection. Also, more than once, we were asleep at 4:00 in the morning, the door buzzer would go off, and then we'd hear John's voice bellowing from Twelfth Street, "Hey, Davis! I know you're up there and you've got some COCAINE! Open up! I'm going to keep yelling until you do!" Had I been alone, I would have opened up, but Emily hated the very idea, and they never did get along. In those days I carried around a "dummy" bottle with a little bit of coke in case Belushi hit on me, because he'd always do the whole thing.

Danny needed a place to park his new Harley and he bought an old bar on the corner of Dominick and Hudson. It had been the Badge Inn for many years, so called because it serviced longshoremen who wore badges. Once he and John put in a jukebox and some instruments, it became the Blues Bar—a clubhouse and antidote for the *SNL* after-party, for the cast, writers, and friends to wind down. In '78, Dan's brother Peter was living in the city. He'd been composing rock-and-roll songs and I'd accompany him on guitar. We'd hang out in the Blues Bar and John started playing drums, and Steve from We Buy Guitars on Forty-eighth Street played bass. We actually did one unannounced gig at My Father's Place on Long Island somewhere. We got paid in cash. I was thrilled.

I smoked very potent, pungent pot at the time, and friends spontaneously started calling us the Stink Band, and we got mentioned in *Rolling Stone*. Ironically, my ex, Jo's, ex-boyfriend, who had poked me in the chest with his finger, sent me a hate letter. He used to play in the Lake Street Stink Band in Minneapolis, so now, not only did I steal his girlfriend but the name of his band, having no original ideas of my own. Not a fan of mine, but who could blame him?

Another time, on my way to LAX from the Chateau Marmont, I stopped off at Fred Segal's, a clothing store on Santa Monica and Crescent Heights, to buy a gift for Emily. I took the advice of a valley girl working there, and when I got home presented the gift-packaged, pink shirt with HOLLYWOOD sequined on the front. Emily burst into bitter tears because it was so tasteless. At least it was the right size.

Since I was making real money (or so I thought), Emily wanted to take a real vacation. It made sense, and I relented, but I knew the momentum with the Blues Bar band would be lost. Ah, well.

We stayed with Emily's friends near Kings Road in London. She took me to the British Museum and showed me the Magna Carta, the Parthenon friezes, and the Egyptian exhibit with mummified cats. We saw a Tom Stoppard play starring Diana Rigg, who could be seen momentarily in her all. We ate in an excellent Indian restaurant. We attended the screening of *The Life of Brian*, where all the Pythons saw it for the first time, except for Terry Jones, who had directed it. None of them seemed enthusiastic about the film, but Em and I loved it. Michael Palin showed us his home (he had a life-size, mock antiaircraft gun in his garden). He took us out to dinner and got us tickets to a Dire Straits concert at the Hammersmith Odeon. We rented a car and drove into the rustic countryside to visit her "ex-beau" Andrea and his mother. He wore an ascot but reminded me of my drug buddy at Callison. We stopped to see Stonehenge the day before the solstice. The constables had erected a cyclone fence around the monoliths to keep out the crowds at sunrise next. The closest pub was in the Druid Motel (I still have the matches).

In 1978, China was not a tourist destination, but my travel agent got us into one of the first tourist groups. However, we were required to fly on an Air Ethiopia DC-8, which stopped over in Addis Ababa—the capital of Ethiopia. The cheap guitar I bought in London did not arrive with the other baggage but we had a nice, new Mercedes bus waiting. As we pulled away from the airport, we saw the lepers lined up along that sorry, dusty road. They were shouting and waving whatever they had at us, as we went by at forty miles an hour, raising a cloud of dust. We were shocked, but sort of excited by the entry into an obviously dangerous place. We checked into the Hilton, which was strategically placed on the top of a hill, guarded by a couple of shy-looking Ethiopian soldiers with World War II–vintage rifles.

The next morning, there was the driver and the Mercedes bus again. He drove us to the ruins of an ancient mud brick church, the ruins of a mud brick synagogue, then the mud brick ruins of an ancient mosque, then lunch at his brother's restaurant. The restaurant looked and smelled good, but we did not drink the water. In traditional Ethiopian cuisine, one gets flat bread as large as a tablecloth, and it is placed on the table. The various dishes are ladled onto the bread before you. They also have a local liquor made from honey, called "tesh." I had two.

We finally got back to the Hilton at cocktail time, but before the drinks arrived, both Emily and I began feeling sick. We dashed to the elevator, whose doors were way too slow. There was a standing ashtray in the elevator that I filled with lunch, and none too accurately. We made it to our bathroom to begin nine hours of tag-team vomiting. I had a tape recorder on which I continuously played a cassette of Bach fugues. Our eyes were dramatically bloodshot from the physical strain, but when we started vomiting blood we looked at each other and started laughing. This could be it. Maybe we were dying. The morning broke and we went down to the breakfast buffet wearing sunglasses and ate only watermelon. Everyone else had been through it, too. As soon as the wheels of our DC-8 retracted from the ground, I started feeling great again.

We landed and refueled at Bombay without deplaning. About a dozen young, uniformed Chinese soldiers came aboard and struggled with their seat belts. Now with the fresh crew, there was no English-speaking Chinese person on the aircraft. Somewhere over the Himalayas we were buffeted by a violent electrical storm and lightning struck the plane. Apparently the soldiers came from a culture where people are uninhibited about expressing their emotions, such as fear. As we made an emergency return to Bombay, the soldiers screamed; Em and I were laughing. The plane could crash into hell for all we cared. As long as it wasn't Addis Ababa. We refueled a second time and landed in Peking the next day.

The tour lasted three weeks, going to some places where they hadn't seen white people since the '30s. We saw an old woman with bound feet, and Uighur horsemen outside of Urumchi playing a type of polo with a headless goat. I got on my hands and knees to drink my fill of water coming out of the ground at an oasis in the Gobi Desert (everyone else watched me with their bottled orange soda in their hands. It was the best water I ever tasted). The Ming tombs were fabulous (and this was before the terra cotta armies had been uncovered). We had Peking duck in Beijing, and went to the Forbidden City, the Summer Palace, and the Great Wall.

On the return, we landed at Addis Ababa, but we did not have to leave the airport. My lost guitar was restored to me, and Emily and I said good-bye to our tour group. We flew to Cairo and checked into the Nile Hilton, guarded by two mean-looking Egyptian soldiers with Uzi machine guns. Posters and banners of Anwar Sadat were everywhere. We rode camels around the pyramids, went to Memphis and to the Cairo Museum, and saw a fifteen-hundred-year-old synagogue that was still operating (but was gone a few years later). The taxi driver who had taken us from the airport to the Nile Hilton was always outside the front door waiting for us. He said his name was Abdul. I told him mine was Johnny. By the third day, he sensed that we wanted to go somewhere out of the ordinary. "Would you like to see King Farouk's palace, Johnny?"

Abdul had been driving two hours through the mountainous white sand dunes of the Sahara. There was no other traffic. Emily looked at me and laughed. Of course we had told no one where we were going with a cabdriver named Abdul. We could easily just disappear. They shoot tourists in Luxor. Finally, we pulled up to an abandoned adobe ranch–style building beside a brackish lake. The screens on the windows were rusted and torn. Inside we found a large room in a marvelously advanced state of deterioration: the stuffed heads of some African animals were still on the walls, but the taxidermy had shrunk back from the teeth. There had obviously been a fire in the large kitchen. A plaque on the wall near the ruins of a billiard table proclaimed that in 1952, Winston Churchill had played the game during a visit with King Farouk. I should have pulled that one off the wall. I wandered upstairs to explore. I must have been high and dehydrated. There was a gorgeous bathroom with a Cadillac of a toilet, and, without thinking, I pissed in it. I could see the rainbow spectrum in the bubbles of my urine as I went to flush and the handle broke off in my hand. Embarrassed, I wandered down a long hallway. At the end I could see some women seated on mattresses. Then I realized King Farouk's palace had been converted into an Egyptian workingman's whorehouse! When Abdul returned us safely to the Hilton, I tipped him handsomely. We were delighted.

Next came Athens, where we checked into the King George Hotel near the Acropolis. We dined at its rooftop restaurant as the sun set, and watched the Parthenon's nighttime lights go on. You could see where the friezes in the British Museum went.

On the island of Ithaki (Ithaca—Odysseus's home) we rented motor scooters and, following a tourist map, found ourselves on the arid unpopulated half of the island, which was much bigger than we thought. Halfway around the island, the unpaved road became very tough. Em was physically challenged to her limit and bitched at me as if it were my fault. When a bungee cord got hopelessly wound around her scooter's mechanisms, I used a pocketknife to make it possible for us to continue. We got back at sunset, and the guy who rented us the scooters and sold us the map was pissed off that our bikes were beat to shit. Emily conveyed her displeasure and he shut up.

While we were gratefully eating and drinking by the harbor, we watched a little girl ecstatically riding a mechanical horse beside the kiosk. When the horse stopped she became annoyed and couldn't get the next coin in fast enough. The old man in the kiosk was beaming.

By the time we got back home, the summer was spent, and the Blues Brothers Band had formed. We went out to L.A. for the Emmys and saw them open for Steve Martin at the Universal Amphitheater. Things were moving very fast. I was twenty-six.

During one show that winter, there was a blizzard and Emily stayed at home. The after-party was near Gramercy Park and some of us took shelter in the apartment of Lorne's supermodel girlfriend, Susan Forristal. So did her sister Kate, a strawberry blonde bombshell. When I first met her, she had a hideously injured foot from a horse-riding accident. She joked about it. I accidentally stepped on it when trying to kiss her. She laughed. She was dating the artist Julian Schnabel while I was dating Emily, and that put us on equal footing; the attraction was real. She lost the foot and named her new prosthetic "Rita." So, in this blizzard, she and I found ourselves in a room alone and spent the night making passionate love. Franni mistakenly walked in while we were in flagrante delicto.

We began an affair. Emily, knowing intuitively, once announced to me that if I was screwing somebody on the side, make sure I didn't

get caught because she didn't want to hear about it. When Kate found a full-time boyfriend, we ended our affair, but I still loved her.

Mr. Mike invited Emily to write and perform in a new project for NBC, *Mr. Mike's Mondo Video*. Despite all the nasty things Michael O'Donoghue said in the press about *SNL*, Lorne still loved him and got him this deal, which he would executive produce as Michael directed, produced, cowrote, and had control over everything but himself. Mr. Mike knew nothing about direction. Emily put her best efforts and hopes on the line. In the end, NBC refused to broadcast, and the videotape was transferred to film and sold to New Line Cinema. At the opening at the Forum Theater in Times Square, first the projector broke down and then there was a sound problem, but it became apparent that Mr. Mike's sensibilities were better realized within the formats of *National Lampoon* or *SNL*. At the party afterward, the depressed principals and their significant others were treated to blue punch and the sounds of an all-girl punk band—the Clits. In my tuxedo, I stepped out and went next door to an amusement arcade with Franken and played the best pinball of my life. Al couldn't believe it. I racked up twenty games and had to leave it to return to Emily's side. She was not a happy camper.

A couple of years later, on another snowy night, there was a party at the "new" Blues Bar near the World Trade Center. Danny introduced me to an ex-girlfriend named Kelly. She was a knockout cover girl. I drove her home and she invited me up to her apartment and nature took its course.

That summer, when Emily was out at our rented house on Shelter Island, I had to come back into the city for business. I was in our apartment and the phone rang. It was Kelly. I told her never to call me there, but she said that she really needed to see me and fuck my

BEFORE *MONDO VIDEO* OPENING; AFTER OPENING © 1980 TOM DAVIS

SIGNIFICANT OTHER

brains out. The next day, before I left for Long Island, I called Emily and told her I was heading back. She asked me to bring her the mail, her Martin Amis book, and the cassette from the primitive answering machine.

I was not actually there when Emily and her best friend listened to the phone messages, but my whole conversation with Kelly was on it. As Emily later described it, their mouths were agape for an eight count before they wailed.

Within three days, Emily moved me into an available apartment on Eleventh Street whose front windows were at sidewalk level. Rhonda Coullet, from the *Lampoon* crowd, had once lived there. She told me there was a beloved old cat buried in the back courtyard I now shared with the Village Vanguard and a Chinese laundry.

A month later, Emily stopped by to see my new digs. There was a photograph of Kelly taped to the refrigerator, which she examined closely and exclaimed. "My God—she looks like your mother at that age!" Then she cried.

Kelly and I lasted a year. We both began finding long blonde hairs where they shouldn't be. I had slept with a blonde keyboardist. A month after we broke up, I saw Kelly's picture in a magazine with David Lee Roth. Last I heard she had married a doctor in New Jersey and had two kids.

11

LORNE

Al and I emerged from the cool stink of the Seventh Avenue subway into the stultifying atmosphere of Fiftieth Street. It was July
1975, and the whole twelve-mile concrete slab of Manhattan radi-
ated waves of heat. Three blocks later we entered 30 Rockefeller
Plaza. If you ever have to work in an office, it may be the best place
in the world. The delicious air-conditioning engulfed us as we
stepped onto black marble in the indirectly lit Deco lobby. All we
knew was that we were to be in Lorne Michael's office at noon. So,
what floor?

We joined the line at the information booth. A tall guy in front
of us asked the uniformed man behind the counter our question. We
introduced ourselves, and the tall guy said his name was Chevy
Chase. He was a writer, too. We walked to the proper elevator bank,

I craning my neck to behold the Diego Rivera murals on the vaulted ceiling and walls. I thought they depicted the laborious construction of Manhattan's skyscrapers, but it is now my understanding that the subject was commissioned as "Human intelligence in control of the forces of nature." Later, I would learn that the empty section above our elevators had once held the images of Marx and Lenin, and old man Rockefeller had them painted over. The mahogany elevators were operated by uniformed, old black guys working the big brass handles. They would be replaced by "modern" automatic elevators two years later, creating untold security and theft problems.

What an odd collection of people outside Lorne's office. We were all checking each other out and wondering what to think. There were Herb Sargent, Michael O'Donoghue (his friends called him Mr. Mike), Anne Beatts, Alan Zweibel, Tom Schiller, Chevy Chase, and Franken and Davis. Finally, the beautiful secretary, Kathy Minkowski ushered us into his office. Lorne was at his elegantly modest desk. From the window behind him you could see the Empire State Building. The other windows looked down onto St. Patrick's Cathedral. I recognized Jim Henson, sitting next to some guy in a suit named Dave Lazer. Then there was Dick Ebersol, a young, tanned NBC exec in a lime green sport coat and loafers with no socks.

Lorne launched into the first of a lifetime series of lectures on comic theory and the history of show business. Chevy sat on the windowsill behind him. There was a potted plant with its own aerosol pump fine-spray water bottle for its shiny leaves. Chevy took the mister, waited until Lorne paused, made the sound of a sneeze, and sprayed the back of Lorne's neck. It was the first Big Laugh, and Lorne loved it.

Lorne wanted to get some commercial parodies filmed in late August (the first *Saturday Night Live* show was slated for October 11). I rode with Mr. Mike and Anne Beatts in a BMW with a sunroof, which they had borrowed from their manager, Barry Secunda. From the backseat, I was amazed to see how quickly the vegetation took over once we left Manhattan and traveled up the Sawmill Parkway, canopied with vine-covered trees. We were going to try to shoot a dozen pieces in two days, and the locations were in Westchester around Millwood, Briarcliff, and Mount Kisco.

Lorne had penned two of the commercial parodies himself. The first appeared to be a recruitment ad. Garrett Morris was in a full-dress marine uniform walking down Main Street "looking for a few good men," the actual slogan in a contemporaneous recruiting campaign. But this was punctuated by a gay guy in a sport coat (Lorne) talking MOS in Garrett's ear, then putting his arm on his shoulder and leading him away.

The other was a parody of a cigarette ad (Lark cigarettes—a roving candid camera would catch members of the public responding to the off-camera cry, "Show us your Larks!" and the people would smile excitedly and wave their packs of smokes). This was *Show Us Your Guns!*

On location, we finally found ourselves spending some time getting to know Lorne. He was from Toronto; he had been half the comedy team of Lorne and Hart, who had a successful comedy/variety show on Canadian national television. Now his ex-partner was a successful Toronto lawyer. Lorne said he hoped Al and I would work for him for the rest of our lives. I started calling him "Boss."

Zweibel and I did a parody of a beer ad. We played depressed patients in a psych ward who brighten up when an orderly comes in with a tray of a dozen bottles of Spud Beer—"the only beer made from potatoes."

Franken and Davis wrote two other pieces, including the *K-Put Price Tag Sticker Gun*. "Imagine—a whole twelve-pound turkey for only ninety-nine cents!" as a fat lady prices her own groceries. "Isn't that amazing?!" Then there was the piece where Gilda and Laraine are housewives shopping in a grocery store (the same as K-Put), where they are encouraged to sample an economical casserole with a higher tuna-to-noodle ratio. They sample. "Mmm—that's good." And when they swallow, they are told by an off-camera voice that they are eating Felina cat food. This was inspired by news reports that elderly people on budgets were really eating cat food.

Chevy wrote a parody of a ridiculous multiblade shaver that began with a caveman who attempts to shave. Al got the part because of his low forehead and poured-cement physique. The shoot was somewhere on top of the Palisades—a hundred-foot cliff overlooking the Hudson River. Knowing Al would take chances, I warned him not to try anything near the precipice. After he put on his caveman fur wardrobe, makeup glued on his beard with spirit gum. The fumes caused him to pass out cold, falling back onto the ground. When he regained consciousness, his first thought was that he must have fallen off the cliff. But the glue had dried and Al seemed fine again, so the shoot resumed. The scene was beside a murky pool among some rocks, where the caveman was to apply some water to his face. On the second take, Al plunged his hands into the water and cut himself on an unseen shard of glass. It was decided Al should be taken to the hospital to have the cut cleaned and be given a tetanus shot. That was the end of the shoot. As Al was being helped back to wardrobe, he was stung by a bee. I remember director Davey Wilson calling Al "a real trouper," but I saw him turn and roll his eyes. Al's performance was saved in the edit. Anne Beatts said if Mr. Mike had done it, he would have quit after the spirit gum.

So, we were well represented in the preproduction commercial parodies. But we were shut out of the first three shows and Al wanted to quit and go back to L.A. He wanted to be in the cast, so Lorne promised us that it would happen in a few more months.

It was the Boss's birthday in November, and we didn't have money to buy him a present. We were still eating soup at home on Eighty-sixth Street, Al's grandparents' apartment. But there, in the back of a closet, we found Grandpa Simon's Shriner's fez, complete with tassel—like Groucho's, or Stan's and Ollie's. We presented Lorne with that, and he was gracious enough in accepting it, but we never saw him put it on, nor did we ever see it after that. What were we thinking?

The first electronic game in amusement halls and bars was called Pong, and a machine appeared in the office. The screen was divided into two halves, each with a "paddle" on the far side that moved up or down according to a knob for each player—so it was hand-eye coordination anticipating where the "ball" would go. You could put spin on it. Al and I became proficient at it. Zweibel wrote a series of Pong pieces where you could hear two dumb college kids talking as they played the game. If the discussion was about girls, and one guy admitted failure, he would miss his shot. Since the Pong game could not be programmed, it required two actors who could recite the pieces as they won or lost on cue. Al and I could do it.

So the Pong machine was brought down to the studio and a television camera looked dead on into the game, requiring Al and me to stand off to either side, making it physically even more difficult. Al had to do it left-handed. A boom microphone was positioned overhead, and they rolled tape in the darkened studio so there would be no light reflections in the Pong screen. We had memorized three pieces. It being exceedingly difficult, we muffed a few times and had to start over because it could only be done as one continuous take. Apparently Lorne had been watching the monitor in his office on the ninth floor overlooking Studio 8H. He came out of the darkness and yelled at us for wasting studio time, turned on his heel, and disappeared. We realized that he didn't understand how difficult it was to do what we were doing, but we didn't want to point that out because then the Boss might can the whole thing. So we aced it, it got on the air, it was well received, and we did three more a couple of weeks later.

Then we were warming up the dress audience, doing some silly routine we used to do at Dudley's involving the nature of comedy and why it's funny to get hit in the face with a pie. Al would always have to be the one to get hit with this shaving cream in an alu-

the
FRANKEN
and
DAVIS
show

minum-foil pie tin. Al would milk the situation by being obviously reluctant to be hit. On this occasion, one of our stand-up microphones tipped the pie so that I missed Al and it flew into the audience, landing upside down on the lap of the wife of a big NBC executive. As we were leaving the studio, Lorne pounced on us: "If I didn't think it would bum everybody out, I'd fire you guys on the spot!"

In those days, if a big piece got cut, there could sometimes be several minutes left at the end of the show. Al and I made a point always to be ready with a Franken and Davis piece to fill that gap. In Elliott Gould's first show on January 11, 1976, Lorne put us on in that "graveyard spot." We did our *Bureau of Whiteman Affairs,* based on the premise of what would have happened if Native Americans had won the war with the white man? It was an interview television show, *Pow Wow with the Press.* We wore feathered headdresses and talked about the genetic problems the white man had with tobacco. "I mean, I enjoy a pipe now and again, but these people can't stop once they start. It's disgusting." Also, some groups of white men objected to stereotyping in movies and the use of their tribe's name for Lacrosse teams, like "the Cleveland Kikes—with the mascot of the little screaming rabbi." This bit was in the show that won us our first set of Emmys, and we received a poster from Native American activist Chris Spotted Eagle, on which he inscribed, "Franken & Davis—Lay it on!"

Then Al hit one out of the park. His brother Owen was covering the '76 presidential campaign and he got a pass for Al to come along on the press bus. Al once asked presidential hopeful Ronald Reagan, "Sir, in California you arrest people for smoking marijuana because you claim it causes brain damage, yet you are also against the mandatory use of motorcycle helmets. Wouldn't you say it's worse to have chunks of asphalt in your brain than marijuana?" Then later he asked President Gerald Ford's press secretary, Ron Nessen, if he would like to host *Saturday Night Live,* and he said yes! Though much of *SNL's* political satire was insulting to his administration (probably more than he knew), Gerald Ford pretaped, "Live from New York, it's Saturday Night!" This was a coup for Lorne. Franken and Davis were now writing top-notch political satire, along with Dan Aykroyd, Jim Downey, and Chevy Chase, in the Ford/Carter debates. For my twenty-fourth birthday, Lorne had twenty-four cases of Heineken delivered to the Eighty-sixth Street apartment.

Paul Simon is probably Lorne's best friend. They were introduced by Edie Baskin, Lorne's photographer friend from L.A., and the daughter of the Baskin half of Baskin-Robbins. She had moved to New York City and was dating Paul. They were a fun couple—he's short and she's about six foot two inches. Edie became the show's photographic designer. Paul's song "50 Ways To Leave Your Lover" was written about their breakup, or so she told me when we dated briefly. Lorne's girlfriend was Susan Forristal, a smart and successful cover girl from Texas. She had dated Danny briefly. Lorne's ex-wife, Rosie Shuster, daughter of Shuster from the Canadian comedy team Wayne and Shuster, was gorgeous and really funny. She and Danny began dating, but surreptitiously, because Dan thought Lorne would be upset, and they were friends from back in Toronto. This went on for months, and, of course, Lorne knew about it the whole time. Lorne is anything but jealous.

The Killer Bees from the first year was Lorne and Rosie's idea. The premise was to put the cast in ridiculous costumes and make them act. The first one was a *Honeymooners* episode with Dan as Norton, Belushi as Ralph, and Gilda as Alice. Franken and Davis were assigned to write up the *Honeymooners* script. It went over all

right, but Belushi hated it. So Lorne and Rosie started writing more just to irk John. According to reviewers and some NBC testing people, the audience didn't care for it either. Lorne said, "I'm going to push *The Killer Bees* down the throat of America," and he did. When Elliott Gould hosted, *The Killer Bees* got their own whole huge sketch and John stole the scene by parodying the villainous bandito in *The Treasure of the Sierra Madre* and making his springy antennae bob during his speeches. The audience went nuts. Lorne and Paul Simon had Bee costumes made up and wore them to the Mardi Gras in New Orleans. *SNL* would be back there in a year. Lorne and Susan bought a magnificent apartment on Central Park, adjacent to Paul's. They had a door between them that was never locked.

Lorne and Danny wrote a brilliant *Alsatian Restaurant* sketch for the Fran Tarkenton show (Al's and my choice for host) at the end of January 1977. Bill Murray and Jane Curtin played first-time patrons in an exclusive, family-operated Alsatian bistro in the West Village. They are charmed by its Old World atmosphere. Danny is the unctuous owner-server who welcomes them, tells them the selection of haute cuisine, takes their order, and disappears through the swinging kitchen door, behind which a screaming argument ensues with his wife, the chef (Gilda). Their terrified daughter (Laraine) tries to entertain the two patrons by blowing into a woodwind recorder, then begging them to help her escape. It had a brilliant ending, with Dan calling for Gilda to present the check, which she stabs into his back so he collapses and dies on the table. There is a pause, Billy pulls the perforated bill off the knife, looks at the total and says to Jane, "Now that's not bad."

The network wanted *SNL* to fill a prime-time special on a Sunday night, and Lorne agreed we'd do a live broadcast from the New Orleans Mardi Gras with a million-dollar budget. The network blinked and we were off. "The Big Easy" was an ironic name by the time it was over. Our challenge was to use real locations as backdrops for sketches, requiring actors to change costumes, sometimes as they ran from location to location. That was difficult enough to do at home in 8H.

We stayed in a funky, grand hotel, the Maison Dupuy, with ancient fourteen-foot doors and windows. I brought an acoustic guitar, which I played for a moment and put down. My next-door neighbor, Laraine, opened the door between our rooms. "Play some more—you sound good." She was my pal.

Alan Zweibel was depressed at the time and Mr. Mike gave him a wine sack with LITHIUM printed on the side.

The highlight of the week was the party with the Morris family. Garrett invited everybody—cast, crew, and writers—to the house where he grew up in a black middle-class neighborhood. It must have been Sunday by the way they were all dressed—and what a family. The food was fantastic, and the boys could go back to the garage to smoke and drink. It went all day. Anne Beatts told me that Garrett said, growing up in New Orleans as a little boy, he knew that where the pavement started, he was not to go beyond that point.

Camera-blocking problems were complicated by the fact that Belushi had fallen in with a motorcycle gang who promptly loaned him a Harley. He could really ride, and he looked like a pirate with his bandanna tied on his head. As he sped by, I said a prayer.

That night Danny took me to meet his new acquaintance, Hunter S. Thompson, who wouldn't unlatch the chain on his hotel room door to let us in. He didn't want to share, I think.

There were ominous signs the morning of broadcast. I saw joyless black ladies in a ramshackle warehouse by the water. They were breaking open oysters with small hammers in their rubber-gloved hands. I had a Bloody Mary for breakfast, bellied up to a bar where two patrons got into an altercation. Like every bar fight I've ever seen, this one lasted two seconds. The loser pulled himself to his feet and ordered another drink. I pointed out that he ought to do something to staunch the copious flow of blood from his nose, and he told me to fuck off, so I did. Walking outside on the sidewalk, I watched as a young woman tried to parallel park and trapped her boyfriend's legs between her bumper and the parked car behind her. He pounded furiously on the trunk of her car. When she finally realized what was going on, she panicked and spun the wheels in reverse. I kept walking.

The show started with Danny as the newly inaugurated President Carter, in party mode, riding on the statue of Andrew Jackson opon his rearing horse in Jackson Square. There were ten thousand drunken revelers who roared at Danny's cue, "Live from New Orleans, it's Sunday Night!" So far, so good. I had written a thing for Belushi on a small balcony of the Cabildo (the original seat of the Spanish government) overlooking the same square now packed with several thousand drunken people. He came out in Mussolini's full-dress uniform, and he was a great Il Duce. The crowd roared when he shouted, "Itsa gonna be *some* party—I'm a tella you!" I'll never forget the image of Belushi hanging on the back of a three-wheeled police vehicle with its flashing blue emergency light, parting the crowd as he tore off his shirt like the Hulk, in order to have the jump on his costume change at the next set.

While there were two Randy Newman songs from a concert hall, the big thing the show was counting on to cut to whenever there was a hangup was Jane Curtin and Buck Henry at a *Weekend Update* news booth looking out on to the Bacchus parade. This became unviable when there was an accident upstream where a car fatally struck a pedestrian, and the revelers began pelting Buck and Jane with more than Mardi Gras beads. Talk about raining on my parade.

Al and I were watching as Gilda, dressed as the geriatric Emily Litella, emerged from a wardrobe tent and tried to run to the next set. The crowd grabbed her and some lout started to do mock oral sex on her. We stepped in and grabbed her back without getting violent, and with Gilda remaining completely cool and focused. Never mind. On to the next.

Michael O'Donoghue had written a thing for Belushi based on

an infamous incident in the late '60s, when the renowned, over-weight trumpeter Al Hirt was once on a Mardi Gras float and got hit in the face with a brick. Naturally, we had a Hit Al Hirt in the Face with a Brick contest, and Mr. Mike employed my throwing arm to stand beside him off camera launching Styrofoam bricks at John's face as he tried to play the trumpet. The wind was blowing and too few bricks were hitting his face, so John was moving his face to catch the bricks. I was laughing hysterically.

After the show I remember being under a bridge near the farmers' market, surrounded by cops, and Danny insisted on giving me a motorcycle lesson. He had to content himself with my getting it only into second gear. By the time I finally decided to head back to my room, I stumbled out of a Bourbon Street bar and nearly fell over a couple fucking right there on the curb. Iko iko.

From a ratings and viewership standpoint, the show was a disaster. Nobody watched it, and I guess it is unshowable even today. I found it unforgettable. Thank you, Boss.

During the first three years Lorne never locked his office, so we could use the beautiful space at night and on Saturday mornings. Sometimes we'd find a bottle of champagne and drink it. One sunny spring Saturday morning, Al and I were in there trying to work through the fatigue and write some *Update* jokes. I opened the window that is a straight seventeen-story drop to the sidewalk entrance facing the skating rink. Lorne had a few toys for his desk that he loved. His favorite was from the '50s—a small metal television truck with a little television camera and cameraman on top, and the NBC logo on the side. For some reason, it was on the windowsill. I was sitting on the other side of the room; the sun must have warmed up some old batteries, and the toy suddenly moved forward and then made a right turn out the window. Al saw it, too. We couldn't believe it. I rushed to the elevators, but by the time I got to ground zero, there was no trace of it for me to retrieve. In the writers' meeting on Monday, Lorne was perturbed and asked where his truck was. I didn't have the balls to tell him what happened, and Al had the intelligence to keep his mouth shut. No one would believe it anyway.

Sorry, Boss. After that he locked the office.

Susan gave Lorne a pair of custom-made red rattlesnake-skin cowboy boots for his birthday, and he really liked them. One day Tom Schiller and I walked into the seventeenth floor men's room. As we stepped up to the floor-length urinals, Tom motioned toward the stalls and winked—there were Lorne's boots under one of the doors. We started a mock conversation where we said as many derogatory things about Lorne as possible.

>Schiller: "What was he thinking of? What a disaster."
>
>I: "I know. Maybe he's starting to lose it, finally."
>
>Still no sound from Lorne.
>
>Schiller: "He's turning into an asshole."
>
>I: "I'll say."

Finally we left and could barely suppress our giggling out in the hallway. A week later it was the Christmas break and when we got back in January, Lorne's office had a new executive bathroom with a shower. I have it on good authority that when the show was produced by Bob Tischler and Dick Ebersol, Eddie Murphy returned to host. In the middle of the Monday writers' pitch meeting, Eddie took his gorgeous girlfriend in there and gave her a good jazzing. That must have been a difficult meeting. When we returned to the show in '86, Boss had commandeered the men's room on the ninth floor with his own personal key.

Lorne was in his office with *SNL* bandleader-guitarist G. E. Smith when I walked in to pop the question. It was early 1978 and I was at the top of my game.

>I: "Hey Lorne, why don't we have the Grateful Dead on the show?"
>
>Lorne: "Hmmm . . . weren't they big in the sixties?"
>
>I: "No one sells more tickets than they do."
>
>Lorne: "What do you think, G.E.?"
>
>G.E.: "They're not happening."
>
>Lorne: "This is TV, Tom. No one knows who they are."

So that week I wrote a live commercial parody where Gilda and Laraine played characters offering testimonials with their names supered beneath them as they spoke—"Donna Godchaux" and

"Candace Brightman" (the real names of the GD singer and lighting director—and my new acquaintances). The piece got on the air. On the following Monday I was summoned into the Boss's office.

> Lorne: "Did you use some real Grateful Dead names in that sketch?"
>
> I: "Yes. I always use real names."
>
> Lorne: "Well, don't do that again. I got all these phone calls."
>
> I: "But you said that this was TV and nobody knows who they are."
>
> Lorne sighed: "Oh, all right. I'll book them in the fall."

The season opener in the fall of '78 had no host. Mayor Ed Koch introduced the show, which featured the Rolling Stones, a major coup for the Boss. Where else were you going to see them live on television? The ratings had been rising steadily—cable television was still in its infancy, satellite television didn't exist, and the three major networks still dominated the airwaves. *SNL* was commanding an excellent share of the ratings, and the fourteen-to-twenty-four-year-old viewers were staying at home on Saturday nights to party with the show.

During the first two years, the writers were each given six tickets per show and instructed by Lorne not to give them just to show business people. By the third year, we each got two tickets, while the Boss filled the audience with show business royalty. (In 2003, each writer got two tickets to every third show, but there were three times as many writers.) But by anybody's standards 1978 was an exemplary year (except for Michael O'Donoghue, who had left the show and was trash-talking to the press. To me he said, "Hey, Davis—not even the Rolling Stones can save your sorry show").

On Wednesday night the Stones rehearsed in a small studio on the West Side. Except for a few roadies, the audience was Howard Shore (Lorne's longtime buddy from Toronto and the musical director and composer of the *SNL* theme), his musical talent coordinator Janine Dreyer, Paul Shaffer, and myself. We sat on wooden crates and watched that band play as hard as I'd seen them play before sixty thousand people. Same thing when they camera-blocked the next day, and by Saturday Mick's voice was hoarse, but that's the way they did it. They had a medley of three songs in one spot in the show—"Beast of Burden" "Respectable," and "Shattered."

Danny, Al, and I wrote a backstage sketch that involved a trailer, the Stones, and Belushi as an embattled backstage manager. The cast played characters trying to get in. At first, design tried cutting up a real trailer to get it up the freight elevators, but they wound up making one out of plywood and paint—it looked perfect, and cost more than the real thing. Al played a Deadhead who sneaks in and is somehow on the top of the trailer. During camera blocking, he told me that he overheard a conversation between Mick and Charlie inside the trailer.

> Charlie: "So when are we going to film this show?"
> Mick: "No, Charlie . . . it's a live television broadcast."
> Charlie: "Really? Live television?"
> Mick: "Yeah. Like Ed Sullivan."

This sketch was cut between dress and air.

Danny and Jim Downey wrote a wonderful Tom Snyder interview with Mick Jagger playing himself (with dignity and a sense of humor). Danny also wrote another *Dave Mable: Danger Probe*. Each episode began with Dave Mable pulling another amazing file from his Danger Probe File Cabinet to set the scene. This week a Hare Krishna (Belushi) and a San Francisco street mime (Gilda) were being interrogated by the Paraguayan junta (Bill, Laraine, and Keith Richards) in a subchamber of *Policia* headquarters. This sketch was at the end of the show, and after the Stones' performance on air it became clear that Keith did not remember the sketch or his part in it, so I donned his uniform and tinted glasses from wardrobe and took his place.

The following Monday evening we got a call from the Stones' road manager. Keith had misplaced his lucky switchblade, which he called his "security"; he thought he might have left it up in the office somewhere. We scoured the place and couldn't find it.

Lorne made good on his promise and booked the Grateful Dead on the show hosted by Buck Henry, which aired November 11, 1978. On the preceding Tuesday, around noon, I met with my heroes in a hotel room overlooking Central Park South. They were all there, being rowdy and jovial. They literally picked me up and stood me on a bed.

> Bill Kreuztmann: "So, Davis—what songs do you think we should play?"
>
> I: "How about songs where Jerry can play pedal steel guitar because it sounds so good on TV?"
>
> Jerry (to the others): "Okay, get him down from there."

They took me off my pedestal and never again asked me for my opinion. What they did choose to play shocked me. Their first song was "Casey Jones":

> *Driving that train,*
> *High on cocaine,*
> *Casey Jones you better,*
> *Watch your speed.*
> *Trouble ahead,*
> *Trouble behind,*
> *And you know that notion,*
> *Just crossed my mind.*

What I discovered was that the drummers, Kreutzmann and Mickey Hart, were the ones who actively wanted to be on *SNL*. They watched the show and hung out with Belushi. Garcia was the one who did *not* want to be on television, but he was going along with the Flow, as was his wont to do. The music camera blocking on Thursday at noon was very nearly a disaster. The Grateful Dead sound crew was rebuffed by union guys who didn't care who they were—*they* did the sound just fine, thank you. Meanwhile, the band was on the stage running through their numbers. Of course, Jerry did it differently every time, occasionally with his back to the camera. Director Davey Wilson was old school hit-your-mark, find-the-lens, say-your-lines. The band was standing there waiting for blocking to end when Davey spoke through the P.A. from the control room:

> Davey: "Jerry—where are you going to be when you do your solo?"
>
> Jerry: "I don't know."
>
> Davey: "Don't you want to be on-camera?"

Jerry: "Not particularly. I don't give a shit."

Davey: ". . . (silence) . . . (click)."

By music rehearsal during dinner break on Saturday, the *SNL* sound guys were still annoyed with the GD crew. I was in the middle with the proverbial tiger by the tail—but I asked for it, didn't I? I was privy to a discussion where putting LSD in the union coffee machine was proposed.

I: "**Absolutely *not*! Those are *my* union guys and that would *not* be cool.**"

GD sound guy: "Okay, Davis—relax . . . heh, heh, heh."

I was in the control room for the first song ("Casey Jones"), and Jerry was red hot. The show was very good. Danny did "Rov-Co Chinch Ranch—make your wife a valuable chinchilla fur coat right in your own home. Isn't that amazing?!" There was a *Samurai Optometrist,* Buck did another *Uncle Roy*—lascivious babysitting for the innocent little girls, Gilda and Laraine. I wrote a *Rasputin* sketch for Belushi as the guy who wouldn't die, and for *Update,* Bill Murray's

Celebrity Interview with Elizabeth Taylor (Belushi), who is eating an entire broiled chicken. There was *Nick the Nightclub Singer* (Nick Sands) set in a cinder block bar in the Nevada desert. Kreutzmann was an extra with a line. Bill Murray told me later, "I got over to Kreutzmann, and as we did our lines I looked into his eyes—and wow! It threw me for a second."

After the show, Lorne was a bit irked that so many Deadheads and Hell's Angels had finagled so many tickets to the show, and that they seemed to be more excited about the music than the comedy. But it was a very good show and "Casey Jones" is featured on a video collection of *SNL*'s best musical performances.

After the show, the party started up in my office on the seventeenth floor. I had a toy gun that shot a light beam, and if you hit a foot-tall cowboy in his photosensitive heart, he would collapse. I thought I had become quite skilled at it until Bob Weir did the last line off a mirror, which he then held up as he turned his back on the cowboy on the file cabinet across the room. He aimed into the mirror and fired the beam so it bounced off and brought down the little hombre with a single shot. Then we headed for the Blues Bar and partied until the sun came up.

My dream had come true. Thank you, Lorne.

The show after next was Walter Matthau, and on Monday, the murders and mass suicide of the San Franciscan Christian cult of Jim Jones was the biggest story in the world. It was my raison d'être as an *SNL* comedy writer to always try to find something funny about major disasters in the news when they happened . . . dark comedy, to be sure. In the pitch meeting I suggested having the whole audience playing dead. Lorne had already received a warning from Standards and Practices not to touch it. Walter Matthau literally got on his knees and supplicated Lorne not to touch it. I found an AP picture of a parrot on a fence with the bodies in the background, and wrote a *News Update* story about the bird, to no avail.

So Al and I jammed on what kind of characters Matthau could play. I said that I had recently been watching Julia Child's show where she actually cut herself with a knife. Al jumped up like Archimedes: "Let's have her bleed to death!" The piece wrote itself in an hour, but after read-thru, Matthau nixed it because it was a "cooking show bit." I insisted that it was not a cooking show bit, but a piece about bleeding to death, spurting blood, etcetera, but our host was too old to sink his teeth into it. The next week our host was Eric Idle, who recognized the skit, and Lorne gave it to Danny, who aced it. We used one of those large insecticide sprayers that looks like a fire extinguisher. It was filled with lots of red dye in water, pumped up so it flowed through plastic tubing that went up Dan's leg and ended at his wrist under the wardrobe. At the right moment, he cut open the tubing with the serrated knife he was using to cut a chicken. Nobody who has ever done that show has done it better than Dan Aykroyd, and we all know it.

A year later, when Eric hosted again, Bob Dylan was the musical guest featuring the new tunes off his Jesus album. The joke that week was "You gotta serve somebody, it might be the devil or it might be the Lorne, but you gotta serve somebody."

I dropped by Lorne's apartment one night. He was watching television with the NBC head of programming, Brandon Tartikoff. They were tuned in to the premier of a Steven Spielberg–produced show called *Amazing Stories*. We saw three stories in an hour of viewing. As it ended, I, mimicking an old Bob and Ray bit, remarked, "The only thing amazing is that so many dull stories could be collected in one place," and then, "Maybe they should call it *Pretty Amazing Stories*." Looking at their faces, I finally figured out, through my toxic haze, that the show was Tartikoff's baby. It was canceled two weeks later, but Lorne knew he couldn't take me anywhere.

I remember Lorne brought me with him to a party at a posh Central Park apartment, and there I met Abbie Hoffman. He was still hiding from the law. In fact, this might have been a fund-raiser for him. I told the man I especially admired the time he dumped a bag of money from an upper tier onto the floor of the New York stock exchange, and brought the whole system to a screeching halt as the floor traders scrambled to rake in the fluttering snowstorm of currency.

Abbie: "You know what was great about that? It was only a bag of one hundred single-dollar bills."

The next year, I beseeched Lorne to book the Grateful Dead again. I crawled onto the table in a meeting room and clenched my hands. I told Lorne I would never ask him for another favor. He booked them. They appeared on the show hosted by Richard Benjamin and Paula Prentiss. They played "Lost Sailor" into "Saint of Circumstance," and later, their arrangement of "Good Lovin'." Reading Phil Lesh's 2005 memoir, *Searching for the Sound,* I was amused that in his recollection, they appeared on *SNL* only once.

Five years of cumulative exhaustion, the departures of Belushi and Aykroyd, and the desire to quit while still ahead led Lorne and the collective "we" that was *SNL* to decide to fold our tent and try something else. Lorne gifted everybody with cigarette lighters that were shaped like 30 Rock with the inscription, NICE WORKING WITH YOU.

When Jean Doumanian, the SNL talent coordinator, was announced by NBC as the new producer of the continuing *Saturday Night Live,* the collective "we" saw it as betrayal by her and the network. Although Jean may not have deserved all the scorn and vicious reviews, she walked right into that buzz saw. She made the mistake of believing that the power went with the chair behind the desk in Lorne's office. Ironically, being a talent coordinator, you'd think she might have known more about it. She did not appreciate that Lorne was more than lucky. He is brilliant, talented, and funny.

Lorne bought office space in the Brill Building on Forty-ninth and Broadway. The Art Deco structure was completed in 1931 and got its name from the Brill Brothers, who owned the clothing store on the first floor (and later the entire building). The Depression made it difficult for businesses to rent new space—except for music publishing, which was evolving out of West Twenty-eighth Street's "Tin Pan Alley." By 1950, you could enter the Brill Building with a song in your head, go to one office to have an arrangement and lead sheet written up, go to another floor to have it duplicated, go to another floor to rent out a studio for an hour to cut a demo using singers and musicians who were hanging around, and then shop it to publishers, also in the building. By 1960, there were 160 music businesses in this building, whose halls echoed with footsteps the likes of Doc Pomus, Phil Spector, Carole King, and Neil Diamond.

In 1980, Lorne bought up the eighth and ninth floors and built his state-of-the-art edit house, Broadway Video (Paul Simon had a recording studio on the tenth floor). He also got a five-picture deal with MGM, headed by the imperious Freddie Fields. Lorne assigned Tom Schiller to write a screenplay, and Jim Downey and Franken and Davis to write another one, and gave us offices. We decided to parody Orwell's *1984*

JIM DOWNEY, ANTICHRIST © 1981
TOM DAVIS

and several other movies of the negative utopia genre such as *THX 1138* and *Logan's Run,* and include a subplot involving the Devil and evangelic End of Days. I like writing fast first drafts, but Downey, who was in one of his depressive, slow-moving modes, insisted on conceiving the whole thing before writing it out. Al was now deferring first to Downey's judgment and, admittedly, his brilliant comic sensibilities, rather than mine. This meant that Al and I took notes as Downey sprawled on a couch and rambled. By the time we submitted our second draft, in March 1982, almost two years had passed.

In the meantime, Tom Schiller, working with Laila Nabulsi as his producer, had written, directed, edited, and finished his movie, *Nothing Lasts Forever.* (Laila had been a close associate of Belushi and the Blues Brothers and produced several Schiller reels.) It featured Bill Murray, Dan Aykroyd, Frank Jaffe, and Imogene Coca, among others, in a delightful feature-length film. However, MGM saw it as an art film that did not test well, and they refused to distribute it. That did not bode well for our screenplay.

We met in the Broadway Video conference room, looking down on the Great White Way with the Rivoli Theater just across from us. Lorne sat at one end of the table with his old friend and adviser, John Head, and Franken and Davis and Downey sat across from Freddie Fields and his guy in a suit with an attaché case. The bad blood between Lorne and Freddie was palpable. Our screenplay was entitled *1985,* the year we intended our *1984* parody to run. The three of us then read the entire screenplay, line by line, in the course of two hours. Mr. Fields did not laugh once. When "The End" was read, he looked at his watch and announced that he had to make some phone calls, and that was that. Only Schiller got his film made, but it's still buried in a mountain of hateful bureaucracy so that for it to be released, someone would have to reimburse MGM.

I showed *1985* to Jerry Garcia, who read it and said, "Sorry—I didn't like it." Lorne said only good things about it, and as late as 2004, his secretary called me and asked if I could send a couple of copies to Lorne, who wanted to show it to some new writers.

Belushi's memorial was held at St. John the Divine on the border of Harlem, 112th and Amsterdam. It's a Gothic cathedral. I rode to it in a limousine with Mr. Mike, Wendie Malick, and Emily. He and I dropped the girls off at the entrance and stayed in the car long enough to snort some heroin.

Belushi was of Albanian extraction, and there was an orthodox Albanian priest. John's mother, ethnically unrestrained in her grief, at one point cried out to his wife, "Judy—how could you!?" as if it were her fault. Danny's eulogy was brave and brilliant. He started out by saying, "I *so* did not want to have to do this." Jim Belushi recalled a childhood moment when he literally was following in his brother's footprints in the snow.

My memory of this event is so flawed that it demonstrates how I sublimated this catastrophe. I remembered sitting with Dan and Judy Belushi in the upstairs lounge on a 747 returning to New York City from L.A.. They were voicing concerns about John "being alone" in Los Angeles. A week later I was in Belushi's Morton Street house where we all huddled in shock when Danny came in and let loose his enormous feelings. I was catatonic. The funeral, the memory of which I had telescoped with the memorial, took place on Martha's Vineyard. I was in John and Judy's house the night before. The simple but elegant structure had once been owned by Robert McNamara. It was snowing lightly as I stepped outside to watch Danny conduct a band of brothers with rifles in a three-shot salute to his dead partner. The next day, I cannot remember the funeral except that John was asleep in the open casket off to the side. On the way out, we all filed past. I touched his hand. It was cold, but I'd seen him look worse.

Outside Lorne and Susan came up to me. She leaned to my ear as if to kiss me, whispering, "You know, Tom . . . we worry about you, too." Lorne asked me if I'd put a joint in the casket. I could have said "yes," but instead I said something like, "My expensive pot isn't going to do him any good anymore."

A couple of months later Lorne and Susan got married on a sunny day at their place in Amagansett, and they invited everybody. Emily and I drove to it in my black, four-door, straight-eight, H-on-the-column '48 Dodge. Al and I had hired one of those advertising biplanes to pull a sign behind it: MAZEL TOV, LORNE AND SUSAN, and then buzz the place a couple of times. Jack Nicholson wore a blood-red silk suit. It became a midsummer night's dream. There were lots of bushes and sand dunes, and a few relationships were made, and some were broken, in the moonlight. Kate Forristal wore a sailor suit bridesmaid's dress and she was the prettiest girl I'd ever seen. As we were kissing in the lilacs, we saw Jack romancing the younger sister of a famous actress. We were all given party favors, which included glass ashtrays with Lorne and Susan's Picasso-like images, as drawn by Tom Schiller.

Franken and Davis toured lots of colleges. The act was tight, and Al asked Lorne for a favor. Would he produce a Franken and Davis concert to be sold as a Broadway Video VHS?

Lorne: "All right."

We found a college not too far from New York City that had a nice new theater. Stockton State was stuck out in the middle of the Blair Witch scrub forests twenty-five miles north of Atlantic City, which is where we all stayed in a big casino (Lorne's choice). Design, Leo Yoshimura, Eugene Lee, and Keith Raymond, got students to paint our backdrop with two dozen folk portraits of Al and me. We taped two shows, back to back. The students were very enthusiastic, but seemed less than sober, if not rowdy. This irked Al, but I didn't care. Our act is preserved, and it was good. Three pieces appeared to be crowd favorites, the first being Al's monologue in which he talked to the audience while hand drawing the continental United States, state by state, with a magic marker on a large piece of white cardboard on an easel. It was a brilliant trick.

Then we had a sure-fire piece that we had written that summer on Sagaponack Beach in the Hamptons. We were throwing the football back and forth when Al said, "How about a piece about what to do if you're drunk and you absolutely have to drive?" I jumped on that idea like a hawk on a mouse. It was written in ten minutes.

Al: "We have a guest with us tonight, who travels around the country, speaking to college audiences like yourself, on what to do if you're drunk and you absolutely *have* to drive. Please welcome, from the Jack Daniel's Distillery, Mr. Frank Wade."

(Tom enters with two glasses of ice and an unopened half pint of Jack Daniel's Black Label. He stumbles on the talk show set and takes his seat.)

Al: "Whoops—welcome, Mr. Wade—have a seat."

Tom: "Well, thank you, Al . . . and let me start by saying that we at Jack Daniel's in Lynchburg enjoy our own product, and we want our customers to enjoy our product for many wonderful years of drinking to come."

(Tom has opened the half pint after using his thumbnail to cut the plastic seal, and pours generously in what is obviously the glass intended for Al. Tom uses real liquor because the audience can always tell it's not iced tea.)

Al: "Whoa! That's plenty."

(Tom empties the bottle into his glass and takes a big slug.)

Al: "Now . . . we've all been taught *never* to drink and drive—"

Tom: "Yes, that is the first thing we would tell you—do not drink and drive. . . . *But* . . . suppose you're at a party out in the middle of nowhere . . . you've been asked to leave, your girlfriend has passed out—what are you going to do?"

Al: "You're going to drive."

Tom: "Of course you are. I, uh, we don't believe the head-in-the-sand is the best way of dealing with this phenomenon."

Al: "So what do I do?—I'm drunk and I *have* to drive."

Tom: "First off—be sure you drive a big American car. Put something substantial between you and whatever it is you're going to hit."

Al: ". . . big American car . . ."

Tom: "Stay away from small foreign imports—Hondas, Toyotas . . . rice burners in general—get yourself a big steel American cage and drive around in it, and that is point number one."

Al: "What kind of car do you drive?"

Tom: "I've got a '72 Lincoln Continental. The thing's a gas guzzler, but it's built like a battleship. Actually, I should have been killed a couple years ago when I wrapped a Delta '88 around a tree, but I walked away with just bruises because I was so loose. If I *had* to be in a car crash, I'd rather be drunk."

Al: "I can't argue with that logic."

Tom: "Take my word for it."

Al: "All right . . . I'm drunk, I'm driving—what other advice do you have?"

Tom: "Don't be one of these people who thinks they can sober up. At least to yourself, admit that you're drunk, and don't be afraid to slow down if you can't see."

Al: "Slow down."

Tom: "Exactly—and don't aim between the lines—you'll just end up weaving—pick one line and stick with it."

Al: "Any rules of thumb?"

Tom: "Do not puke and drive. You could choke to death. If you're going to get sick, pull the car off to the side of the road, put it in park, turn it off, walk around to the front bumper, and hang on—just remember to turn off the head-lights if it's at night."

Al: "Well, I'd like to thank you for joining us tonight, Mr. Wade. Where are you off to next?"

Tom: "I'm speaking at SUNY Albany at one o'clock tomorrow afternoon—actually I think I'll drive there tonight—I got a couple of good hours left in me, and I hate getting up in the morning."

Al: "I'm sure you do. If there's anyone in the crowd who needs a ride to Albany, might they accompany you?"

Tom: "No problem. I can fit three or four in the back, and if somebody wants to ride shotgun and crack the cool ones, I'd enjoy the company."

(Al shakes Tom's hand)

Al: "Thanks again. The kids loved it."

Our showstopper was our Rolling Stones parody of the opening number of their tour in 1982. My old pal Bill Buchen was

Charlie Watts, and Jon and Sally Tiven were Bill Wyman and Ronnie Wood, respectively. I was a convincing Keith: leather jacket, long silk scarf, mascara, cigarette, and playing loud. As we started "Under My Thumb," Franken came running out as Mick Jagger, wearing yellow football pants and Capezios, and was so good, it was scary.

Unfortunately, Franken and Davis at Stockton State never sold very well at all. In fact, one would be hard-pressed to find a copy on the Internet or anywhere. Even on eBay. At least our act was preserved for posterity. Thank you, Lorne. Maybe it would be re-released if one of us became president, or shot a president.

The Boss decided to return to TV in January of 1984. He called it *The New Show.* According to Hill and Weingrad's book, *Saturday Night,* "It aired on NBC Friday nights at 10:00 p.m., presumably on the theory that the same audience had now grown more sedate and might actually be sitting at home, perhaps minding the kids."

But there was a structural fault that doomed *The New Show*—it was taped before a live audience on Monday. However, it was shot like a film, cutting between multiple takes to be edited somehow before Friday. The live audience couldn't laugh at it, and would leave before the taping was half through. For them it was not a show, but watching the making of a show. So we had the worst of both worlds:

March 22, 1982

Mr. David Letterman
c/o NBC
New York City, New York

Dear Mr. Letterman,

I was appalled at the performance of two of your guests on the
Wednesday night, March 17, 1982, program. Apparently, the segment
concerning what should be done about driving while drunk was supposed
to be humorous. I can't say that I found it amusing.
The two men talked about their children in the segment. I
wonder how funny they would find it had one of their children been
killed by a drunk driver. I can tell you from personal experience,
it is not funny. It is a horrible experience, and one that no parent
should have to go through. Losing a child is a nightmare, but particularly when the life of a 26 year old son is taken because someone didn't have the decency to stay sober.
My nights are long now - I don't sleep very well because all
I can see is my son's body lying on the pavement. It's that very
reason that I watch late night programs such as yours. But, I
can assure your of this - I'll never watch your program again if
that kind of presentation is to be shown. Losing one viewer may
not matter, but I hope you will reconsider the choice of material
presented on your program.

Sincerely,

Mrs. Betty Prude

Mrs. Betty Prude

satire -
MADD
irony

it lost the spontaneity of a continuous performance, and there wasn't enough time to edit it properly. It had to be "sweetened" (laugh track). Nonetheless, there were a few remarkable comedy sketches that will probably not be seen again until they break open the inner chambers of Lorne's pyramid. The show with John Candy hosting stands out. George Meyer wrote a sketch about a guy who runs a food repair shop. A customer enters. "Yeah—I dropped this piece of toast with jam on it." John Candy: "Oooh . . . yep—there's the dog hair. Okay, I'll wear my magnifying visor and clean this up using tweezers. You can pick it up tomorrow morning." Then there was *The Time Truck* by Tom Gammill and Max Pross, where Dave Thomas and John Candy drive their truck into a time warp. Al and I wrote a black-and-white film parody of *The Hustler,* with Kevin Kline as "Fast Eddy" Paul Newman, and John as "Minnesota Fats" Jackie Gleason. Their performances were brilliant. The joke was that when they finally came to shoot, neither one could sink a ball. Cut to: montage of clock hands spinning, shots being missed, characters watching, mopping their brow, etcetera.

Here's one I wrote for Dave Thomas, Buck Henry, Teri Garr, and Jeff Goldblum:

THE NEW SHOW
FLOONT ARTNEY DAVE/BUCK/EXTRAS/Jeff V.O. TD 3/17/84
(FULL-FRAME TITLE SLIDE: FLOONT ARTNEY, PRIVATE EYE)
(MUSIC: FLOONT ARTNEY THEME)

        JEFF V.O.:
    And now it's time for another episode
    of *Floont Artney, Private Eye.*

(CUT TO: BEDROOM WITH BODY ON THE FLOOR. HOMICIDE
DETECTIVE, DAVE THOMAS, IS CONFERRING WITH TWO OTHER
COPS AND A CRIME PHOTOGRAPHER. ENTER BUCK AS FLOONT.)

        DAVE:
    Floont. Floont Artney. Why is it
    whenever we find a body you show up
    five minutes later?

                    BUCK:
          I don't know. Lucky, I guess.
          Tell me, Zudd—

                    DAVE:
          That's Sergeant Baatnip to you, Artney.

                    BUCK:
          . . . OK . . . Who's the stiff?

                    DAVE:
          Nessilfar. Chark Nessilfar.
          President of Twooz Industries.

(THE COPS COVER THE BODY WITH A SHEET.)

                    DAVE:
(SPEAKING TO ONE OF THE COPS.)
          Hellshrit, bring in Mrs. Nessilfar.

                    BUCK:
          What do you think?

                    DAVE:
          Looks pretty cut and dried to me.
          Another rubout by the Leeplashlie
          gang.

                    BUCK:
          It's too simple. I don't like it.

(ENTER TERI AS FEMME FATALE.)

                    DAVE:
          Sorry to disturb you, Mrs. Nessilfar,
          but I wanted to ask your permission
          to set up a twenty-four-hour guard for your
          safety.

                    TERI:
          What's with the gumshoe?

                    BUCK:
          The name's Artney—

                    TERI:
      I read the papers. It's just
      that there's a stink that goes
      with you and I don't want it in
      my house.

                    BUCK:
      Sorry to impose while you're so
      "upset," but before I go . . .
      Does the name Rard Duts ring a bell?

                    TERI:
      He was a friend of my husband,
      I believe. Disappeared on vacation
      in the Amazonian Svetlands. What's it
      to you?

                    DAVE:
      What are you getting at, Artney?

                    BUCK:
      It's just that I've been doing
      my homework, Zudd. This is not
      Mrs. Nessilfar's first marriage.
      It seems eight years ago she was
      Mrs. Karpil Ploynair.

(TERI LAUGHS DERISIVELY.)

                    TERI:
      Floont. Are you trying to convince
      Sergeant Baatnip that Duts, Ploynair
      and Nessilfar are all tied up with
      Twooz?

(MUSIC: DRAMATIC STING)
(CUT TO: FULL-FRAME TITLE SLIDE: FLOONT ARTNEY,
PRIVATE EYE)

                  Jeff V.O.:
      Floont Artney, Private Eye, will
      return after this message from TRW.

(FADE)

The ratings were the worst in the time slot. That's when I learned what schadenfreude was. The reviewers, the struggling *SNL,* even network execs took pleasure in watching Lorne's Spruce Goose go into the mountain. Lorne was even spending his own money to hire more editors, and people in show business *only* spend other people's money. After several broadcasts, Lorne called for a pow-wow in the upstairs room at Hurley's. We got drunk and decided to fall on our sword before we got canceled.

I was dating a beautiful blonde client of Broadway Video, Bea Doering. Her mother and father were surgeons in Greenwich, Connecticut. They had fallen in love after World War II; her mother's ancestral Brittany home had been occupied by German high command, and her father, Ernst, had been a sailor on a U-boat and a POW. I asked Ernst about Hitler Youth. "Oh, Tom, it was all about girls. They had these coed overnight campouts with a bonfire, beer, and the moonlight."

Bea had very preppy friends in lime green Lacoste Bermuda shorts, and we went to Yankee games and Nantucket. She left me for her old boyfriend, just as I discovered the new receptionist at Broadway Video who was also her friend. After one date, Beth Young asked Bea if she was done with me, and Bea gave her blessing. Beth grew up in Marin and Mendocino counties, north of San Francisco. Carolyn "Mountain Girl" Garcia recognized her as one of "the pony girls" of Stinson Beach at the end of the '60s, making her eight at the time, ten years younger than I. She was tough and street savvy. We lived together for six years. Beth—where did you go?

Franken was sprawled on a poolside lounge. Lorne was seated comfortably in the shade of an umbrella table. I was in the pool, it being a gloriously hot day in Amagansett, July of 1985.

> Lorne: **"You guys like Laila [Nabulsi], don't you?"**
> F&D: **"Yeah, sure . . ."**

Lorne: "NBC has approached me, and I'd like to executive produce *Saturday Night Live,* and have you guys and Laila produce the show. What do you think?"

F&D: "All right. Sounds good."

Lorne: "Bernie's got this gay comedian for the cast. He's very funny."

F&D: ". . . gay guy . . . Cool."

Lorne: ". . . and we should have a funny black woman."

F&D: ". . . black woman—of course."

Lorne: ". . . and I've already got Anthony Michael Hall and Robert Downey, Jr."

Tom: "Who?"

Al: "C'mon, Tom. Don't you remember we saw *The Breakfast Club* when we were in Chicago?"

Tom: "Oh, right. Young people."

Lorne: "Exactly. You like Randy Quaid?"

Tom: "I fucking love Randy Quaid!"

Two weeks later I was in the Comedy Store in L.A. for the first time since 1974, when Al and I were blackballed for helping organize a stand-up comedian's strike. Now he, Laila, and I were the big shots in the audience, for whom they all were playing and jockeying for position. I didn't know how to feel. The three of us saw Dennis Miller and figured he might be right for the *Weekend Update* slot. Lorne would have to look at him. We went to the Groundlings the next night. It was the L.A. version of Second City where Laraine Newman was discovered by Lorne. We thought this fellow, Jon Lovitz, was hilarious. Al and I went backstage to tell him so, as he was getting out of costume and standing in his underwear. We told him Lorne would have to see him, and he was thrilled.

In Chicago, Laila spotted Nora Dunn, who was waitressing in the restaurant below our audition hall. I saw a young, gangly, funny actress, Joan Cusack, in a tiny club across from Wrigley Field. It wasn't until she was hired that I was informed she came from a prominent show business family.

I also lost a few friends in this process. Knowing the spot was already filled, I neglected to invite a Chicago actress whom I had once dated. Big mistake. Also Jan Hooks, who joined *SNL* a couple of years later, was told by our talent coordinator that I said she was "too old." Thanks a lot. Dave Lander, whom we knew from '74 at the Pitschel Players (he had been in the Credibility Gap with Harry Shearer and Mike McKean), was flown out to New York, told he was hired, then told he wasn't. That was Lorne's doing, but he was my friend.

Then there were three producers trying to get shit done starting in the morning, but the executive producer would come in around 5:00 p.m. and change the decisions. As a result, no one would act on any decisions until the Boss came in.

Then there was the cast of many colors, which had, on the one hand, Randy Quaid, who was talented, funny, professional, and selfless, and on the other hand, the clueless Anthony Michael Hall and Robert Downey Jr., who behaved, at the time, like school bullies with a substitute teacher.

Damon Wayans was on the writing staff but was quickly making his way into the cast. We all realized he was brilliantly funny. But he saw what was and was not going on, and deliberately got himself fired. This happened when he was improvising in a sketch all the way through dress rehearsal, and Lorne told him to be professional and read the lines as written. On the air, he did not, and Lorne either had to change the show around him, or fire him. We supported his decision, but were depressed that the big one got away.

At some point, I suggested to Lorne that we could fire Herb Sargent to try to put new fire into *Weekend Update,* and give Dennis Miller, whom Herb despised, someone to play with. Lorne was shocked at my suggestion, saying, "Tom, someday you're going to be Herb, too." Lorne would fire us both within a couple of years.

The first show under Lorne's returned aegis was hosted by Madonna. She was wonderful, and I thought we got away with it, but by Monday, it was clear we had not. For the reviewers, it was as if they had taken all their *New Show* reviews and simply substituted *SNL,* and a whole new generation of "Saturday Night Dead" bylines was flourishing. Garcia was in town. I called him up and asked if he had seen the show. He said, "Yeah. I thought it was fun watching those people try to do that show." That was the nicest thing anybody said. The ratings had dropped through the course of the broadcast.

That was the Battle of Bull Run. The rest of the year was like the bloody Civil War. Later in the week I went to see the GD at Madison Square Garden, where I saw the keyboard player backstage:

> **Brent Mydland (sarcastic): "Hey, Davis. Thanks for the tickets."**
> **I: "Huh?"**
> **Brent: "I wanted to go see** *Saturday Night Live*—**I called up your number, and your girlfriend told me to fuck off."**

I couldn't win for trying. Beth had been having a shitty week, too.

Then Kate Forristal died in the spring of '86. A few years before, she had become paralyzed in a freakish one-car, low-speed accident in Mount Kisco, near where the first commercial parodies had been filmed. She had been the passenger, and bumped her head just so, on the dashboard. Her friend, the driver, never spoke to her again. I visited her in the Mount Kisco Hospital. She was lying facedown on a massagelike table so one had to crawl underneath to talk to her face. Under there she introduced me to her best friend, Kim Altobello, and encouraged us to date each other. Al and I had done a special performance for her in that hospital. Kim recently challenged my recollection. "You don't remember the first time we met. You and Al came to her hospital room when she got her foot amputated. I was there having just returned from Italy where a boyfriend had beaten me and my face was banged up. Kate and I were both pretty glum—I mean what do you say to each other— 'Gee, you look great!' You did your interpretive dance, and then you guys did the brain tumor piece. The performance made us giggle—but it wasn't your humor that was so engaging as much as how happy you and Al looked in your lives. I didn't want you to leave that day and I guess I didn't want you to leave any other time either."

We all believed Kate would recover from the paralysis, but she knew better, and accepted the situation before anyone else. She became wheelchair bound, with very limited use of her arms and hands. In the fall of '86 there was an incident where one of her caretakers lost patience and abused her. She told me she was considering suicide and I told her I would understand. She had never been a big reader and was not going to be another Stephen Hawking.

Once, she was at her sister Mary's apartment when I came over for a visit. Mary had just decided to quit drinking, and asked me not to imbibe in front of her. Kate laughed and said, "Don't be ridiculous, Mary. Do I ask you guys not to walk in front of me?"

Apparently, Kate had been hoarding her pills. They found her in her wheelchair wearing a T-shirt that read, "I came. I saw. I took valium."

Kate's funeral was held in an alcove of St. John the Divine. I rode in Lorne's limo with Edie Baskin. When we got there, Lorne went up to offer condolences and respect to Papa Forristal, who was  shooting daggers at him. Lorne and Susan were in the process of getting divorced. The casket arrived half an hour late, and we were all saying, "How typical of Kate." Mr. Mike eulogized her (at her request). He described her as "reckless" and recalled taking her out dancing after she had her foot amputated. Papa Forristal didn't like that, but I know Kate did.

Then the book by Hill and Weingrad, *Saturday Night,* came out. Lorne summoned me to his office.

> Lorne: "Who told those guys you and Franken took LSD to write the *Nixon/Final Days* piece?"
> I: "I did."
> Lorne (irked): "Why did you do that?"
> I: "They were asking about drugs and I felt uncomfortable talking about anyone else, and I thought better to talk about a psychoactive drug than narcotics."
> Lorne (sarcastic): "Great."

The '85–'86 season is generally considered the worst in *SNL* history. We elitists from the original show had gotten our comeuppance. Those who had suffered at the show in the previous five years felt vindicated, and the press took obvious pleasure in piling on (bad reviews are usually more interesting). Lorne wrote the final sketch in the final show of that season: Al and I were shown tending bar in Hurley's (via live cameras), and Studio 8H was on fire as Lorne was leading Dennis Miller and Jon Lovitz to safety.

> **Dennis Miller: "But Lorne—what about the others?"**
> **Lorne: "Never mind."**

Of course the producers were blamed and sacked by the network as Lorne promised to produce the show in his old hands-on method. While I understood that this was inevitable, my pride was hurt and I took a sabbatical, which included an extended period with Garcia, doing a rewrite on our screenplay of Kurt Vonnegut's *The Sirens of Titan*. Al, with his family responsibilities, had to return as a writer. Despite myself, I sent Al two sketches that got on the air. One was for Garry Shandling as a passenger on an Arkansas airline where smoking was no longer permitted, but you could chew and spit tobacco (Jack Handey off camera with a bucket of brown fluid and a turkey baster). The other was for William Shatner, a parody of *The Ballad of the Green Beret* where he played Oliver North in *The Ballad of the Mute Marine*. A month later I saw Phoebe, Al's mother, who asked me if I had seen Al's sketch about *The Mute Marine*.

I returned to the show as a writer in January of '88, and was given my own office as far away from Lorne's as possible. Things had changed and I hadn't. There were several people having babies, and Lorne's favorite writers were Bonnie and Terry Turner, who already had a fifteen-year-old daughter. Franken also appeared to be their champion. Dana Carvey (I thought it was Danic Harvey) was immensely popular with the Church Lady character. As I took a seat in the writers' meeting with Jim Downey, now head writer, he asked me what I thought of the show.

> **I: "It's great—but what is it with this Ruth Buzzi Church Lady shit?"**
> **Jim: "Gotta love ya' for that, Davis."**
> **He laughed. Then I took a joint out of the breast pocket of my flannel shirt and lit it up. There was a collective gasp from all the young writers.**
> **Jim: "Uh, Tom—there's no more smoking in the office."**
> **I put it out.**

Al was in his own office and working with young writers mostly on the subject of substance abuse and twelve-step programs. I hated the Stuart Smalley stuff—why the gratuitous over-the-top gay shit?

> Al (on the phone, August 3, 2007): "The Stuart character comes from Al-Anon. When I first joined I was asking questions like, 'I find it hard to turn life over to an all-loving higher power because of the Holocaust.' And then there was this guy who was saying [in Stuart's voice], 'I want to thank God that I have an apartment, and I can't leave my lover—I just can't do it,' and it was there that I discovered that I could learn from people stupider than I am. My mother had always taught me to learn from people who are smarter than you."

From an interview in the *Los Angeles Times,* October 28, 1994, Al is asked a lot about Al-Anon. "What have you been addicted to?"

> Al: "Well, in twelve-step jargon, I've sort of been addicted to codependent attitudes. Deriving my self-worth from things outside myself. Addicted to other people's feelings. I used to be the person who needed to control things, otherwise I didn't feel safe. That sort of classic codependent behavior. It was harder to define than [if] I was addicted to alcohol or cocaine."

Stevie Ray Vaughan and his brother Jimmie were the musical act one week in February 1986. The sound rehearsal was at 11:00 a.m. on Thursday, which was when I got a call from 8H asking, "Tom, have you got any whiskey up there?" As a matter of fact, I had some in my desk. I went down there and shared what I had. Jimmie Vaughn showed me some chording at my request. On Saturday, during the music rehearsal at dinner break, I was sitting right in front of the band when Mick Jagger came and sat next to me. We were both blown away by Stevie's Hendrix-like ability. Lorne appeared and stood beside Mick. On the air, after their last note, I approached Lorne.

> I: "Now that was some kick-ass music, wouldn't you say?"
> Lorne looked at Stevie leaving the stage, clicked his tongue, and shook his head.
> Lorne: "Another alchy."
> Boy, was I in trouble.

Not only were my sketches getting in less and less, but the young writers soon recognized that it was not advantageous to have my initials next to theirs at the top of the script. Lorne read all the script directions at read-through, and his enthusiasm for an idea, or lack thereof, was apparent. Another writer, John Schwartzwelder, felt similar discrimination, and we complained. So, initials no longer appeared on the scripts—except Lorne's. Schwartzwelder was an excellent writer but got fired at the end of the year, widely recognized as caused by his addiction to tobacco and his penchant for wearing western shirts. He went on to work at *The Simpsons*.

During this period of my decline leading up to 1994, I did manage to get some memorable sketches on the air. When Steve Martin hosted in '87, I came up with a new twist on the *Jeopardy!* game show, which I called *Common Knowledge,* and wrote with Franken and Downey:

> Steve (à la Alex Trebek): "Questions for our show are selected by educators from Princeton University, to reflect a broad range of history, science, and culture. Answers for *Common Knowledge* are determined by a panel of one hundred high school seniors from around the nation.
> Steve: "His assassination sparked World War I . . ."
> Nora (as contestant Jean Kirkpatrick): "Who is Archduke Ferdinand?"
> SFX: buzzer.
> Steve: "The answer is Lincoln. Who is Abraham Lincoln . . . Les?"
> Kevin Nealon: "Let's go to state capitals for one hundred."
> Steve: "New York State."
> Kevin: "New York City."
> SFX: ding ding ding.
> Steve: "Correct."
> Kevin: "State capitals for two hundred."
> Steve: "New Jersey."
> Kevin: "New Jersey City."
> SFX: ding ding ding.
> Steve: "Whoa, you're on a roll, here, Les."

When John Malkovich hosted the show in 1989, he was in my office when I pitched a favorite idea of mine, and told him that it would get on only if he championed it. He did. It was a family barbecue on a patio deck when a big bird flies through the set and hits the sliding-glass door, then falls to the deck where it squawks piteously with a broken neck. Franken was the live voiceover for the bird, which was both a model-on-wire and a hand puppet made by Bob Flanagan, SPFX (special effects). Malkovich's character concludes he should put the animal out of its misery. He picks up a croquet mallet and tries but fails to dispatch the bird, which screeches in terror. Nora, the mother, takes the children inside so they will not be traumatized. John gets an air-pellet gun from the toolshed and pumps it up, putting the gun to the animal's head as its breathing is labored. The gun fires and renews a round of hysterical squawking and flopping about. Nora sticks her head out, "Do you need help?" John Malkovich: "No!" Out of frustration, he grabs a Garden Weasel and begins wailing on the screeching creature. Cut to: inside the kitchen, Nora is distracting the kids by reading to them from the newspaper. The camera pulls in on the back page where there is a picture of the bird with the headline: "California Condor Released Today."

I was completely out of the loop now. I was standing innocently outside Lorne's office when someone informed me that the Boss was talking to a new member of the cast. Apparently the young comedian from Canada had submitted a tape of himself doing several characters, and Lorne hired him, fait accompli. Sure enough, a young man emerged from Lorne's office seeming like he didn't know what to do next, kind of lost and lonely. I knew that Lorne liked everybody to figure things out on their own. So I walked up and introduced myself; he said he was Mike Myers. I invited him to join me in a trip downtown to my West Village apartment, where I figured we could have a smoke and go out for dinner. He accepted.

My pot was notoriously potent and as he took a toke I could see that he was just being polite. I put the joint out but it was too late. I watched him melt into my overstuffed armchair. I started talking about sketch ideas, including one I pulled out of the air, about a German performance artist (in my mind like Klaus Nomi). Mike was a bit freaked out. Had I seen his tape? No, I hadn't (sometime later when I saw his Dieter character, I realized it must have been on Mike's tape, and weirdly I had channeled the idea). He almost ran from my apartment. We never collaborated or socialized. Once, when his father died, he asked me for one of my joints.

Rob Schneider and Robert Smigel wrote a very funny sketch, *Head-wound Harry*. A guy with a horrific head wound comes to a party as if nothing is wrong. I suggested to them that they have the head wound topped with real shrimp, and have the character sit on a couch. Then a blind person with a Seeing Eye dog enters, and the dog eats the shrimp, unbeknownst to Harry. It got one of those *huge* laughs on the air. I live for that.

Christian Slater championed a sketch of mine. Victoria Jackson was the housewife in an evangelical Christian family, and Slater appears to her as Jesus. It went over very well, but between dress and air, Victoria announced that the scene was blasphemous and her own religious beliefs made it impossible for her to do it. The next week I showed it to Sally Field, who loved it. I cast Phil Hartman as Jesus: her character constantly prays to Jesus about everything ("Dear Jesus, please help my daughter with her math test," "Jesus, help my husband drive his car carefully," "Jesus, help me get my shopping done quickly so I can get home in time to watch *General Hospital,* and please help Luke and Laura get back together again"). Poof! Jesus appears before her in the kitchen.

> Phil: "Yes, Gretchen, it is I, your personal savior—can we sit down for a minute?"
>
> Sally: "Oh Jesus! I love you so much—praise your name! My best chair is in the living room!"
>
> Phil: "This simple kitchen table will be fine . . . now Gretchen . . . I hear everybody's prayers all the time . . . and I was wondering if you could perhaps just pray to me about the really important stuff—life, death, temptation—and not bother with the mundane stuff. It would just make things a little simpler on my end."
>
> Sally (upset): "You mean I shouldn't have asked you to help Jennifer in her math test?"
>
> Phil: "No—I don't mind helping Jennifer—but things like influencing your soap opera, or asking me to be sure your soufflé won't fall—I'd rather you figured those things out on your own."
>
> Sally (panicked): "Does this mean I won't go to heaven?!"

Phil realizes that she'll never get it, so he gently explains that he's going now, and she won't remember anything of it, and poof!—he disappears. Sally returns to normal and starts praying about *General Hospital* again.

I married Mimi Raleigh in 1991. She's a brilliant veterinarian. Lorne couldn't make it to our wedding, but he sent a basket with beluga caviar, a bottle of Cristal, and a beautiful pair of white silk pajamas with the note: "Dear Tom—now, more than ever, it's important to look good in bed."

I wrote another piece that didn't get past read-thru *Sexoffenderville*. A couple looking for a new home is attracted to the low rates in Sexoffenderville, where each person they meet is very pleasant, but is required to inform them of something, like they once were convicted of improperly touching a troop of Boy Scouts, etcetera. It wasn't until afterward that I realized that my major character's name was Henry—Lorne's newborn son's name.

In January of 1994, my isolation at *SNL* was complete. I had not gotten one single sketch on. Finally, I wrote a live commercial parody for *Cat Hats*—fur hats made from cats, with the tail on the back and the flattened face on the front flap. It was getting laughs, and seemed like a shoo-in, but after Saturday run-thru, Lorne, without speaking to me, instructed wardrobe to remove the faces on the hats. Of course, it failed in dress rehearsal and was summarily cut. Defeated at last, I walked home in the rain while the show was on the air. The next week, I entered Lorne's office to speak to him alone. I told him that since I was not getting my stuff on the show, perhaps it was time for me to leave and try something else. Lorne shook my hand. When the season ended, there was no "Good-bye, Tom" cake and champagne. Oh, well. Two weeks later I got a call from Ken Aymong, the unit manager.

> Ken: "Hi, Tom, I'm sorry to tell you this, but you're not going to be invited back next year."
> I: "Ken, I told Lorne three months ago that I was leaving the show—he didn't mention that?"
> Ken: "Oh geez, Tom, I'm sorry."

In 2002, Danny invited me to come to an event at which he was to appear as emcee in Las Vegas. I sometimes assist him at the larger events, such as rock festivals. This was something else. The casino industry was unveiling *Saturday Night Live*–theme slot machines—the Church Lady, Hans and Franz, the Blues Brothers, the Czech Brothers, and the Coneheads. Laraine was there. Apparently, if you had your face on the machine, you got paid; but you *really* got paid if you were a producer, or manager of the producer, or a performer. Bernie Brillstein was sitting there with Lorne. This must have been some real money. The *SNL* band played and Kevin Nealon performed; there were ice sculptures and a lavish buffet. The next day, Danny was invited to fly on Lorne and Bernie's jet to L.A. Danny had his FBI friend and me in tow, so we were invited, too. We got to the Vegas private airport, and FBI opened a book he was reading, *How to Stop Terrorism*. Lorne approached us and said to him, "Shouldn't you have read that a couple of years ago?"

On the plane, I was having a conversation with FBI about how stupid NBC was during the first five years, never to have spent the money to tape the dress rehearsals—all those sketches with John and Gilda that didn't get to the air for one reason or another. Lorne spoke to me from across the noise of the aircraft. "No, Tom, that was *my* doing—I didn't want the network to be able to do any editing or censoring for Mountain and Pacific."

When Dan Aykroyd hosted the show in 2003, he brought me along. It was great fun writing and getting stuff on again; it was a terrific show. I thought Lorne would choose it for an Emmy submission, but he went instead with the Al Gore show, which Al Franken had come back to work on. It did not get a nomination.

Lorne once told me that he'd just met Hoagie Carmichael. He said the aging star of the '30s and '40s told him that he still wrote and performed as he'd always done, but that pop culture had only a passing interest in his art, as an object of nostalgia.

12

JOHN BELUSHI

Davis, I'm the Jerry Garcia of comedy!

—John Belushi

© 1976 TOM DAVIS

In the first year, we did twenty-six *SNL* shows, stretching into July. The Emmys were being held two weeks later, and *SNL* was nominated all over the place. NBC didn't want to pay to fly out the writers. There were eleven of us, including the last-minute addition of Danny, because he had, indeed, written more than anybody. They were reluctant to give Danny a writing credit because they thought the rest of the cast would want one, too. After putting us all through that, they flew us out, and Danny refused to go.

We were thrilled to be there. A year before, I couldn't get arrested. Now I could. Lorne won Best Show, Chevy won Best Actor, and then we won for Writing. At the announcement, we rose from our seats, walked to the stage, and accepted the weighty statuettes; somebody said something, and we were whisked away backstage and ushered into a press gallery where the first question was, "How much of that show is actually written?"

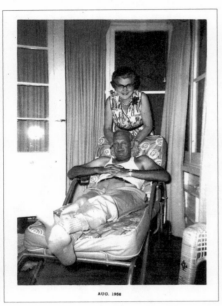

AUG. 1956

When I returned to New York City, I called my parents. My beloved grandfather, Palmer Johnson, had died two days before the Emmys, and they had decided not to tell me and spoil the event. I was furious; my grandfather's death and funeral were more important to me. He had always stuck up for me, and didn't take any shit from my father. He was a second-generation Swede, a blue-collar worker who took me fishing. He had a manicured lawn and liked to listen to Twins baseball on the radio and drink beer. Grandma had found him in his chair in the garage, next to his boat and workbench. She thought he was asleep.

Shortly thereafter, in August 1976, Danny invited Belushi, Franken, and me up to the Aykroyd homestead in Ontario. Al and I rented a car and parked in front of John and Judy's second-floor walk-up on Bleecker Street. As we entered their apartment, John was still half-dressed and laughing heartily at the television. Jacques Cousteau was narrating his show, as his son was sent scuba diving with a camera into the Zambezi River to photograph hippopotamuses swimming. "As yoo can zee, deez cantankerous kreechers are quite grazefool een zee watear, but zare vooloominoos excretions queekly make zee watear opaque." John howled with laughter and rolled on the floor.

Six hours later, we were crossing the border into Canada where, for the first time in my life, we were stopped by Canadian customs. When asked our occupations and purpose for visit, now knowing not to say "comedians," we said, "We work in television and we're going to visit friends." This, apparently, was high profile for such scruffy-looking young people. Next, we all discovered that John had not brought his wallet, so not only did he have no money, he had no ID. As they went through the trunk, they discovered Danny's Emmy, which we were delivering because he did not attend the event. They thought we'd stolen the object, and that's when John lost his patience. Of course, I was the one holding the dope, but finally one of the officers recognized him and waved us through.

One Wednesday at 3:00 a.m., I was walking past the open door of Lorne's darkened seventeenth floor office when I heard Belushi's voice. "Davis! Get in here!" The only light was reflected from the huge spotlights that illuminate Rockefeller Plaza, and there were John and Bill Kreutzmann, the Grateful Dead drummer, snorting coke off Lorne's desk. Apparently the band was recording at some studio in town, and John had found them. He delighted them, despite knocking over some drum equipment and getting in the way as only he could. He introduced me to my heroes. Thank you, John.

During the second year of *SNL,* Danny and John made money on the side by appearing at corporate shows and conventions. I never saw one of these shows, but I know Belushi did his samurai and Danny would end the show by sawing the lectern in two with a chain saw. They did one of these productions in a ballroom in the Sheraton Hotel on Seventh Avenue and Fifty-fourth Street. On the lobby walls were three-foot-diameter circular relief state seals from all fifty states. As they were making their exit, Belushi ripped the Seal of Minnesota off the wall and carried it back to my office where he presented it to me. I was thrilled. Today it hangs prominently on my library wall.

When Karen Black hosted, she showed up for the Monday pitch meeting holding her infant

3 ft Dia.

JOHN BELUSHI

son. Belushi walked into the meeting late, walked over to Karen, and offered the baby a cigarette from his pack, getting an interested response from the tiny hand. A few minutes later, as each writer was taking his turn offering ideas, Karen pulled out one of her ample bosoms and began breast-feeding the little tyke. Belushi: "Hey—I'm next!"

One night, after *Animal House* had taken the world by storm, things worked out where it was just John and I walking through the West Village. We got a table in a restaurant, ordered dinner, and started drinking. It seemed John wanted to challenge me to a drug-off, so the conversation quickly became, "Okay . . . what have you got?" I had some acid, which we consumed on the spot. As we were getting off, I came to understand that he had a beef with me. He had come so far so fast, and I had not recognized his achievement. This was true. Except for the Grateful Dead, I had a conscious philosophy that celebrity, money, and power were ephemeral and were important only as they figured into the world of ideas in which I lived. Even as a child, I never thought of asking people for an autograph or having my picture taken with them, like a tourist at the Eiffel Tower. This may explain why I now live alone in the woods. I was never really in show business—I only did shows. I saw John as my contemporary, and I wasn't going to kiss his or anyone else's ass. He would just have to accept that about me and get past it. But on this night, it was driving John nuts. That's when he finally said, "Davis—I'm the Jerry Garcia of comedy!" I thought it was the acid talking. We went barhopping and then wound up back at his new place on Morton Street (I called it Goering's Palace). At some point, Keith Richards showed up, and we went to the basement to play—John on drums, I on guitar, Keith on bass. Keith reached over and tuned my instrument as we played.

When John died, I got a Grateful Dead sympathy phone call. When Jerry died, they got one from me. A couple of months later I heard Bill Murray say in conversation, "I think what got John is when he switched from Marlboros to Merits."

13
A NIGHT IN THE BUNGALOW

Memories, like dreams, are significant only in their
proximity to the real thing.   —Tom Davis

The Chateau Marmont was built on the Sunset Strip in 1929.
There's a picture of Humphrey Bogart planting a rosebush in its garden. Though it changed hands in the '80s and was given new furniture and a face-lift, the rooms still have the metal-framed
crank-open casement windows and the original tiled bathrooms.
Many have a furnished kitchen with a gas stove, a refrigerator, and
a table and chairs, and a small closet where an ironing board folds
out.

For many of my favorite friends and contemporaries, "the Chat"
was the hotel of choice. Doug Kenney stayed there, as did Michael
O'Donoghue and Tim Mayer—those *Lampoon* people. They would
subtly draw little rats on the landscape paintings that adorned the
walls of almost every room.

The poolside is where Lorne Michaels sat with Tom Schiller to read script submissions to find writers for an as-yet-unnamed late-night comedy show in June 1975. That's how Franken and Davis got hired.

I remember when Keith Richards was on my floor. Late one night as I walked past his door, I could hear him playing through a small, warm-up amplifier. I pounded on his door until he stopped. Then I shouted, "Turn it up!"

In those days it was the custom in Hollywood to fly out talented young people from New York to pitch ideas for movies and television. Most old-school producers and executives were from New York. They would pay for a first-class round-trip flight and a hotel, and at lunch on Wednesday you'd pitch to him. Then you'd pitch to his boss on Thursday, meet again in his office before noon on Friday, and fly back on the red-eye Saturday night. It was smart to treat writers like that. Then if you *do* work with them, you could really screw 'em later. So we stayed at "the Chat." Not like today (though how would I know?).

I was playing pool with Al at Broadway Video when Joe Forristal (Kate and Susan's brother) walked in and said, "Belushi OD'd." I asked if John was going to be all right. "No. He's dead." We couldn't believe it. We ran to the television and turned it on. There was the image of ambulance attendants dollying a gurney from the back of one of the Chateau's bungalows, with a shrouded, rotund figure covered by a sheet. I knew exactly where that was and what that was. They loaded John into the maw of an ambulance.

A couple of months later, Al and I went to L.A., and I specifically requested *the* bungalow, which had two bedrooms. We flipped a coin and I got *the* bedroom. Our friends Carrie Fisher and Eric Idle came over in the spirit of an impromptu wake—a grief thing. We four were seated in the "living" room, exchanging stories about our fallen friend, when we heard three loud banging sounds, like someone pounding his fist against the roof of the bungalow. We were all startled and had that flash that it was Belushi, and then we laughed. But we started talking about how weird it was. Then it happened again. Al and I jumped up and ran outside to see if anyone was out there. Al even climbed onto the roof. Nothing. We searched the bungalow, looking for the rational source. There was a large air duct in *the* bedroom, and we speculated that the thermostat could have been turned up and the duct could have made the sound as it expanded with the heat. Still, we all thought it was weird.

Danny told me that Judy told him that when she had John's grave moved to a private location, the cemetery guys dropped the casket, and she saw John fall out . . . and he looked pretty good, considering.

TOM DAVIS

14

TIMOTHY LEARY

> Never play the part of victim. Always question authority.
> —Timothy Leary

In 1980, Franken and Davis signed with a college booking agency, Brian Winthrop International, Ltd. Their talent list included G. Gordon Liddy and Timothy Leary, whose shows involved a "debate" and Q&A. Al and I entered the second-floor Winthrop office space over Sixty-something and Broadway. Today was office-party day— a chance for the bookers to meet the people they were booking, which was good for morale.

The first person we saw was G. Gordon, the former district attorney of Dutchess County, New York, and a former FBI agent and Watergate burglar also known for busting Timothy Leary at Millbrook. When Liddy wouldn't turn state's evidence or even testify, Judge Sirica gave him hard time. Now both he and Tim were out of prison and generating some income.

I walked up to G. Gordon Liddy and introduced myself. He smiled and shook my hand, saying that he had seen a tape from an *SNL* broadcast a few weeks before where I played him. He congratulated me, saying he thought it was very funny. It had been a *Weekend Update* "remote" with reporter Laraine Newman. We were satirizing a story from Liddy's widely read autobiography, *Will*, where he demonstrated his superhuman resolve in front of White House staffers by holding his hand over a candle flame. As G. Gordon, I was interviewed by Laraine, while barbecuing my hand on a Weber broiler and applying BBQ sauce. As Laraine finished, I ate one of my fingers (some BBQ rib meat stuck between my fingers).

COURTESY OF BROADWAY VIDEO

In the next room, all the pretty girls were huddled together facing inward. At their center sat the good doctor Leary holding court, a cigarette in one hand and a paper cup of champagne in the other. I listened to him skillfully direct the conversation, drawing opinions out of his youthful admirers and challenging them to pursue their thoughts. Finally, he saw me standing there, smiling. He walked up and shook my hand.

 Tim: "Hello. I'm Timothy Leary."

 I: "I know. I'm Tom Davis and I've got great smoke and coke."

 Tim: "Let's go."

By the time we had walked the several blocks to his room at the

Mayflower Hotel on Central Park West, we were fast friends for life, which for Tim would be another sixteen years.

Timothy Leary's life's work was meant to appeal to people's better instincts. But as sometimes happens, some people's worse instincts can be psychedelically realized, and Tim chose to ignore that for what he considered the greater good. He was misguided, as is every prophet, and that is a destiny he embraced. He was a psychologist who *did* the acid as a whole world of shit went down. For most people, getting high on LSD means being unable to function socially as you ride out the experience—and not answering the phone or driving a car. He read, wrote books, lectured and debated, gave press conferences, and played the political/legal enforcement game as a master, all the while under the influence of powerful drugs. He was an absent father, a short-term husband, and a snitch. But to me he was a professor, a liberal father figure, a brilliant conversationalist, a free thinker, and a fun-finder. He was my friend.

Alan Rudolph directed a documentary about Liddy and Leary, *Return Engagement*, which captured their act fairly well. During their "debate" they would provoke the bipartisan crowd. G. Gordon had a routine about the Millbrook bust where he said that Tim had been wearing only a shirt, and he had to follow him up stairs, "which is why, if you were a husky in a sled-dog team, you would want to be the lead dog."

Tim referred to an episode from Liddy's book where he claimed to have taken a big bite out of a dead rat that had been thrown at him by another prison inmate, establishing his nonintimidation. "Gordon—I'll eat one of your rats if you'll eat one of my brownies."

Then there is an interview on the porch of the suite on top of the Chateau Marmont, overlooking Sunset Boulevard. Liddy and Leary and their wives are having breakfast and answering the questions posed by our agent, Brian Winthrop (if that really is his last name). But the girls steal the show for a couple minutes, taunting their husbands about women on the road.

> Tim: "Sorry—I'm not going to play the fidelity game."
> G. Gordon: "I don't like no-win situations. I plead 'not guilty.'"
> Mrs. Liddy: "You always have. That's why they gave you twenty years."

The first time I met Barbara Leary was at their house on Won-
derland Avenue in Laurel Canyon. With her close-cropped red hair
and cigarette holder, she was like a spoiled, audacious, sometimes
rude, young Katharine Hepburn with a rack. She did not hold her
drugs well, and she was a sexpot at a time when Tim was in his six-
ties and admitting, "You know, I never have been a great lover." I saw
the Grateful Dead, who reported a backstage encounter they had
the week before with Tim, Barbara, and her teenage son Zack.

Mickey Hart: "Man, Leary's wife was really hitting on me."
Bill Kreutzmann: "She was all over him—it was weird."

Barbara finally left Tim for a Brazilian billionaire in 1992. Zack
stayed with Tim. Several months later, before a gathering of friends

BARBARA AND TIM © 1981 TOM DAVIS

at the kitchen table, Tim was extolling her virtues. "Wasn't Barbara
wonderful?" Everyone was rolling their eyes.

I: "No, Tim. She was a terrible human being."

That changed the topic of conversation. I could be a sharp-
tongued questioner of authority, too.

Tim said, "Tom—I love your women!" He had been to the Twelfth
Street apartment several times, and invited Emily and me to his book
party for *Flashbacks* at Andy Warhol's Factory. Next he appreciated
Bethany Young, with whom I lived for six years on Thirteenth
Street. He also became good friends with my wife, Mimi, herself a
doctor of veterinary medicine. Once, when we were staying at Tim's

house on Sunbrook, above Beverly Hills, I produced a fifth of Johnnie Walker Black Label, and subsequently Mimi and Tim got into a vehement argument about something existential that didn't interest the rest of us. The next morning, they were laughing at the breakfast table. "If two Irishmen can't get together to drink whiskey and argue about God," Tim said with delight, "then the world can end!" Perhaps, but that was the last time I brought scotch.

Though I had met her only twice before Tim died, Rosemary Woodruff (his wife during the '60s) and I became friends after he was gone. What a beautiful, intelligent, healing woman she was. During the series of upheavals that was his life, aside from his children, Rosemary was hurt the most. Because she never snitched, she had to remain in hiding under an alias from 1970—when she aided the Weathermen who masterminded Tim's escape from prison—until 1994, when all charges against her were dropped. Apparently, she could not only forgive Tim, she could still love him.

At a premiere of a documentary on Tim's life, at the National Arts Club on Gramercy Park in New York City, Rosemary commented, as we were walking out, "For once Tim came across where his heart was bigger than his ego."

She took her friends Denis Berry, Donna Scott, and Mimi and me, up to Millbrook where she had received special permission from the Mellon family to revisit the storied grounds. A solitary caretaker admitted us to the unoccupied estate. Rosemary basked in the memories. Beaming, she showed us the smaller guesthouse where people who were struggling with their trips would be segregated from the rest. On the perimeter she pointed to a massive oak tree, in which a certain artist had lived for a year and a half. No evidence of the tree house remained.

I attended the fifth and final Timothy Leary memorial and potluck, thrown by Rosemary and Denis in their house in the redwoods near Santa Cruz. Even Ram Dass showed up, as well as a couple dozen other friends from different eras, including an old German hippie named Brummbauer. He had apparently visited Tim and Rosemary when they were in exile in Algeria. In his German accent he recalled, "We were walking in the desert after taking enormous amounts of LSD. Timothy got it into his head that because we were so high, we could beat the house at the casino in Algiers. Of course, when we got there, they wouldn't even let us in. So we went to a good restaurant where we sat down, and Tim went through this laborious process of ordering a steak. It had to be the biggest, thickest, juiciest steak, broiled medium rare with sautéed mushrooms and onions. When it arrived, nobody could eat it because we were too high."

Seven grams of Tim's ashes had been shot into space, along with Gene Roddenberry's and twenty-four others'. But there were plenty of ashes left, which Rosemary mixed with glitter and placed in a

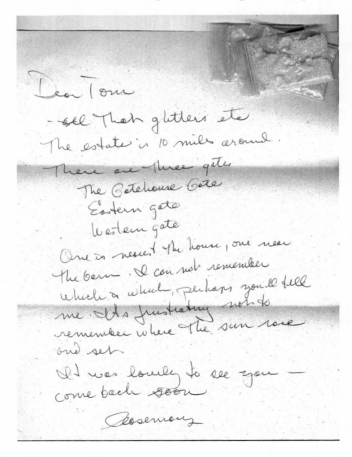

Dear Tom
- see That glitters etc
The estate is 10 miles around.
There are three gates
    The Gatehouse Gate
    Eastern gate
    Western gate
One is nearest the house, one near
the barn. I can not remember
which is which, perhaps you'll tell
me. It's frustrating not to
remember where the sun rose
and set.
It was lovely to see you —
come back soon
        Rosemary

bowl on the table alongside some plastic gram bags and a spoon. We were all invited to help ourselves. I still have three grams of Timothy in my cupboard. I was instructed to throw the ashes over the fence around the Millbrook estate. I haven't done it yet.

My host was extolling the limitless wonders of the Internet, including interactive books:

> Tim: "Wouldn't you like to talk with Tom Sawyer?"
> I: "No. I like reading the masterful words of Samuel Clemens. Would you want to use a hammer and chisel with Michelangelo as he labors on the Pieta?"
> Tim: "Of course I would!"

> Tim (mock macho competitive): "I'll bet I can love you more than you can love me!"

> Tim: "Whomever or whatever I want to put into my body is none of the government's business."

> Tim: "Never answer the phone after eight o'clock."

There was a bogus antique sign in Tim's computer/dining room: IRISH NEED NOT APPLY

> Tim: "Someday there will be a statue of me in the town square of Millbrook."

> Tim: "Do you actually know anyone who has finished a book by Bill Burroughs?"

Taped to his refrigerator several months before he died, was a minimalist Christmas card bearing the following scrawl: "Tim—why don't you do something to surprise us all—maybe even yourself?— Bill Burroughs"

We were chatting on the phone and he asked me what books I was reading. I announced that I had just begun an attempt to read

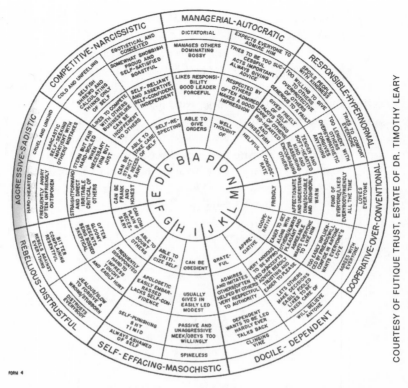

FIGURE 6. Interpersonal Check List Illustrating the Classification of Interpersonal Behaviors into Sixteen Variable Categories. *Interpersonal Psychology*, 1958, Timothy Leary.

the Bible from cover to cover.

> Tim: "Oh no—there goes another one."
>
> I: "Relax. You don't have to worry about me. Maybe you'll feel better if I read you something really good that I just found in it."
>
> Tim: "Okay . . ."
>
> I: "Here's Timothy 1, Chapter 1, 'the law is not made for the righteous man, but for the lawless and disobedient, for the ungodly and for the sinners, for the unholy and profane, for murderers of fathers and murderers of mothers, for manslayers. For whoremongers, for them that defile themselves with mankind, for menstealers, for liars, for perjured persons, and if there is anything that is contrary to sound doctrine!'"

Tim (laughing): "Whoa! That was wonderful! Thank you for that."

I really never did get past Leviticus.

After a lecture in Manhattan one summer night, Tim dined with Mimi and me in a restaurant, in front of which was parked my 1962 Buick Special convertible. As we were saying good night, Tim decided to ride with us to our house upstate. As dawn was about to break, we sped past the Millbrook exit on the Taconic Parkway, where two large wild turkeys seemed to be standing at attention. Suddenly, Tim turned around to Mimi in the backseat and grabbed her hand, saying, "I sense the presence of your mother." Mimi burst into tears. Her mother had died fifteen years before, but had attended Radcliffe when Tim was at Harvard, and she had been a staunch admirer. I have no idea how he could have known that. We arrived at my house as the sun rose above the horizon. We sipped screwdrivers at the kitchen table as Tim read aloud from the opening pages of *Ulysses*.

The conservative public still blamed Tim for the drug use of the '60s and he'd say, "Oh, I'd love to be able to claim credit for that!" He also loved being compared to Socrates, who was persecuted as the corrupter of youth.

I: "They want you to take the hemlock."

Tim: "Or keep me from taking it."

In 1993 I told Tim the news that Bob Haldeman, Nixon's chief of staff, had died.

Tim: "If you can't beat 'em—outlive 'em!"

Tim said he was often mistaken in airports for Dr. Benjamin Spock. He was delighted, of course, though he identified himself with Felix the Cat and his wonderful bag of tricks.

Tim: "Life is all about finding the right toxins in the right amount."

During a discussion of the subject of cloning, Tim said, "Isn't it marvelous that the Egyptian Pharaohs may achieve their plans for immortality—the thieves and grave robbers take the gold and jewels, leaving behind the really valuable stuff—the bloody rags in the corner."

Tim: "Quentin Tarantino is brilliant, but he's an asshole."

Tim had only one rule in his house—no one was permitted to talk about O. J. Simpson.

We had just been seated at a table in a trendy, crowded Beverly Hills restaurant and Tim asked if I had any cocaine left.
I: "Yeah . . ."
Tim: "Well, dump it out on the table."
Tom: "No, Tim. Not here."
The next day I reminded him of the nonincident.
Tim: "Oh no. I didn't say that, did I?"

Tim's friend, Lindsay Brice, a very attractive fine-art photographer, said she accompanied Tim on a trip to Johnny Depp's Sunset Strip Boulevard nightclub, the Viper Room. "The place was crowded but a large table had been reserved. After a while, Tim announced that it was time to go. As we got up to leave, Tim said that his wallet was missing. Everyone started crawling around under the table and the lights were turned up. Then he discovered that it was in his pocket. I believe he put us through all that just for fun." Lindsay is my girlfriend today.

We would exchange old jokes. Here are three I heard first from Tim:
1. **A hunter is stalking prey in the woods. He sees a bear drinking from a creek and he shoots, but the bear disappears. The hunter tries to pick up the trail when, suddenly, the bear comes up from behind and smashes the rifle on the rocks. The bear knocks him to the ground, kicks him in the ass, and disappears. The hunter staggers to his feet, brushing off his torn jacket, and says, "Goddamn bear—I'll show him!"**
    The next day the hunter drives a tank into the woods but gets stuck in the big trees. Suddenly the turret door is ripped off, and the angry bear reaches in and pulls the hunter out. Then the bear makes him go down on Mrs. Bear while he fucks him in

the ass. The bears piss on the hunter before they walk away.

On the third day the hunter is flying in a fully armed Apache helicopter. As he flies low over the forest ridge, the bear reaches up and pulls down the helicopter. The bear rips open the cockpit window, pulls out the hunter, and says, "This isn't about hunting, is it?"

2. (As told to me in the crowded Imperial Garden Japanese restaurant by the Chateau): A guy is standing in line at a sperm bank. A beautiful woman takes her place behind him. He looks at her and asks, "Making a withdrawal?" (joke-teller Tim takes a sip from a glass of water, so when he speaks, it leaks out down his chin) "No—a deposit."

3. How does a nigger drink champagne? (Tim gleefully pantomimes pouring a celebratory bottle all over his head).

4. I: If they make a movie about you what actor would you like to play your part?
   Tim: Why, Grace Jones, of course!

Tim, to my wife and me: "You mean you haven't tried ecstasy (the drug) yet and you're still married?"

Tim had a blind golden retriever he called Beau and a cat named (by Barbara) Armani.

Tim's sense of humor was never more evident than in his flowery, silver-lining descriptions of disaster. Take, for example, these excerpts from a letter from the bowels of Folsom Prison, as described in *Timothy Leary: a Biography,* by Robert Greenfield:

> After head count and mail delivery, he went to dinner, which was "always a gossipy occasion for dramatic tales: rape in the mattress room, drug busts in the kitchen, heroic crimes, daring shoot-outs." At eight-thirty, Tim padded down the cell block in rubber sandals to stand "under the steaming water, a soapy moment of lifebuoy buffoonery. Then, with the warm, clean bodies of California's most vicious killers all tucked into their beds, one by one we spi-

raled down the creamy whirlpool of sleep." As others slept, Tim wrote letters on his typewriter and boiled water for "a rich cup of hot chocolate and powdered milk." Climbing into bed, he arranged "the four soft pillows into a comfy pile," turned on his lamp, and browsed "through the dozen wonderful books that had been loaned me." Around ten o'-clock, he snacked on a hot grilled cheese sandwich, chips, and pickles prepared by his next-door neighbors, "a jolly veteran of forty years federal and state time and his paramour, a willowy soft-skinned 'lady' of thirty." After the older con "removed his dentures and climbed" into the other's bunk, "toothless cries of pleasure filled the air."

In January of 1994, Tim and Mimi were by the window of my seventeenth floor office at NBC. It was my last year at *SNL* and I didn't have one word in the air show as it was about to be broadcast at 11:30. But I believed I had to suit up on game day even if I wasn't going to play. Such was my devotion. As the cold opening started, I shushed them to be quiet. Tim smiled at me in a disappointed kind of way. When the opening and credits started, I turned back to them.

I: "What?"

Mimi: "Tim and I were discussing the fact that he has been diagnosed with an advanced stage of prostate cancer."

Design for Dying, by Timothy Leary with R.U. Sirius:

I was told by two wise and gentle medical doctors at Cedars-Sinai Medical Center in Los Angeles that my prostate gland had become the host of a healthy, robust, spectacularly ambitious cancerous tumor . . . DNA has designed this complex gland as a procreative tool for the reproduction of the species, with no regard for my personal health!

These thoughts led to a humbling conclusion. DNA apparently uses me and my body as a lumbering, complicated vehicle to carry around the precious, delicate genetic code locked in my sperm. She (DNA) has cunningly located her fertility and

sperm-mobility equipment in a protected and
bustling area of my body.

"I want to keep all my options open," Tim would say. "That's the
beauty of death by design. I might decide to go to the frosty freeze,
or perhaps to the barbeque. Why let fungus eat the tangle of den-
dritic growths of my nervous system when there may be more
choices in the future?"

I was in Tim's kitchen making lamb chops, baked potatoes, and
salad as he was having a high-level meeting with a few cryogenics
people. One of them approached me and started a conversation that
soon turned toward its purpose. "You know—your friend may be
waiting too long. His rate of deterioration may now diminish his
chances of reanimation. And you know, when the time finally
comes, this road will be jammed with press and police, delaying our
efforts to quickly get him into the liquid nitrogen. If you could influence him to work with us more, it would be in his best interest."
Ultimately, Tim chose not to be cryogenically preserved. "I don't
want to wake up to see one of them with a clipboard looking at
me"—although they did go so far as to have a cryogenic "bath" prepared against the house by the patio, as if they would take the whole
body. I believe they were planning to saw off his head.

In preparation for his last birthday celebration, I saw Tim use a
funnel to pour cheap vodka into empty Belvedere bottles. Later, at
the party, through the cheery haze of nitrous oxide I saw a perfectly
preserved Tony Curtis with a white pompadour, wearing a navy-
blue blazer, and a gorgeous starlet on his arm.

Rock star Trent Reznor, from the band Nine Inch Nails, became a
frequent visitor to the house on Sunbrook. Tim admired his exceed-
ing capacity to ingest cocaine. We were at a concert in an auditorium
at Universal and it was *loud*. We stepped out into the lobby for a
breather and a cigarette. A teenager who did not recognize Tim as
anything but an old man approached him with amazement.

Teenager: "Wow, man. How do you like the music?"
Tim: "It's the best concert I've ever been to."
Teenager: "Wow, that's so great!"

TIMOTHY LEARY

Tim had to alter his house to accommodate his increasing debilitation. He gave me the tour. "You see, Tom, over there is my living room, and here is my dying room. I'm considering broadcasting my death live on the Internet. What do you think of that?"

DEATH BED NITROUS BALLOONS, 1996.
COURTESY OF TOM DAVIS

I: "Geez, I don't know, Tim. Dying is one of the most intimate acts. It's when you're most vulnerable. That, and there's the groans, gasps, and gurgling noises—all that sort of thing."

This was another option Tim did not choose.

The last time I saw him, Tim was in bed in the dying room. I was saying good-bye before heading to LAX. As I walked to the door, I looked back at him.

Tim: "Don't look at me that way. I'm not ready to de-animate yet. By the way, is there anything of mine that you'd like?"

I looked at the bookshelf beside me, and almost at random I grabbed an old book, *Dark Laughter* by Sherwood Anderson.

I: "How 'bout this book?"

He waved at me dismissively.

Tim: "Take it. How about my lava lamp?"

I: "You know, it's Mimi's birthday soon. Would you like her to have it?"

So Mimi has Timothy Leary's lava lamp. On two occasions it produced lava lumps that bore a striking resemblance to Tim's head and face.

15

INCIDENTS AND COINCIDENCE:
DEATH CAMPS, FRANKEN, AND THE BEATLES

© 2009 LINDSAY BRICE

In the future, everyone will have fifteen minutes of
anonymity.   —Tom Davis

In July 1970, Franken and Davis headlined at Dudley Riggs's Brave
New Workshop. This was our first Franken and Davis show (Franni
was in the booth for light and sound). On opening night we did a
lot of Nixon material. Al's Nixon was influenced by David Frye and
probably several other comedians, but Al's Nixon was the best because of how the character thought. He was brilliant. We even did
a Q&A with me fielding the questions:

> Tom: "Mr. President, the woman in the back row asked,
> 'What quality do you value most in other people?'"
> Nixon: "Idol worship."
> Tom (pointing): ". . . yes, the man in the Twins cap . . . I be-
> lieve the question was, 'What did we learn from the sixties?'"
> Nixon: "Aim for the head."

The audience was eating it up. We did a travelogue show with a guy from the National Rifle Association who brought along slides from his latest hunting trip, where he'd shot a cow. We did the commercial parody for the only personal feminine deodorant to come in a roll-on, and our flagship bit of the local news on the day of the night of World War III.

We had the audience with us for the whole show, until we ended with Lowell Thomas interviewing a G.I. (Al, with a thick southern accent) who had been one of the first to liberate the death camp at Dachau: "One of my buddies said, 'Boy, them Joosh girls aren't very pretty,' and I said, 'Well your sister wouldn't look so good if she was all bald and skinny.' I had a Hershey bar I gave 'em, and boy did they eat that up."

Our audience filed out in silence as we played the instrumental part of GD's "Dark Star" for house music. So we cut that piece that didn't work and found appropriate house music. Dudley loved the show.

In 1977, Al and I were very impressed with Italian director Lina Wertmuller's *Seven Beauties*, starring Giancarlo Giannini. The art film was a dark comedy that spends half its time in a Nazi death camp. My new girlfriend, Emily, argued vehemently with Al that the movie was insulting because it was misogynous. The next day we were in a cab when we noticed the numbers tattooed on the old driver's arm. Al had the balls to ask the guy if, in the camp, there had been a sense of humor. He said, "No."

Nevertheless, inspired by the highly successful dramatic television miniseries *Holocaust,* starring James Woods, we started to toy with a movie idea where two boyhood friends meet again in a death camp, one a Jewish prisoner, the other a guard.

Elliott Gould hosted *SNL* yet again in February 1980, and Al and I had a new *Franken and Davis Show* for it with Al's parents (it would be their second appearance). The piece made it through Saturday afternoon blocking (in costume for the first time). We were following our F&D *SNL* formula of having an animated opening sequence with theme song, à la Jack Benny. Typically we'd come out in silly costumes that implied we were going to do some huge production, we'd have a fight, and as our show theme played we'd cut to a bogus commercial, then cut back to us waving good night in front of the curtain. But this time we were wearing accurate SS uniforms (with the skull and crossbones, and swastikas). On cue, the elderly, arthritic Joe and Phoebe came out in '30s street clothes and overcoats, with the yellow Star of David armbands and a suitcase. They expressed their concern that the piece might be perceived as offensive. Then Al exploded into a tantrum and kicked his parents off the stage.

As soon as we were finished blocking, a PA instructed us to go to Lorne's office. Bernie Brillstein, who managed Lorne, the cast, and half of Hollywood, was there. We entered with Elliott in tow—he had been summoned, too. He intro'd the piece and, as a veteran host, had veto power. As Al and I stood there in SS uniforms, Lorne told us that Standards and Practices had a problem.

> Al: "With what?"
> Bernie: "Geez, Al, you're playing with really sensitive stuff."
> Lorne: "How do you feel about it, Elliott?"
> Elliott (as always): "I have no problem with it."

Then we knew Lorne had a problem. After all, we were the guys who wrote, with Jim Downey the *Superman* parody—What if Superman had landed in 1930s Bavaria instead of Kansas? We had a spinning headline, "Uberman Rounds Up 6 Million in 8 Hours." That got us a threatening letter from the Jewish Defense League. But still, we argued for this one. That's what we did.

Lorne asked to see Joe and Phoebe. As they entered in the costumes, Bernie was almost in tears, "You guys—you can't do that!" Lorne agreed with Bernie and announced the piece was cut. As Joe and Phoebe turned and left the office, they were obviously dejected (of course they had told everyone they knew that they were making another appearance). The door closed, and we saw Lorne was pissed.

Lorne: "Don't ever do that to me again."

Al: "What?"

Lorne: "Make me cut your parents."

After the season ended, Al and I decided to go to Dachau to see for ourselves. To treat ourselves to some adventure, we booked round-trip tickets on the Concorde SST to London, with a return from Frankfurt. We decided to spend a couple of days in London before going to Germany.

The Concorde was cool—I got a Bloody Mary served to me at the ticket counter—but the interior of the aircraft was surprisingly small. The windows were the size of a two-egg omelet, through which you could see the blackness of space. Before we began our descent, the digital "machometer" on the bulkhead registered 2.2.

I took Al to the British Museum and walked him right up to the Magna Carta. In one minute of examination, Al found in the massive document a law that stated that if you were indebted to a Jew, and he died, the debt was no longer due.

Lorne and his future wife, Susan Forristal, were also there in London, and invited us to dinner at a four-star Chinese restaurant, along with Eric Idle, and Paul and Linda McCartney. As dinner ended, Al had the savvy to pick up the tab, putting it on our business American Express card (our corporation: Bogus Productions). Two years later, when we were being audited, the IRS guys found that receipt (which we had written off). They were so impressed that we had Chinese with Paul and Linda that they immediately suspended the investigation.

Lorne and Susan invited us all over to their digs at the Savoy Hotel. McCartney was dominating the conversation, 90 percent of which I recognized from his recent interview in *Rolling Stone*. When he was finished, the handsome couple graciously bid all a good evening and exited. A few minutes later, Al and I followed suit. As we walked the marbled hallway toward the elevator, Al said, "I liked Paul, but that Linda sure has a stick up her ass." As we turned the corner, there were Paul and Linda waiting for the fuckingly slow elevator. Silence on the way down. Time to leave London.

We flew to Munich. That night we got thrown out of a touristy discotheque for doing push-ups and stretching exercises on the dance floor (we hated disco music). The Industrial Museum was worth it. At an open-air flea market, we looked for Nazi memorabilia while munching wurst and drinking beer. There wasn't much, but people were very helpful. I found an aluminum Luftwaffe belt buckle; Al got a chromed mantelpiece of that eagle atop a swastika. The next day we rented a yellow Mercedes and hit the autobahn. Al was laughing at the fantasy of being busted trying to break into Dachau at night with a German shepherd. We almost missed our exit. Suddenly we were in Dachau, the town. This made us laugh, because, what else is Dachau known for—pastries?

The signs seemed too few to us, but we finally found the death camp and pulled into the parking lot. As we got out of the car, we heard bells and read banners, half of them in English. As serendipity would have it, we had arrived on the thirty-fifth anniversary of liberation day!

AL AT THE KREMATORIUM © 1980 TOM DAVIS

As is my habit, I was carrying a Polaroid camera. We passed through the "Arbeit Macht Frei" gates and headed for the crematorium. We started to wander, and discovered the many rows of cement foundations where the barracks had stood, as noted by a single sign. We were angry all of a sudden. The damn Germans tore down the evidence! We found a woman who was the resident curator/archivist, and answerer to ignorant, emotional tourists. She explained that Dachau had remained as a refugee camp until 1962. Since the barracks had all been fitted with radiators, insulation, new walls, and running water, the decision had been made to tear them down, leaving only the original foundations. We would have to go to Auschwitz to see everything. "Oh." Had we seen the film yet? "Ah . . . no."

In the small, unadorned theater, we saw images we had never seen before. In the row of seats behind us was a family from Texas, with a sixty-year-old man wearing a veteran's hat and a ribbon pinned over his heart. The woman next to him had a small child. At one point, in a thick southern accent, she said excitedly "Look, Daddy! There you are! Look, it's Grandpa!" I turned around. Tears were streaming down his face.

Tuesdays on show weeks were all-nighters for the writers. One Tuesday night in late 1991, Lorne returned from dinner with George Harrison in tow. George wandered through the offices and met with the writers and actors, who were all thrilled to meet the man. Apparently he sat down at the piano in the writers' room and proceeded to play and sing to the happy group. Al's opened office door was fifteen feet away.

> Al: "I was coproducer at that time and I think George had perhaps too much wine. He played for two hours, no work was getting done, and there was no telling how long he'd be there."

So Franken rose out of his chair and said to the two young writers with whom he was working, "Watch this . . ."

He walked over to his door and slammed it shut. George Harrison got up, excused himself, and disappeared into the night.

That still makes me laugh just to think about it.

16
MORE GD

Time is a stripper, doing it just for you.
— Hunter/Garcia, "Cats Under the Stars"

The Grateful Dead was an experiment. Some people got it, some never will. I couldn't get enough. Did you know Jerry when he was king of the hippies?
— Steve Parish

Once a month the band had a meeting at their rehearsal hall with all employees. As described in Dennis McNally's *A Long Strange Trip,* "Bill Graham attended the meeting because he was a board member of the band's charitable arm, the Rex Foundation. He made a suggestion, and had it dismissed as 'commercial' by Willie Legate. Everyone plainly agreed with their superintendent. Graham looked away, presumably muttering to himself, 'The janitor?'"

This janitor once wrote a note to the band and pinned it to the bulletin board at the studio: "Bad-mouthing someone in his absence is an art form, deliberately cultivated here ... Optimistic descriptions of situations are sometimes passed out to anyone nearby who is prepared to play the role of patronized fawning multitude. The optimistic description is given with the understanding by all concerned that if it should change within the hour or the week, that the adjustment will not be relayed; in other words, that anything you're told is meaningless. In the words of the prophet: if you don't know by now, don't mess with it. And I want you to know that there is no hope. Insanity, sickness, and death are coming."

Jerry once told me:

1. He knew what Weir was going to play before he played it.
2. He didn't realize how good Phil Lesh (the bass player) was until he heard one of his tracks backward on a tape in the studio.
3. He was the only one in the world who could control Mickey Hart (the other drummer with Bill Kreutzmann).
4. His favorite film was *The Devil and Daniel Webster*. He told former manager Jon McIntire it was *The Grapes of Wrath*.
5. His favorite feature on *SNL* was Mr. Bill.

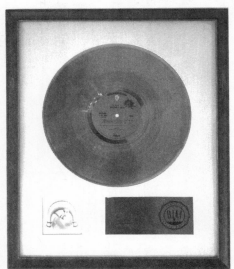

Bill Kreutzmann offered to trade one of his gold records for one of my Emmys. He invited me to his home, which he'd acquired from Spencer Dryden, the Jefferson Airplane drummer. It was a beautiful, contemporary, wooden, two-story affair with high ceilings and windows, nestled in one of those rolling green foothills in Mendocino County. We celebrated our exchange by shooting a Winchester rifle at an old Zildjian cymbal suspended from a tree limb down the driveway.

It was Christmastime and I saw among the Christmas cards one from Ken Kesey. I picked it up and read the inscription, which spoke to the grief for his son who had died some months earlier in a wrestling team school-bus accident. He wrote, "Your music has never meant more to me. Love, Keez."

Mickey Hart told me that on one of the Grateful Dead's first trips to New York City, he bought an issue of *Drummer* magazine in the West Village and didn't realize it was a gay porn publication until he got back on the band bus.

The Grateful Dead never paid for advertising.

At a New Year's Eve concert, the crew was giggling about the LSD that was put on the mouth end of Jerry's nonfiltered Camels.

Jerry held an amazing library of songs in his head, stretching from bluegrass, rock, and R&B, to big band, jazz, and classical. I once took a toke and handed it back to him. "How is it that you can remember all that chording and lyrics?"

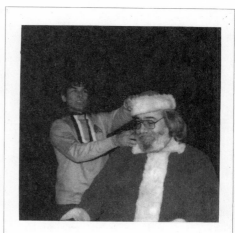

Jerry: "Oh Geez—I could never do it if I had to 'remember' all that stuff."

Annabelle, Jerry's teenage daughter, loved Phil Collins, and wanted to be a drummer. Jerry took her to see him, for a show and backstage, but he said he would not buy her a drum set until she practiced with drumsticks on one of those rubber pads drummers use to warm up with before a show. He eventually did buy her a drum set, but she then decided she didn't want to be a musician, so she sold the drums to buy cartons of cigarettes that she shared with school pals.

I took the Jerry Garcia Band to dinner at one of my favorite places in Little Italy—Umberto's Clam Bar, which no longer exists. I made sure Jerry was seated in *the* chair, and then informed him he was in the exact spot where Joey Gallo got it. Jerry was delighted.

Annabelle, then twelve, was along with us. She said her father had told her she "was going to get some culture by visiting Little Italy."

Annabelle: "The way you guys played 'Dancin' in the Street' really sucked tonight, Dad."
Jerry: "Oh really? Sorry, sweetie."

I called up Jerry.
Jerry: "Hello?"
I: "Hi, Jerry. What are you doing?"
Jerry: "Watching the hands on the clock spin around."

Jerry's open-minded generosity did not extend far enough to accept the Doors. Apparently there was some old backstage incident with Jim Morrison vomiting. As we finished watching Oliver Stone's movie starring Val Kilmer, I asked Jerry how he liked it. "It's better than the real thing."

On hearing me try to explain my guilty feelings about dating a friend's girlfriend two weeks after they split up, "Davis—we all know what you did."

On the subject of multiple girlfriends, "That's your body trying to tell you something."

Jerry: "We fucked up all the big ones—Monterey Pop, Woodstock, Egypt. At Monterey we came on between The Who and Hendrix. The Who blew everyone away, broke their instruments, and then we came out and went, 'Plink, plink, plink,' and then Hendrix came out and ended up lighting his guitar on fire—we were pathetic."

I asked Jerry about roadie Kid Candelario, "We went to do our soundcheck at the Carousel Ballroom and we were amazed at how well the dance floor had been buffed and polished, and asked who did it. They brought out Candelario and we hired him on the spot."
Dennis McNally, in *A Long Strange Trip*, wrote: "Then there was

the time that a rookie driver burned out his truck's brakes in the Sierra Nevada and had his life and load saved by Bill 'Kid' Candelario driving the truck behind him. Candelario managed to get his own rig in front of the first one and gradually slowed down until they both could come to a halt."

I was backstage with the band before the show at Madison Square Garden when promoter John Scher entered the room with a weird look on his face: "You guys—I'm really sorry to have to tell you this—but we just received a phone call from a frightened woman who says her boyfriend is jealous of her love for the Grateful Dead, and he's coming here with a gun to shoot Jerry." John Lennon had died a year and a half earlier.

> Scher: "Do you want to call off the show?"
> Everybody turned to Jerry, who was suddenly very annoyed.
> Jerry: "No."
> Candelario: "Boy, Jerry—you must be shaking in your Adidas."
> Weir: "Jerry, would you mind not standing too close to me?"
> Lesh: "I know—let's open with 'Don't Murder Me!'"

Jerry told me that the band was once on the road over Thanksgiving, so they all sat down to a long table with turkey and the works. Suddenly, a shaky, disturbed young man burst through the door. He had a handgun, which he pointed at Jerry. Everybody stayed cool and talked him down; Big Steve got up and slowly approached the young man and took the gun away.

> I: "Gosh—what happened then? Did you let him sit at the table?"
> Jerry: "No. Parrish beat the shit out of him."

At the Burning Man festival in 2006, I was talking to Carolyn "MG" Garcia, who told me this story about Ramrod: "I'd just come from a meeting with Bill Graham. Ramrod was walking past me carrying an amplifier and I mumbled, 'Bill Graham can be such an asshole.' Ramrod stopped and said to me, 'Ken Kesey, Bill Graham, and Jerry Garcia are the three biggest assholes in the universe.' Then he turned and continued on his way."

When Jerry died, Ramrod quickly assessed the situation. In rock and roll, there are no pension plans or life insurance, and Ramrod had been with the band since 1967. He went over to Jerry's house and took the famous, custom-made "Wolf" guitar. Before Ramrod died in May 2006, he bequeathed it to his son Rudso, who recently sold it for over a million dollars.

Rhoney Stanley is my friend and upstate neighbor. She is an orthodontist, but in the late '60s–early '70s she was a significant other to Owsley Stanley, and mother to his son, Starfinder, now a successful veterinarian. Owsley, a brilliant eccentric and now ex-patriot, is arguably the greatest name in the history of LSD manufacturers, except perhaps for Sandoz (who knoz?)

> Rhoney: "Owsley was religious about purity, and made us perform a strict protocol. We had to wear biohazard suits and work in windowless rooms in yellow light (LSD degenerates in white light). *We* were the contaminants, although we didn't wear respirators—we'd stop when we started getting high from breathing it in. But we considered it a sacrament whose purpose was to inspire transformation."

McNally, *A Long Strange Trip:* "His [Owsley's] standards were so exacting that he rejected a significant proportion of his yield. Between 1965 and 1967 he made about 450 grams of crystalline LSD. A gram produces 3,600 quite strong (250 mg) doses, so his total was around 1,250,000 hits. He gave away at least half."

> Rhoney: "When you write a book, you want people to read it. When you make music, you want people to hear it. When you make LSD, you want people to take it. When you take LSD and make music before a crowd on LSD, there is transformation."

Owsley became closely associated with the Grateful Dead, sometimes designing their elaborate sound systems, always with the quest for purity, with little concern about cost. It was a connection that fueled the psychedelic movement of Northern California.

Tripping at Grateful Dead concerts, I found that I would have wonderful series of comic ideas. I learned to carry small notebooks and pens. The next day I would find that about one in ten ideas was good, about the same ratio as without the stimulants—but I had a hundred ideas.

The Grateful Dead signed up with Clive Davis of Arista Records in 1977. Their first album for him was *Terrapin Station,* on which the title song played the whole second side of the LP, at one point employing the Martyn Ford Orchestra. I told Jerry that I met Clive Davis at a party, where I told the man how much I enjoyed hearing the band perform "Terrapin Station" at Madison Square Garden. Clive: "Really? How could they do it without the orchestra?" Jerry groaned and said, "You shouldn't have told me that."

The GD song "Jack Straw" has a lyric sung by Bob Weir: "We used to play for silver, now we play for lives." Belushi came up to me and sang, "We used to play for silver, now we play for Clive." At another concert, I told this to Jerry, who thought it was hilarious, and the joke quickly spread through the band and crew. Weir employed the joke lyric in performance several times thereafter.

Jerry was in town and I took my gorgeous girlfriend Kelly to visit him in his hotel room. Jerry liked pretty girls; they were always welcome. I played Jerry a tape of my band that I produced, and he said, "Why don't you open for us (The Jerry Garcia Band) at the Tower Theater?" Philadelphia is Grateful Dead country in the style of Long Island (young, macho, drunk, and vocal). In my band we had a great, beautiful female singer, Syd Straw, and Kelly, who wasn't so good at singing, but she was such a knockout, I figured who cared? We looked great. Franken wore spandex pants, a sleeveless sweatshirt, and Capezios. He did not take music seriously at all. I didn't take myself seriously as a musician, but suddenly I was trying to play guitar and sing opening for the Jerry Garcia Band.

At the Tower Theater they started booing before we could plug in. Al made a running joke about how we were Jerry's friends, so they should indulge us. This made them boo even more, which Al thought was funny, but it threw Kelly. I had sent a message to the sound board before the show to mix her down, but maybe it never got there. Introducing our fourth number, Al announced, "Now the moment you've all been waiting for—our last song!" (huge cheer). As we came off the stage, Steve Parish said, "Hey—you guys almost had it there a few times!" Jerry said, "It sounded like a band."

That was the last time I ever talked about my music to Jerry. I think that was his intent from the beginning.

© 1983 OWEN FRANKEN

17

TRADING PLACES

It is better to know some of the questions than all of
the answers.
                                        —James Thurber

When Lorne and the collective "we" at *SNL* exited from the 8H
stage and studio on May 20, 1980, we truly believed it was the grace-
ful end to our show—quitting while we were still ahead after a five-
year run. That was probably a little arrogant, as we were, but it was
certainly ignorant. It was NBC's show, of course.

Lorne had bought two floors of the Brill Building, built a state-
of-the-art edit house, and landed a five-picture deal with MGM.
He'd assigned Jim Downey and Franken and Davis to write one of
the screenplays. The three of us wrote a parody of Orwell's *1984,*
which we titled *1985,* the year we intended our movie to be released. Lorne gave us a corner office in the back of the building,
looking down on a forest of rooftop water towers and ventilators.

Al and I were doing our stand-up act at colleges all over the country in the winter of 1982, and we were talking to Lorne about taping a live performance. John Belushi had about a month to live. Don Novello and he were in Marin County, writing a screenplay titled *Noble Rot*. Dan Aykroyd called me up to say he was shooting a movie with Eddie Murphy from the current *SNL*. Rick Moranis and Dave Thomas were supposed to appear in the picture, but they had a previous commitment. As replacements, Danny suggested Franken and Davis to the director, John Landis (*Animal House, The Blues Brothers*).

They were shooting in some ancient studio in the West Fifties in Manhattan. We showed up, as instructed, at 7:00 a.m. In those days we were still on the *SNL* cycle of working through the night and sleeping through the morning. They put us through makeup and dressed us in blue jumpsuits and caps and put us in a trailer where we slept until noon. We got up and entered the studio to watch the laborious process that is movie making. We were released an hour later when the director was sure he wouldn't get to us that day. I asked Jamie Lee Curtis if she'd like to go for a drink after the shoot. She said maybe later in the week. Landis said hello only in passing. He was a busy guy.

For two weeks we followed this same pattern, which was fine with us because we were getting paid and this was our big break. We were asleep in our trailer when there was serious knocking at the door, which opened to reveal a production assistant in down vest and hiking boots. She was clutching a walkie-talkie and a cluttered clipboard.

PA: "The director wants you on the set."

I: "But we haven't met with him yet—should I have a haircut?"

Al: "Nobody's shown us a script yet."

PA: "He wants you on the set now."

The set was the interior of an Amtrak train bar car. It was a New Year's costume party with lots of extras. John Landis, the center of all the action, was standing with his hands on his hips, watching us approach him.

Landis: "So—what do you want to do?"

I: "Do I need a haircut?"

Landis: "No. Hair's fine."

Al: "What are our lines?"

Landis: "There's no script for you. You're supposed to be the funny guys. Make it up."

I: "You want us to improvise?"

Landis: "Here's the deal: you guys are two dumb jerk-off loser baggage handlers that have crashed a costume party and you're hitting on pretty girls."

It was clear the director was not afraid to use broad strokes. In this scene in the movie, Al and I, in our blue uniforms, sit across the table from two girls. With the camera rolling, I said, "Imagine how embarrassed I was when I saw that someone else came in the same costume . . ." Landis liked it, so he used us some more, offering us a line or two to cover the action when our characters walked from one 'train' car to the next. Then he had us burst into a compartment, and then back out, excusing ourselves when we saw another character with a gun (the late Paul Gleason). Finally, we did a scene in the baggage car with a "real" gorilla in a cage.

A few days later we were all at the Newark Amtrak station to shoot exteriors. Al and I improvised a scene where I'm driving an electric baggage tractor, towing a baggage trailer with the "real" gorilla in the cage. It is our introduction in the film; Al is complaining that it's his turn to drive the tractor, and we argue. Silly, but it worked. But we never did get to see Don Ameche or Ralph Bellamy.

The next year, *Trading Places* was released and became an instant hit. Landis approached us with an idea for a screenplay. He flew us out to Hollywood and put us up at the Chateau Marmont. We met with him at his offices at Universal. A few weeks before, there had been the terrible accident on John's *Twilight Zone* set, in which a disabled helicopter killed Vic Morrow and a little girl. John told us that the pilot ran away, and he was the first on the scene, turning off the helicopter motor and seeing the horror. Did we know Vic was Jewish? Anyway, he had the desire to make a comedy segment film (like *Kentucky Fried Movie* or Woody Allen's *Everything You Always Wanted to Know About Sex * But Were Afraid to Ask*). It was clear we wrote great comedy sketches for television, now how about a movie?

The next day Landis invited us to his house, about a half mile up the hill from the Hamburger Hamlet at the top of Doheny at Sunset. Walking into the foyer of his home, we saw his display of gorillas, featuring a couple of great gorilla suits and a life-size model of a gorilla in a glass case. His wife, Deborah, who does wardrobe for all his films, their young daughter, and Al and I got into his car, and he took us all to lunch at the Hillcrest Country Club. John explained to us that this was the country club that Groucho Marx and his friend built when they weren't accepted at other clubs because they were Jewish. As they were making the golf course, oil was discovered, and the wells are still pumping it out twenty-four hours a day. John gave us a walking tour, including the men's locker room, where, to our delight, George Burns was playing pinochle in his shorts, garters around his calves to hold up his black socks, and smoking a cigar. It reminded me of the photo of Lucille Ball, Desi Arnaz, Bob Hope, Groucho, Milton Berle, and George and Gracie that hung in the writers' room at *SNL*. (We had been putting black X's over the dead ones—Uncle Miltie saw it when he hosted and he didn't think it was funny.)

Landis got us some development money and we spent a couple of months writing several pieces, about a hundred pages, and sent them to John. He was nonplussed by our material and amazed that we couldn't write more, faster. "If I were writing this, I'd have written four hundred pages by now. I need lots to choose from. C'mon, you guys. I mean, really."

Whenever someone says they don't like your stuff, it's deflating. We had written some good stuff, we liked it, but he was the director. But then when we thought about it, the best part of *Animal House* came from the mind of Doug Kenney, and Belushi's performance was shot out of a cannon. The Blues Brothers came from the mind of Dan Aykroyd, and the film's weakest points came from the sensibility that if it's funny for six police cars to have a pileup, then it's really funny if a hundred pile up—and that was Landis. However, *Trading Places* was his baby and a good break for us, so, to stay on good ground with John, we pulled out of the project, taking our material with us, including the title, *Shameless,* and we gave back the development money. Giving back the money was stupid—in show business, no one ever gives back money.

In 1987, John's segment movie was released, *Amazon Women on the Moon,* and it was terrible. Whenever you can't get good reviews to use in your ads, you make them up and attribute them to fictitious magazines. In this case, newspaper ads and the marquis in Times Square included the quote: "Shameless"—*Showbiz Journal.*

Our next misadventure in the screen trade began in September 1984, with a meeting in the Russian Tea Room, an excellent Russian restaurant that was next door to Carnegie Hall (RTR is currently reincarnated, I'm told). Al and I assumed our reputation had preceded us, and the elegant movie/network lady, Diane Sokolow, was approaching us because we were so talented. But I felt that lunch might be all there was in this deal, so I had the borscht, blini with caviar, and two fresh OJ screwdrivers. She had the Salade Niçoise. We said yes to another meeting, with the producer of this newly hatched project. That was Tova Laiter, a recently nationalized Israeli who was a protégée of Bob Cosgrove, a Hollywood mogul. He got Tova a deal as first-time producer with Universal without having any real idea what the movie would be about, other than it would be titled *Datenight.* We didn't know how it was possible to get a deal with just a lame title, but we figured maybe it didn't hurt to be Jewish. It would be months, and even years, before I would discover the

whole story. But since the project seemed wide open, we figured maybe we could make it into something with our sensibilities. What did we have to lose?

Tova and Al developed an amicable working relationship, but I found her voice

TRADING PLACES

TOVA © 1984 TOM DAVIS

cloying: "*Datenight*! I love eet! Eets going to be a new Amereecaan Grafeettee!" We met with two directors, and over my objection, Al and Tova chose Dennis Klein. He was a protégé of Ron Howard, and as I recently read in Bernie Brillstein's memoir, *Where Did I Go Right?*, he was represented by Bernie, who managed the larger half of Hollywood, including still, at that time, Dan Aykroyd. Dennis was amiable enough, but he was a compulsive eater of second-rate food, didn't smoke or drink, projected an indeterminate sexuality, and at this point of his career had never directed a film. He kept saying, "I want to do *your* picture. If we're still friends after this is all over, that will say a lot."

DENNIS KLEIN © 1984 TOM DAVIS

Al and I began writing the story around several characters in a small town in Minnesota in the course of one Saturday night. We wrote ourselves in as a side plot: rock musicians on tour in a van, who hustle girls, smoke pot, and get in trouble at the motel after the gig. Of course, the director and producer insisted on the obligatory final scene where all the characters have breakfast in a pancake house as the sun comes up.

Somehow, during one of the many script meetings with Tova about what we would have to do for "my movie," she let it slip out that Columbia was desperate for Dan Aykroyd to come up with *Ghostbusters II*. Then I realized that it was worth $7 million to jerk off Dan's friends Franken and Davis, while getting some other people started in moviemaking—and who knows, maybe Tova could pull it off with her chutzpah. So Danny was the dark matter holding this whole universe together.

Al didn't share my alarm about the direction in which this production was going, which was south. I thought that if Dan's cachet got us into this, maybe it could get us out of this dilemma. Maybe he could get Tova fired and have Al and me produce it.

Danny and his new wife, Donna Dixon, were actors on location for John Landis's movie in progress, *Spies Like Us*—in the middle of Norway in the middle of winter. I flew SAS to Stockholm and connected with a flight to Oslo. On this flight I was impressed with the Norwegians' seemingly genetic inability to hold their liquor. They were a bunch of yahoos. I went to use the toilet and was amazed to see it was filled to the brim, with a Dairy Queen turd on the top. It wasn't just repulsive, it was a bad sign. I spent a day and a night in Oslo wandering through the huge park filled with Gustav Vigeland's sculptures, dining on reindeer meat in an old high-raftered restaurant, and getting drunk by closing time with a Norwegian professor of history (the bars close early, so everyone really goes for it). I took a train that climbed over precipitous, snow-covered mountains through the night, heading for my goal just below the Arctic Circle. There was a crazy woman speaking angrily to herself while drinking a bottle of peppermint schnapps; the rest of us avoided eye contact. In the morning I boarded a ferry and moved up a spectacular fjord to a town where I hired a taxi for the final leg, finally arriving at the hotel where everyone was staying. I went to the set where they were shooting in deep snow. The Aykroyds were pleasantly surprised to see me, and Landis greeted me warmly. That night after dinner, I finally got Danny alone.

> I: "Dan, this *Datenight* movie is a disaster—you got to get this woman fired."
> Dan: "Davis—I can't do that."

Of course, he was right. I was being ridiculous and would just have to make the best of it. I spent another day watching Landis and his masterful crew and then I disappeared as quietly as I arrived. A couple of weeks later I reported to the *Datenight* production offices in Chicago. We had wanted to shoot on location in St. Cloud, Minnesota, but the Minnesota Film Board thought our script was obscene.

Starting the first day of principal photography, Director Klein literally refused to talk to us. Al said that he was probably nervous and wanted to establish his authority. The director of photography, who would talk to us, had visions of grandeur and supreme confidence in his own talent. "Moviemaking is the sport of kings!" No, I thought, that's horse racing. When I saw the dailies, my stomach knotted up, but I held my tongue. I resolved to sit back, try to enjoy myself, and maybe learn something. Al liked what he saw, and for the first time we didn't agree on something big.

In the script, our band's name is Badmouth, and Jerry Garcia designed a logo that was painted on the side of the van. I asked him if he would produce the band's "live music" for the bar/pickup scene.

Al and I met Jerry and Big Steve at O'Hare and headed for this little recording studio in the middle of nowhere outside of Wheaton,

JERRY GARCIA WATERCOLOR, 1984

Illinois, Belushi's hometown. In the backseat, I lit up one of my best and handed it to Jerry. Suddenly, a state trooper glided up alongside us. Sensing the officer's presence, Jerry kept the joint down, turned, smiled, and waved. The trooper smiled and waved back, then accelerated into the future.

We checked into a new, luxurious hotel, almost empty except for my real-life band (playing themselves in the movie), and my old friend Pat Hayes from the Lamont Cranston Band, whom we'd flown in from Minneapolis to play Al's part on guitar. In the studio the next day, we laid down the tracks for the first song. I was having trouble with my solo, so Jerry plugged his Steinberger into the sound board and ripped a great solo in one take. My favorite moment in the film.

Jerry was making a lot of trips to the bathroom, and that evening we ran out of coke. So I took Pat, my drummer Bill Buchen, and the car into Chicago. We parked in the blues and reggae nightclub district, where I had seen Willie Dixon a few weeks before. Pat knew his way around and was recognized by harmonica player. Those two got up on the stage with the house band and had a stunning blues harp duel that got the crowd to its feet. When the music stopped I was talking to a beautiful waitress who took us to her home where

her boyfriend sold me some coke. I arrived, victorious, in Jerry's room before the sun came up. He said, "Davis—you're amazing." He was right.

We finished the session on time and on budget, and just as Jerry was running out of dope. I gave him my straw, which had enough residue to get him back to San Rafael. Did Tova thank me for a job well done? "I heard dat Jerry Garcia was smawking freebess in thee bethroom." Somebody snitched.

In postproduction for *Datenight*, like every other Hollywood B movie, some hack arranger wrote a discolike song called "Blown Away," featuring a fledgling female rock star. She was featured in the video along with clips of the movie, the soundtrack release, and the movie credits theme. For our appearance in the video, Al and I suggested the image of the two of us being literally blown away into a brick wall.

So, in a studio in Hollywood, we found ourselves suspended about ten feet above a concrete floor. We were dangling from wires connected to leather harnesses under our tuxedos. My balls were being smooshed as the crew lit us and everything was being prepared for action. A wall of Styrofoam bricks was behind us. Al asked the special effects master if he had to be careful, or could those cables hold his weight no matter what?

　　　　　　　　　　　　　　　　TRADING PLACES

SFX master: "Yup."

So Al experimented, gyrating his body and bouncing up and down; his cables snapped and he landed on his back, groaning in pain. Everyone rushed to his aid. They covered him with a blanket and called an ambulance. I heard the director sternly say to the SFX master, "I thought you said the cables couldn't break!" The master said, and this was the first time I heard the phrase, "That was then. This is now." Everyone was thinking lawsuit and that Al would have to have ramps built over the steps to his house, when Al stood up, brushed himself off, and said, "I'm all right." By now my testicles were bow-tied around my prostate. The pain was so great, my voice was reduced to a whisper, and I couldn't get anyone's attention. Al finally looked up at me. "I'm okay, Tom . . . What's that? Lah durr . . . ? Oh—LADDER!" We both recovered and finished the shoot.

A couple of days later we were in a production office at Columbia to ask about distribution plans and look at the poster, etcetera. We couldn't get anyone to look us in the eye. Someone finally came up with "the poster." It was the worst poster either of us had ever seen, the title of the film was now *One More Saturday Night,* and it said "Starring Al Franken and Tom Davis." Franken threw a fit, and finally the guy holding the poster had had enough. He informed us that the film was going to open in two theaters to meet some legal requirement: one in Times Square and one in Sacramento. He said that if it tested well, then a new poster could be made.

While Al was in front of the theater in Sacramento with a bullhorn, trying to exhort the theatergoers to buy tickets, I was in the wilderness of northern Minnesota with my fishing buddies. A week later the two of us went to the opening at 1:00 p.m. in a crumbling Times Square theater where the poster was just hand-scrawled Magic Marker text on white cardboard. There were only two other people in the audience—two black guys who complained through the whole show, "What the fuck is dis shee-it?" It opened in those two theaters and never played anyplace else. The video sucked, too.

I don't always agree with Leonard Maltin's assessment of movies in his annual bestselling *Movie and Video Guide,* but I think he was right on the money when he wrote,

> *One More Saturday Night* (1986) C-95m. BOMB D:
> Dennis Klein. Tom Davis, Al Franken, Moira Harris,
> Frank Howard, Bess Meyer, Dave Reynolds. Un-
> funny comedy written and starring the nerdy duo
> from TV's *Saturday Night Live.* Unlike one of their
> TV skits, this feature, about various goings-on dur-
> ing a Saturday evening in Minnesota, runs an hour
> and a half. Forget it. [R]

To this day, Al will defend that film.

Several months later, Lorne called me into his office. "There is this woman, Diane Sokolow . . . her son's best friend is dying of cancer and he's a huge Grateful Deadhead—do you think you could get Jerry to call him up?" I groaned. Jerry was just recovering from a diabetic coma and I couldn't do that to him. I said no. Ten days later Lorne told me that the young man had passed, and Lorne had attended the funeral where they played the Grateful Dead song, "Brokedown Palace." To this day my heart aches that I didn't try to get Jerry to call that kid.

In the summer of 1990, I got a rare phone call from Lorne. "Tom— would you like to make *Coneheads* into a movie?" It was obviously a rhetorical question because he had to have asked Aykroyd first, but I was thrilled to hear it. Danny and I had always envisioned the characters' background story as huge sci-fi stuff that couldn't be done on television. Lorne was on a run, coming off the resounding success of *Wayne's World* and the birth of his first son. So Dan and I holed up in the Chateau Marmont and wrote the first draft.

My first feelings of trepidation came when Lorne hired a director who had done only children's movies. Lorne started talking about crossover audiences, something about how our original *SNL* fans were now having children, so he wanted to make a movie that's not too scary. Then he hired Bonnie and Terry Turner to "help" Dan and me with the rewrite. Bonnie and Terry were protégés of Al Franken, by this time my ex-partner, and they were Lorne's favorite writers on the show (Lorne always has favorites). However, their sensibilities were not compatible with mine. Poor Danny was caught in the middle between his loyalty to me, and his professionalism in the screen trade, which he'd built up in the last fifteen years in Hollywood, where the executives at Paramount were also his friends.

I approached Lorne in his lair overlooking the *SNL* studio. "*Coneheads* is about sex and violence, Lorne, and nobody knows more about the Cones than I do," I said.

> Lorne: "Nobody knows more about the *Coneheads* TV sketch than you do."

Back on the other coast, I discovered the script had been rewritten so that the scenes on their home planet, Remulak, had been reduced to a big gladiatorial event in a stadium. I had written in restaurants, streets, and homes. Then I saw the cones. They had been reduced because they didn't fit in the frame! That was always the big joke—The Heads! The Heads! And then they'd decided not to use Laraine Newman as Connie, getting instead a nubile fledgling actress to play opposite Chris Farley, thus breaking up the old team. This is why the first rule in Hollywood is get rid of the writer. Now *I* was the troublemaker.

Dan and I were called into the executive offices where he was literally pulled in a door that closed on me. Inside though, while he was inside being read the riot act, Bernie Brillstein solemnly told me to sit back, smile, talk up the movie, and I would be made rich like everyone else. My part, the dentist, went to Jon Lovitz, who was wonderful, but that was supposed to be my big acting break.

On opening weekends, the Hollywood numbers guys always know by 7:00 p.m. on Friday whether or not a movie is a success. *Coneheads* was a disaster. The old *SNL* fans did not show up with their kids, and young people were bored with it. So much for your crossover audience. It became fodder for Leno and Letterman. "Hey—are they starting to make another one of those *Coneheads* movies yet?"

Danny and Lorne immediately went on to do other films. Bonnie and Terry became very successful Hollywood producers of *Third Rock from the Sun* (the television show starring John Lithgow). That pretty much left me holding the bag.

Lorne gave me a watch for my birthday.

18

MICHAEL O'DONOGHUE

My piece is brilliant—what piece of shit are you working on?
　　　　　　　　　　　　　　　　—Michael O'Donoghue

Late July 1975, it was our second day as writers for a new live comedy show produced by Lorne Michaels. We had heard of him in L.A., where we'd resided since '73. Our friend Matt Neuman and his girlfriend, Marilyn Miller, had worked on a Lily Tomlin special that Lorne had produced. Now the team of Franken and Davis had just moved to New York City with a six-week contract. The two of us were paid the minimum, as one writer. The day before, Lorne had told us to write up stuff for television. Later, I would learn that Lorne never even read this material. He wanted us all to let go of our act, and any other old trunk-scripts. This was our first job as writers, and Al and I should have been intimidated, except that our act was as bright and funny as anybody else's. Our stand-up comedy experience had taught us how to get a live audience to laugh, and we had that confidence.

Nobody seemed to know what was going on. Waiting outside Lorne's office, I walked up to the "old" guy Herb Sargent, who was talking to the *National Lampoon* guy, was who wore dark wire-rims and was dressed like Clifton Webb in *Laura*. I was twenty-two, wearing jeans, boots, a Grateful Dead T-shirt, and shoulder-length hair. I had a pair of dark wire-rims, but I only wore them when I was out in the sun. Phrases like "far-out" and "fuckin' A, man" were part of my vernacular. That would change quickly. Sargent and O'-Donoghue were examining the stories from two newspapers—the *New York Times* and the *New York Post*. I amiably commented, "Ah, what's the difference, anyway?" Michael bared his teeth like a cornered rat and proceeded to get pissed off at me. Herb held up his hand to intercede and turned to O'Donoghue. "So? . . . he doesn't

know."

Fuck, I had to get out of there and smoke a joint. Franken came with me. We wound up in the bushes outside St. Patrick's Cathedral. As we reentered the office, I smelled really good pot coming from somewhere else. Like Bugs Bunny following the vapors of cooking carrots, I wound up outside O'Donoghue's office. I knocked on the door.

"Yeah?"

"It's Tom Davis."

"Oh—c'mon in."

I sat down. We smoked his dope and started talking about everything, and we laughed. Michael told me the show was going to be an enormous hit, and after two years it would go "down the dumper," which is when he would leave. Our conversation happily went all over the place, including favorite literature. He recommended three books for me—*The Magus* by John Knowles, *The Last Temptation of Christ* by Nikos Kazantzakis, and *The Sirens of Titan* by Kurt Vonnegut. Mike and I became lifelong friends, which for him meant another twenty years. He was then thirty-three.

Franken never really hit it off with Mr. Mike. Still a few weeks before the first show, O'Donoghue was talking with a gaggle of writers when Franken came up to him with a rejected script that he thought was worthy. Mike took the script, opened the window, threw it down seventeen stories onto Forty-ninth Street, then returned to his conversation. A few days later, when we asked him how much he was getting paid, he asked us what we were getting. When we told him, he laughed and said his cats were getting paid more than that.

Mr. Mike went first class or not at all. Because I was going globe-trotting with Danny over the holidays in late '76, Mr. Mike, with Anne Beatts, took my girlfriend Emily and me for an early Christmas goose dinner at Luchow's on Fourteenth Street. Established in 1882, the dining was grand, eight-course, and very German in the dark oak paneled room. Reservations had been made ten days in advance. Inside the door, customers waited patiently to be seated, but Mr. Mike strode up to the maître d' and shook his hand, slipping him a twenty. We were immediately seated at a table between the active fireplace and a classically decorated real Christmas tree, as a guy in tails serenaded us with a violin. Mounted boar and deer heads watched us savor our holiday repast.

Mr. Mike was always pasty white and rather sedentary—except in East Hampton playing badminton. This lawn sport requires quickness, not strength. He kicked my badminton ass.

Some of my favorite O'Donoghue stuff included:

1. A *Starsky and Hutch* police show parody with miniature police cars being crashed by hands that also squirted lighter fluid and set them aflame. "This week's episode: *If He Hollers.*"

2. Host Ralph Nader explaining to a visitor the presence of a blow-up party doll in his apartment as part of a vigorous series of consumer safety tests.

3. Old stock footage of a whale being harpooned and pulled alongside a ship. "And now . . . the Song of the Harpooned Humpback Whale . . . (screaming)."

4. Mr. Mike got Jerry Rubin of the Chicago Seven to do a commercial parody for stain-resistant wallpaper. "Up against the wallpaper." I told Mike how much I admired Jerry Rubin and Abbie Hoffman and he said, "Yeah, Davis—but just remember that these guys encouraged a lot of people to go out and get their heads knocked in by the Chicago police while they watched it on TV."

5. *Minute Mystery.* A dead body lies on an apartment floor as crime photographer Mike Mendosa (Aykroyd) does his job and speculates with a cop (Chevy) whodunit. Then the camera pans around the set at bizarre and arcane objects as if one could solve the mystery by seeing them. All the objects came from Mr. Mike's real apartment at 23 West Sixteenth Street, which also contained reflective mirrored shelves with collections of armies of toy rhinoceroses and tacky objets d'art. His meticulous wooden office files of his life's work were labeled with cuttings of female anatomy from Victorian pornography. There was a painting of a leather-jacketed bobby socks girl beating another ponytailed girl with a belt. There were several folk art items framed on the wall, signed by serial murderers Richard Speck and John Wayne Gacy. He had two fireplaces, one of which suffered a chimney fire and the firemen chopped through the wall to be sure it was doused. There was a leopard-skin upholstered dry bar. Gilda Radner gifted him with a framed photo of the anal rape scene from the television miniseries *Roots,* with Gilda's surprised face pasted over the victim's. O'Donoghue was delighted to receive from Al and me an antique vibrator ("muscle relaxer") in its original case with all the attachments that we found in the back of Al's grandmother's apartment.

6. An obit in the *New York Times* of a real man known as "Professor Backwards" caught Mr. Mike's eye. Apparently this guy had an act where he demonstrated a unique ability to talk backward. He was shot to death by a mugger in Miami. In O'-Donoghue's *Update* joke, bystanders ignored his cries of "Pleh! Pleh!"

7. In a parody of the 1958 sci-fi classic *The Fly*, Mr. Mike wanted the scientist with the genetic transporter machine to accidentally become half man, half tuna melt.

When Mr. Mike broke up with Anne Beatts, we all knew it because it was a tempest. We could hear him ranting with her on the telephone behind his closed office door. During this time he literally smashed several rotary telephones by beating them with the receiver. This is hard to do. I've tried. Digital phones are much easier to break.

After Mr. Mike left the show, Lorne had silk jackets with the then-signature *Saturday Night Live* embroidered on the back. He thoughtfully had one boxed in tissue paper and sent to Mr. Mike. The box with the jacket was mailed back after he had apparently plunged a large butcher knife through it fifty times.

Mr. Mike once had a downstairs neighbor who didn't like him and complained about any kind of noise. At that time he had two cats that had just outgrown kittenhood, and Michael was leaving for the weekend. He left the animals with food and water, and also moved furniture and rolled back the Persian carpet to reveal the hardwood floor. There he spread catnip and released a bag of one hundred marbles.

Steve Allen, one of my heroes, who should have been an *SNL* host, had his own talk show on NBC for a while in 1977. One day I had my office television on the NBC feed as they were taping at about 11:00 a.m. Steve introduced, with generous praise, his next guests, John Belushi and Michael O'Donoghue, from the sensational *Saturday Night Live*. It was obvious that John had been up all night, and Mr. Mike was clearly enjoying the surreal spectacle as it ensued. Steve graciously tried to cope with the situation when John suddenly kicked over the coffee table before them on the set. Michael giggled, and Steve turned to him.

"Mr. O'Donoghue . . . you clearly do a lot of the show under the influence of drugs . . . what happens on those days when you can't get dope?"

Mr. Mike: "Do you mind if I go out and smoke a joint before I answer that?"

Mr. Mike and I collaborated on several pieces that went to air. The worst was *Green Cross Cupcakes,* a surreal, live-commercial parody for a mass-produced, unappetizing snack. This was when we were broadcasting from an ancient studio in Brooklyn, while the Elections Unit commandeered 8H for the '76 election. Our sketch had a '50s family saying, "Mmm . . . delicious" and "they *don't* cause cancer!" Then it cut to Mike and me, dressed in hooded radiation suits, carrying between us a stretcher upon which dozens of cupcakes were arranged as in a product shot.

"Why take chances when it comes to cupcakes? Cancer freeness never tasted so good."

It ended by cutting to a cage of hungry rats into which was thrown a cupcake. However, instead of devouring the sweet treat, the rats were terrified, and piled into the opposite corner. We hadn't rehearsed with real food, because we wanted them really hungry. Maybe the cupcakes should have been made of cheese. Fucking rat handlers should have known. The audience was confused and silent. *Green Cross Cupcakes* became director Davey Wilson's term for "no laughs," like, "Don't you think that might be another *Green Cross Cupcake?*"

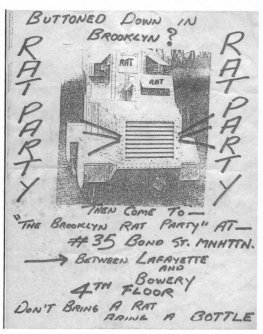

Danny threw an after-party and photocopied invitations celebrating the "Rat piece."

The best thing Mike and I did took a year to get done. We wanted to use the show to do a '50s-type sci-fi movie parody, where a giant creature causes death and destruction to the audience, cast, and crew. Davey Wilson's mantra at the time was, "You can't do that." Now, I loved the guy. Davey was old school. He had worked the Catskills after he won the Funniest Guy in New Jersey award in 1947, doing an act in which he wore a Boy Scout uniform. He worked on the production staff of *The Colgate Comedy Hour,* where Herb Sargent was a writer. Davey made his bones working up through the early days of television. Sometimes, I think to amuse himself, he would make up show business stories to tell us, like Carol Channing is a man, and Danny Thomas had a wax thumb, which is why he always held a cigar. His original thumb was crushed in a car door, if you believe that. It was Davey who started a rumor that Danny Thomas and Charles Laughton both liked to eat human shit. Many giddy late-night hours were lost imagining a different *Make Room for Daddy.* Davey died of an aortic aneurysm in June 2002 while it was his turn to perform in a game of charades. I'm told it took the other players some lengthy moments before they realized it was the real thing.

Anyway, Leo Yoshimura and Eugene Lee from set design would always say, "Sure. We can do that." So Mr. Mike and I went to them to figure out how to get our sketch done.

We found two teenagers (I remember one's name was Billowitt) who were stop-action animators who would work for cost. They were good, too. We took them up to the eleventh-floor outdoor platform where there was a goldfish pond and some gardens. We had them take a still photograph at night, looking down onto Forty-ninth Street, with the conceit that it was looking down from a picture window in Studio 8H (which we would estab-

MICHAEL O'DONOGHUE

lish with breakaway wooden window panes in front of a chroma key). At first we wanted a *Tyrannosaurus rex,* but after looking at the boys' painstaking work, we decided to make it *The Attack of the Atomic Lobsters.* So they made new footage of giant lobsters on Forty-ninth, climbing up the side of 30 Rock.

Finally, on the Robert Klein show of January 28, 1978, we set up our lobster ending for the show by working in a shot of our 8H window during Klein's monologue, and placing a story in *Weekend Update* about radioactive waste dumped in the Atlantic. Some unusually large sea creatures had been sighted, with lobsters the size of helicopters, and people reading in the dark by the light of glowing mackerels. Near the end of the show, giant atomic lobster calls interrupted a sketch and an intro to the musical guest. Chevy had prerecorded the lobster call with *National Lampoon Radio* sound engineer Bob Tischler. Finally, the lobsters attacked, breaking through the window. Huge lobster claws jutted in the frame of a handheld camera that stayed on Robert, who described the carnage as soldiers fired rifles and audience members fled in terror, etcetera. John Belushi, in a bee costume, got beheaded.

> Klein: "Oh my God—he had his whole life ahead of him . . . at least two or three more years."

From the book *Mr. Mike: The Life and Work of Michael O'Donoghue,* by Dennis Perrin:

> The show's announcer, Don Pardo, yells out to Klein, but he too is devoured. The credits roll over lobster roars and static. Two voices, O'Donoghue and Davis, assess the situation. O'Donoghue has a plan: The only way to stop the beasts is to eat them. They'll need millions of gallons of boiling water, enough to fill Central Park pond. Also, enormous lemons, helpings of butter, nutcrackers, and bibs. The plan becomes a dinner menu, and O'Donoghue and Davis argue about the proper dessert (a swimming pool full of jello? A rum raisin cake the size of a tennis court?) and what constitutes an appetizer? Their voices fade into the static.
>
> "Atomic Lobsters" came off on air nearly without a hitch, but in dress rehearsal there were audio and visual problems, and this sent O'Donoghue into

hysterics. Tom Davis watched as his colleague threw scripts into the air, kicked chairs, screamed about incompetence, and generally raised total hell. Audience members exited hushed and intimidated by this mad display; they steered away from O'Donoghue's tantrum, an outburst Davis felt was justified. O'-Donoghue wanted the piece done right for the live show, and for the most part, it was.

"Atomic Lobsters" proved a fitting epitaph for O'Donoghue's time on the show.

When the original *SNLs* were meat-cleavered down to one hour for the E! channel, I saw this show, and everything about the *Attack of the Atomic Lobsters* was gone, except Robert Klein's shell-shocked farewell over credits, with smoke in the air, dead bodies lying around, and lobster calls. Fuck whoever did that, and their pets.

19
CHRIS FARLEY

Al Franken to an inebriated Chris Farley in a room full of writers and production staff: "You know, Chris, we've already got one dead fat guy."

If Chris Farley had stayed in his hometown in Wisconsin, he might be alive today. But John Belushi and the notoriously hard-living Del Close were his heroes, and Farley had the talent. What doomed him was his own success. Fate is a fickle mistress. Several of us who lived through the Belushi tragedy saw this one coming with the sort of dread and hopelessness one feels seeing a puppy beside a major highway.

I knew he was going to be a star in the spring of 1990. He had that quality where you can't take your eyes off him, even though he was not yet accomplished in his own craft. The fact that he was nearly illiterate accentuated his boyish appeal, but denied him the tools he would need to survive. He took an immediate liking to me, in part because of my association with Belushi and the heady days of the original show. This did nothing to slow my declining influence at *SNL,* and may have precipitated my firing, as Lorne and his burgeoning young staff sent Chris to rehab after rehab.

Despite his size, Farley was remarkably nimble and athletic. One of his first appearances was in a sketch I wrote based on an idea from my old friend Bill Buchen: if there was a mobile-home park on Manhattan, the trailers would have to be set on end. The set was delightful, but Chris's entrance from the top of the ninety-degree-askew trailer home, scampering down through the sideways kitchenette, got the piece on the air.

Jim Downey and I wrote the first *Chris Farley Show,* with Martin Scorsese as his guest (November 16, 1991):

> Chris: ". . . ah . . . uhm . . . you know in *GoodFellas* . . . when Joe Pesci says, 'What do you mean I'm funny? Do I amuse you like some kind of clown?' . . ."
>
> Scorsese: "Yes . . . ?"
>
> Chris: "Well, um . . . that was awesome."
>
> Scorsese: ". . . thank you."

During the after-party in a fancy restaurant on West Seventy-ninth, Chris and I walked over a few doors to the Dublin Bar to have a few drinks without the crush of the crowd. When I saw him throw back shot after shot of tequila, I thought, "Uh oh—this guy's going to have to quit." Of course, it was just the proverbial tip of the iceberg before the *Titanic.* He could not even give the appearance of moderation. Subtlety was not an arrow in Farley's quiver. On two separate occasions, I met him in the Fiddler's Green on West Forty-eighth just before closing time, and seeing him in such an obvious state of intoxication, begged him not to return to the office. He'd agree, but twenty minutes later, there he'd be, making the younger male writers laugh by hitting himself so hard the red welt on his face was in the shape of his hand, or by doing a painful pratfall. I'm told he once took a shit out the seventeenth-floor window. I wasn't laughing.

Chris once left his wallet in his first-class seat on a flight to L.A. It contained a quater of an ounce of cocaine, and somebody managed to keep it out of the papers. In another instance, he put a Ninth Avenue heroin dealer on the security list, and the person showed up at 8H asking for Chris. Not cool. Then Chris came back after a Christmas break with hideous stitches all over his arms, he said from walking through a plate-glass door. Nobody laughed at that.

So, during the season's-end party in 1994, I pulled Chris off into a quiet corner of Rockefeller Plaza and confronted him (and you know you're in trouble when *I'm* the one intervening).

> I: "Chris—this Belushi thing you're doing is getting kind of creepy. You don't want to die the way John did, do you?"
>
> Chris: "Oh—that'd be cool!"

I wept before him.

> Chris: "Hey, Tom—you're crying."
>
> I: "Yes, Chris, I'm crying for you."
>
> Chris: "Wow. Thanks, man."

Chris eventually left the show to make movies in Hollywood, but returned to host in September 1997. Chevy appeared in the cold opening. I watched the show, and the next day I paid a rare visit to Chevy's home.

> Chevy: "Boy—how long do you think that guy's going to last? I give him two months."
>
> Chevy nailed it. On December 18, I pulled into my driveway after sunset, and my wife came out to meet me.
>
> Mimi: "I have some bad news."
>
> I: "Chris Farley."
>
> Mimi: "Yes."

I was angry with him, and did not cry—I'd already done that.

At the wake at St. Malachi's Church on West Forty-eighth Street, Dan Aykroyd did a remarkable imitation of Chris's motivational speaker character and made everyone laugh. The priest told us of Chris's work with the homeless, and the visits he made to hospitals to cheer convalescing parishioners. Downey (in absentia) composed a letter read by Marci Klein, recalling the Christmas party in Lorne's office when Chris showed up as an overly exuberant Santa Claus who scared Jim's young son, but then won the child over. Lorne spoke, and sweetly recounted his youngest son's love of Farley, and his child's question about the wake, "Is that where everybody says nice things about Chris?"

I will remember him dancing so hard at a Grateful Dead concert at Madison Square Garden that he shook the lighting booth. I will remember him coming to my wedding and charming all my family and friends. I will remember we all loved him.

20
MORE DANNY

The greatest gift of all is generosity of spirit.

In the second season of *SNL,* there were two high school kids, a boy and a girl, who somehow were always inside NBC hanging around the elevators and the studio. Being a nice guy, Danny would say hello to them. Then Lorne got a call from a truant officer complaining that those kids were absent from school, and Lorne informed Danny. Entering the party after the next show, Dan spotted the boy near the entrance with a small group of other underaged young people. Dan became angry and went right up to him, "Goddamnit, you got me into trouble by being absent from school, and I won't stand for it. If I ever hear that you've been truant again, I'll personally bar you from being anywhere near the show!" Then he strode into the crowded restaurant. As I passed by the kids, I heard the boy explain to his friends, "Ah—I had a fight with Danny."

★　★　★

I was wearing a Palestinian burnoose, dark glasses, a sweatshirt with a UFO with a red blinking light on it, and an elegant Paul Samuel black sport coat (a hand-me-down from Danny Aykroyd). It was Halloween 2006 in the Red Dot Restaurant in Hudson, New York, and I was out in the back courtyard where a circular wood-burning fireplace and chairs are provided for tobacco-appreciating patrons. A guy who was not wearing a costume was quizzing me with "what do you do?" A few minutes later I was getting *his* story. In 1978 he was working for SIR (Studio Instrument Rentals), a prominent midtown Manhattan sound studio, and they serviced the musical equipment needs for *SNL*. Apparently he was standing with some speakers and cables out by the 8H elevators during a broadcast. Belushi came storming out of the show in costume and makeup, clearly agitated about some sketch that didn't go right. Pacing like a caged animal, he punched out the glass in a fire extinguisher case. Danny emerged from the studio to find him. When he saw what John had done, he said, "I'll show you how to do that." He stepped over to the matching extinguisher case on the other side of the entrance and smashed his fist through the glass. Then they both walked calmly back to the show with their hands bleeding.

The day after the *SNL* Mardi Gras prime-time special in 1977, Danny explained to me that instead of flying, he had driven to New Orleans in an America DriveAway Service car he had to deliver to a man in Yazoo, Mississippi, just above the Louisiana border. We had spent the whole day sleeping and now we were plying ourselves with fine cuisine. By the time we got it together, it was 9:00 p.m. and raining heavily. Danny and his old friend, Benoit ("Ben-WAH"), were in the late-model Caprice; I drove a rental with Bill Murray in the passenger seat. Danny had a lead foot, and following those red taillights through the inky deluge in the deepest part of the American South was testing my driving skills. I was afraid I was going to lose him. Billy told me I was doing great and that Danny would pull over and wait when it was time to make a turn.

At two in the morning we arrived in downtown Yazoo City

where Danny found a pay phone under the only streetlight standing before a closed-by-suppertime Tennessee Williams general store, across the street from a one-room post office. Five minutes later we were invited into the funky kitchen of an old black couple. The naked lightbulb shone at the end of a cord dangling from the ceiling. She opened the refrigerator and took out long-necked bottles of beer, and then she made ham and eggs as Billy played chess with Hank Aaron in overalls. We stayed until the sun came up and the rain stopped. Danny drove the rental all the way back.

After the Grateful Dead appearance on *SNL* in November '78, the Blues Brothers were invited to open for them at the New Year's show, to be the swan song of Winterland before it was torn down.

The Blues Brothers band was especially wary of being dosed. They were all meticulous about opening their own drink containers. Talking to him sometime later, Steve Cropper told me he thought it must have been in the ice water in the coolers, and they absorbed it through their skin while securing virgin bottles and cans. However it was, they were red hot. "I thought I was going to swallow my harmonica," Dan recalled. I remember watching their performance from Candace Brightman's lighting booth. She handed me a bottle of Rémy Martin. I took a few pulls off the frosted green glass bottle of cognac. It seemed as thick as honey.

Bill Murray arrived in jeans, a rumpled jacket, and a three-day growth, having hitchhiked up from Los Angeles. He was immediately adopted by the GD family.

After the Blues Brothers, there was a forty-five-minute break until the countdown at midnight. An FM station, KSAN, and a local television station were broadcasting live from the event. There was a television camera set up in the balcony with chairs and a microphone, with the crowd and the stage in the background. Somehow, Al got in there. I did not join him. I felt too high to perform on camera. He had no such doubt. I was told that he went on for over half an hour as if he were a network anchor at the '68 Democratic convention: " Senator Ribicoff has just concluded his address—uh oh, Mayor Daley is making his way through the crowd to the proscenium." Several people told me later that he was hilarious. I wonder who's got *that* tape? I'd love to see that Blues Brothers performance again, too.

I got lost backstage. There was a room there, and I was crawling around on my hands and knees watching the carpet undulate when Jerry entered with a huge snifter of the honeyed cognac.

"Hi, Davis—are you having fun?"

I: "Hey, Maestro . . ."

Jerry: "Here—have some of this."

Then, suddenly, I was alone again, and I could hear the music roaring out front.

Meanwhile, the Jefferson Airplane had a bus to shuttle guests to and from Winterland and their legendary HQ in the Haight. John and Danny spent several glorious hours over there.

When the show finally ended, Emily and I walked out into the dawn and across Geary Boulevard to our room in the Miyako Hotel. She drew a hot bath while I opened a bottle of vodka and made fresh-squeezed screwdrivers. It was the peak of something wonderful, and Danny was at the core.

He married Donna Dixon, one of the most beautiful women in the world. As June ended in 1982, she called me. She even sounded like Marilyn Monroe. "Davis—Danny's thirtieth birthday is coming up and I'm throwing a surprise party. Can you make it?"

There must have been fifty of Dan's best friends that showed up. Donna had booked every available motel room in the nearby small Canadian town.

Danny was building his lifetime family home on property his great-great-grandfather had originally acquired on a beautiful lake scoured out of limestone by the last retreating glaciers. The lodge was half-built, but a large Quonset hut had been assembled to harbor his growing collection of cars and motorcycles. His father, Peter, had feigned a sprained ankle to occupy Danny long enough for all of us to crowd into the Quonset hut, the steel doors slid shut and latched from the outside. I cracked everyone up by saying I smelled gasoline being poured around the outer walls of the structure. Finally, Donna and Peter finagled Danny into opening the door. I think he knew something was afoot, but I'm sure he couldn't have anticipated the scope of the operation.

Then there was a softball game. Danny's friend John Alexander, an artist/painter and boyfriend of Rosie Shuster, was pitching when Donna came up to bat. Legendary drummer Steve Jordan was at catcher's position. Donna popped the ball up to Alexander, who stood underneath it to make the grab as she ran to first base. Jordan put his hands on his hips and shook his head saying, "If you were a real man, Alexander, you would have dropped that ball."

Then there was a macho volleyball game that included vicious repartee. We all took off our shirts in the summer heat. The Blues Brothers started picking on their manager, Michael Kleffner, who was much bigger than Belushi. Horn player Al Rubin got everyone to giggle by calling Kleffner "Triple Bypass." The bassist Duck Dunn said in his sarcastic southern drawl, "Nice pair of pants—you should have bought two pair—one to shit in, and the other to cover it up."

Donna called me through Lorne's ninth-floor office at *SNL*. "Hey Davis—I want to do a surprise for Danny and you're the only one in the world who can do it."

In February 1993, Donna was pregnant with their second child, and the question of the hour in the Aykroyd house was, is it a girl or a boy? Apparently Donna had just gotten the test result and the next day she wanted me to manipulate Dan into being in Times Square on the ticket island, between 11:45 a.m. and 11:47 a.m. looking up at the huge "zipper" news screen where the message would read, "Danny—it's a girl!" Tom Schiller would tape Dan's reaction from a surreptitious vantage point on the corner of Forty-fourth.

I was over at their place when I mentioned to Danny that I was meeting a guy in Times Square who had some exquisite bud. Then Donna came in and asked Dan to run an errand for her in midtown so that's how we got Dan into Times Square at 11:44. As Danny and I stepped onto the box-office island, he suddenly stepped in front of me.

Dan: "Davis! There's a guy with a camera taking pictures of us. It's a bust."

MORE DANNY

I: "Really?"

I couldn't find Schiller among the hundreds of milling people, but no one can find the lens better than Dan.

Dan: "Let's get out of here!"

I had to grab his arm to keep him from bolting. "Davis—what are you doing?"

I: "Dan—look up there."

I pointed at the screen where the message was starting. Dan was still riveted to the cameraman.

Dan: "It's a police camera!"

I: "Dan—look at the message on the big screen!"

Dan: "What . . . ?"

As he read the message, I saw all the gears in his head downshift through the layers of the ruse. He broke into a big smile and started laughing. I was nearly in tears from the changes I had just put him through. But I was the only guy in the world who could do it, and I did it.

The telephone rang. "Davis—I've got a gig with the Rolling Stones." Two days later, in August 1994, I found myself in an elegant house in a suburb of Toronto. Danny and a production crew were listening to *Voodoo Lounge,* the Rolling Stones' new album to be released in a few days, as their tour started. It sounded *good.* Danny and his crew had been hired to tape a short piece on the Rolling Stones for television magazine shows. It would be done the day after next, during sound rehearsal in the afternoon at RFK Stadium in Washington, D.C., before their full dress rehearsal.

Danny shot an intro where he's on his Harley with the Toronto skyline in the background. He invited the viewing audience to come along with him to see the Rolling Stones. He took off on his motorcycle and disappeared. Cut. Danny drove back and loaded his bike onto an eighteen-wheeler full of equipment. Then he and I stashed his wardrobe in Donna's Mercedes with Virginia plates, and we drove all night to D.C. and crashed at a motel near the stadium.

By 11:00 a.m. we arrived at the business entrance to the aging venue, an ugly steel and concrete monstrosity built in 1961 as home to the Washington Redskins, and the scene of some great rock and roll. We were given multiple laminated IDs and shown to Dan's trailer, among the dozens. Now he and I started jamming about what exactly we were going to do. Danny scrawled a couple of the ideas onto a legal pad and handed it to a production assistant, and then he donned his motorcycle outfit and headed back to the gate where the crew was waiting. The director suggested Dan argue with a fat security guard, who, he thought, would be funny chasing after him. I could see this production was going to be fast and loose.

The stage was a huge metal sculpture like a battleship's deck, with a lighting tower that looked like a colossal robot cobra. An enormous, state-of-the-art television screen was suspended over the stage. I saw that our low-tech production could have Danny on the screen as some giant talking to Mick.

Mick: "Who are you?"

Dan (covering one eye with his hand): "I am the Cyclops Polyphemus, keeper of the stadium."

Mick: "So you have come to help us celebrate the beginning of our tour?"

Dan: "No. I clean up after the show."

Mick: "What song shall we play?"

Dan: " '2000 Light Years from Home'!"

Mick: "No. You get 'Brand New Car.' "

So they launched into that solid rocker from *Voodoo Lounge*. I was amazed at how good the sound was onstage. I saw a roadie looking at me kind of funny.

I: "Is it okay if I stand here?"

Roadie: "Sure. Stand anywhere you want."

Later, I was standing by myself inside the stadium's vaulted archway when Mick's dark-windowed limo drove slowly by. Several minutes later another roadie came up and told me Mick Jagger wanted to talk with me. He led me through the security point to the band's area and opened a door. I pushed through a curtained area into a large dressing room with fluorescent lights and Mick Jagger cross-legged in a director's chair beside a glass table with an ice bucket and some wineglasses. There was also his attractive female assistant.

Mick: "Hello, Tom, come in. Would you like a glass of wine?"

Tom: "I certainly would."

Mick: ". . . and you know Miranda?"

I *did* know Miranda. She had dated Lorne Michaels in the mid '80s.

Tom: "Hi, Miranda—how are you?"

Miranda: "Nice to see you."

Mick flattered me by praising my work at *SNL*. The white wine was good.

Mick: "Have another glass. Have you got any jokes for me?"

I: "As a matter of fact, I was thinking of a Washington, D.C., joke. How's this: 'Washington, D.C. is like Hollywood without the talent.'"

Mick was amused. I tastefully thanked him for the wine and got up to leave.

Miranda: "I'm going to give you our fax number in case you come up with any more jokes. Is there anything we can do for you?"

I: "Two tickets to Madison Square Garden?"

Miranda: "Of course."

Dan brought me to another green room. Ronnie Wood was drinking a Guinness and inspecting a rack of T-shirts and other apparel that would go on sale at each venue. Apparently he oversaw their design. Most of the shirts were awfully busy. His twenty-year-old son was obviously proud of his father and seemed like a splendid fellow.

Keith Richards was accompanied by a young man whose job appeared to be constantly rolling hash joints. A caterer brought Keith some exotic taco: "I've found it's healthier to eat a little bit several times a day." He'd also been working out with a trainer. While most people get fat when they get old, this band was still remarkably hungry looking.

Charlie Watts entered as in a dapper dream, dressed completely in white: silk shirt, vest, puttees, Capezio ballet shoes, and a golf cap. As I stood there chatting with him, a guy from wardrobe came up and thanked him for flying in his parents. When he walked away, Charlie said, "We see to it that all our people are well taken care of."

That night Donna arrived and, except for a dozen or so Stones children, we danced around the infield of the empty stadium while the band performed the entire show. They played all out, and sounded *great*. They even did an encore with the fireworks, some of which were shooting out the holes in the stage where I had been standing.

On July 30, 2003, I had a gopher-hole Stones gig with Danny— the SARS Benefit outside of Toronto. "Gopher-hole gig" is Danny-jargon for emceeing a big event where he would station himself under the stage, next to a ladder leading to an opening from which he could pop up through the stage floor like a gopher from its hole. There was a big lineup of bands: AC/DC, Rush, the Guess Who, Justin Timberlake, Blue Rodeo, the Tea Party, and Kathleen Edwards, who I thought stole the show. The Rolling Stones flew in from Sweden, where they were on their world tour.

Danny took me and his friends Wally, Dave, and Matthew, backstage into the Stones' compound. Ronnie Wood invited us all into his trailer and made us espressos from his own personal machine. He announced that he'd quit drinking, and now enjoyed a lot of really good coffee. As we stepped out of the trailer, Keith Richards came over and hugged Danny. Then Mick Jagger came striding by in a terry-cloth robe and a towel around his neck. As he approached, I said "Hi, Mick," and he walked past me as if I didn't exist. His snub was so well performed that everybody giggled, and Keith and Ronnie shrugged at me like, "Hey—that's Mick." I realized that Miranda didn't work there anymore.

I don't remember if I witnessed this or read it somewhere, that backstage, Mick and Keith got a message from John Popper, the harmonica player/lead singer for Blues Traveler:

"Dear Mick and Keith, It has always been my dream to jam with the Rolling Stones, and I'm here tonight . . ."

Mick said, "What—and have dueling harmonicas or something? Fuck him."

Nearly half a million die-hard Canadian rock fans were gathered on this former air force base on a blazingly hot day in July. It's always the big guys who pass out with sunstroke first. If this show had happened in the United States, some people would have died. The Canadians, bless them, provided free bottled water to the crowd, who booed Justin Timberlake off the stage. I must admit, that made me laugh. During their set, the Rolling Stones invited the shunned young superstar to join them onstage for a rendition of "Miss You." I thought that demonstrated the Stones' (probably Mick's) savoir faire, although I had to laugh again, because "Miss You" is the worst song they ever wrote.

The phone rang.

> I: "Hello?"
>
> Dan: "Hey, Davis—I got another gopher-hole gig—Harley-Davidson's throwing a hundredth anniversary celebration."

The corporate jet banked over Milwaukee in its final approach. Looking out the window by my elbow, I could see the natural harbor on Lake Michigan and the large outdoor venue, Veterans Park, where the show would take place. There must have been a hundred thousand motorcycles parked in surrounding lots, fields, and the downtown area. Many of them had those iridescent paint jobs that made them glitter in the morning sun like swarms of tiny, bejeweled insects. Being the last day of August 2003, the cloudless sky promised it would be a hot one.

We checked into the Victorian Pfister Hotel in the center of the city famous for brewing, the pride of Wisconsin, a dairy state. The dining room featured "The Butter of the Day" to spread on bread, steak, fish, vegetables—everything except the salad. The Badger State also had the highest per capita rate of obesity (I now understand that Alabama has now taken that cake).

In the backstage area we entered a mobile home to meet the grandson of the original Davidson. He was about sixty years old, with well-coiffed gray hair and beard, a Harley-Davidson beret, Harley-Davidson boots, and a monogrammed Harley-Davidson T-shirt of the type that brings in more revenue than the machines themselves. He had planned this event, which featured several acts, including Kid Rock and a "Special Surprise Guest" to cap everything off. The Special Surprise Guest was his big secret. He wouldn't even tell Danny, his emcee, and warned us that if we discovered the secret—not to tell anyone.

There is a rule in show business—never bill "Special Guest" or "Big Surprise" because the audience is going to spend all day hoping it's the Rolling Stones.

The labyrinthine backstage had a series of event tents around which walkways had heavy rubber mats to cover the tangles of electrical cables that snaked everywhere. We had a cooler in our tent that had beer and soda, but no food. Finally, when we inquired, a tray of bologna and mayonnaise sandwiches was presented by a high school girl who, I would guess, was working for free. Kid Rock threw down one of these sandwiches, jumped on a new display motorcycle, announced he was going for a cheeseburger, and roared off toward civilization.

I assisted Danny from his "green room" under the stage at the bottom of some stairs leading to his gopher hole. We had a couple of folding chairs and a cooler; tarpaulins were tied to the steel pipe strut/supports to afford us some privacy. I kept track of the rundown and helped Danny phrase intros with some humor. From our gopher-hole vantage point, I could see only the performers' feet.

Kid Rock was the last act before "The Special Surprise Guest." Mr. Rock impressed me with his energy and fearlessness. When his set ended, grandson Davidson himself went out to introduce the finale. When he shouted into the PA, "Ladies and gentlemen—Elton John!" we could hear the collective groan of a hundred thousand sunburned bikers. "What da fuck? Not even Bob Seger!"

Elton has the reputation for playing any event where they'll pay the price—even bar mitzvahs. If he had been properly billed, the biker throng might have been more open-minded, but when he broke into "Tiny Dancer," you could see thousands turn and start the painstaking process of mass dispersal.

Kid Rock saw what was happening and came out to sing with Elton for "Saturday Night's All Right for Fighting." I had to poke my head up through the stage to see this one. There was Kid, dancing on top of the rhinestone-studded piano, his long hair stringy with sweat, screaming out the lyrics into his cordless mic. He got the audience to turn back around and cheer. After the last song (no encore), Dan finished his responsibilities by saying, "Good night! See you in another hundred years!" Then we made our break on loaned-out bikes. Danny jumped on the lead motorcycle. I rode on the back of Wally's, and Dan's pal Dave brought up the rear as Danny got the sea of people to part before his headlights. Several angry police officers converged on our convoy. Then they saw it was Danny, who likes cops. Two minutes later we had two squad cars with lights flashing to escort us back to the hotel.

In the hotel bar, I was drinking gin shaken on ice and served straight up with a twist. Wally was cracking up as I entertained a table full of bikers with my routine, "Yes, Hitler was a monster, but he did a lot of good things—the autobahn, methadone, the best artillery and uniforms . . ." Dave lured Wally and me upstairs with a big hash joint. We went to my room, which had an adjoining door to Danny's suite. Dave lit up the honker and handed it to me. As I used my lung capacity to full advantage, a beeping alarm went off. I looked up at the ceiling—we were standing beneath a smoke detector. Like a bear swatting a beehive out of a tree, I ripped the annoying appliance off the ceiling. That's when the real alarm went off. Now there were wires hanging from the ceiling—it had not been battery operated. Wally ran to the window and looked down. "Wow, Davis—the whole hotel is emptying out into the street!" Suddenly there was frantic pounding on the door. I admitted two uniformed hotel security guys. They saw the dead detector lying on the floor.

> Security guy #1: "What's going on here?!"
> I: "I smoked a joint under the smoke detector and ripped it out of the ceiling. I'm very sorry."
> Security guy #2: "Aw geez . . ."
> Danny entered from his suite.
> Danny: "What happened?"
> I: "I fucked up."
> Dave: "Davis pulled the detector out of the ceiling and set off the hotel fire alarm."
> Dan: "Oh, geez."
> He pulled a wad of bills out of his pocket and started handing out twenties to every hotel person and fireman who came in, "Here. Sorry—false alarm. Hi—sorry."

Dan told me a week later that Harley-Davidson was past due paying his fee, which included two new, cream-colored Harley-Davidson police motorcycles, complete with the lights and sirens. That was taken care of and Dan gave Wally one of the police bikes.

21

HEPBURN HEIGHTS, THE DEN OF EQUITY

Until it seemed I must behold
Immensity made manifold;
Whispered to me a word whose sound
Deafened the air for worlds around,
And brought unmuffled to my ears
The gossiping of friendly spheres,
The creaking of the tented sky,
The ticking of Eternity.
　　—Edna St. Vincent Millay, "Renascence"

I got into my rented car at SFO and drove toward San Bruno, took Nineteenth Avenue past San Francisco State, through the park, and across the Golden Gate Bridge into magical Marin County.

As I exited at San Rafael and headed up the hill, I was filled with anticipation about beginning our project. Kurt Vonnegut's novel, *The Sirens of Titan,* was both Jerry Garcia's and my favorite book, and he had recently purchased the film rights. Now he and I were going to adapt the work into a screenplay and see if we could get it made into a movie. It was early December of 1983.

For most of the '80s, Jerry lived on the topmost road, Hepburn Heights, overlooking this town nestled between Mount Tamalpais and the Bay. The Grateful Dead office was a house on Lincoln down by the highway. "Front Street," their warehouse and studio, was on

Front Street. Hepburn Heights, he told me, was given to him by some former rock promoter who had pressed and distributed a live recording of a performance without the band's permission. Jerry's problem was that the recording and the mix were shitty. Anyway, the fellow had become a real estate agent and owned that house, and I'll bet the issue was resolved without lawyers (although GD lawyer Hal Kant was a world champion poker player). About that time, Ben and Jerry's ice cream came out with a new flavor—Cherry Garcia. Jerry tasted it and didn't like it. He considered a cease and desist for about twenty seconds, and then decided to let it go. "Aw fuck it, anyway." (In the early '90s, Jerry's lawyer convinced him to make a licensing deal with the ice-cream people so he could retain power over the use of his image in perpetuity. As I write this, a huge chain of restaurants is currently using a caricature of his image on billboards across the country, prompting his estate to respond. His lawyer was right.)

The house was set up like a duplex; the downstairs had its own kitchen, living room, bed, and bath. It was amazing how few possessions the man had, considering the millions he'd generated and pissed away. His closet had a few old flannel shirts; his dresser a pile of unopened black T-shirts. The only thing framed on the wall was the hand-illustrated and calligraphed lyrics by Robert Hunter to their song, "Blues for Allah." Jerry never graduated from high school, but was extremely well-read from years of touring.

I: "You mean you've read the entire Bible?"
Jerry: "I know it well. Haven't you read it?"
I: "No. I figure that's something I'll read when I'm in prison."
Jerry: "Well, what do you think a hotel is?"

But in his home at Hepburn Heights there was but a smattering of books that different visitors had left for him. Nothing had been moved since my last visit several months before (I'd heard that the only time he picked up the place was when Bob Dylan came over). The most prominent thing on his bookshelf was the complete music publishing of the Beatles. There were two armchairs in front of the television, which was always on—even when he was gone for months at a time, and between them a small glass-topped table.

As I entered, I put my duffel bag on the bed. Jerry slept sitting up in his chair. He hadn't slept in a bed for years. Sometime in 1977, sitting in my office at 30 Rock watching the network feed on my telelvision monitor, I saw the taping of a *Tom Snyder Show* (the interviewer and eccentric broadcast personality; Danny used to do him on *SNL*). His guests on this day were Ken Kesey and Jerry Garcia.

> Tom Snyder: "Mr. Kesey . . . it's well documented that you've taken all these drugs since 1964 . . . do you think it's done you any harm?"
>
> Ken (spazzing): "Yah—niikt, sp-, spa- . . . ah . . . don't know . . . aah!"
>
> Tom (turning to Jerry): "Mr. Garcia . . . when was the last time you had a good night's sleep?"
>
> Jerry: "What year is it?"

Jerry's guitar from the '70s ("The Wolf") stood neglected in "my" bedroom. I had brought a fresh set of strings; Jerry let me pick on it, which I would do only when he wasn't there.

I sauntered into the television room; I was carrying my briefcase.

> I: "Hey Jer—you wanna talk about *Sirens*?"
>
> Jerry: "Sit down, Davis. Relax. Let's get high first."
>
> We took our seats like hungry lumberjacks at a smorgasbord.
>
> Jerry: "You got some coke?"
>
> I (like Curly): "Soitanly!"

Jerry dumped a ▮▮▮ of the ▮▮▮ and a pinch of ▮▮▮▮▮ into about a half inch of water in a small beaker. He held a Bic lighter under it and wiggled it around until the ▮▮▮ congealed with the ███████████, forming a translucent ███ floating on the near-boiling water. This could be collected with the tip of a butter knife, but there was a special pharmacist's instrument he used for the purpose. The ███ was deposited onto ███████████████████ ████████████, where it became a white crusty ███ Holding the flame under the foil would cause this to turn into a ██████████. Then out came the ███████████████████████████████ ███████ which, when added to the liquid and heated, would mix into a ████████████████████. Using a pencil, we fashioned straws out of more foil, which we used to inhale the smoke produced by the ████ held under the ███ tray. Much of the substance would collect in the straws, which later would be unrolled and likewise ██████████.

I had brought along several cassettes of *Bob and Ray* radio shows from the '50s and '60s. We laughed at these for hours at a time.

A mouse showed up and sat on his haunches to look at us. "That's my friend," Jerry said. "So am I," I thought to myself.

We left Hepburn Heights to go to a Grateful Dead gig in Berkeley (getting up to go, I accidentally put on his blazer while he put on mine. When we realized the mistake we made like old-time comedy "Gimme that coat! Why . . . I oughta . . ."). At that time, Jerry was driving a gray BMW given to him by a coke dealer. He parked

in the yellowed DO NOT PARK HERE space at the rear door of the auditorium. As we went in, Jerry gave me his laminated pass so I could get around. When we left after the encore, keyboardist Brent Mydland said to me in his withering sarcasm, "Say hello to Jerry for me." As Jerry became increasingly addicted, he had begun to withdraw from everybody, as they, in turn, became increasingly worried. I found myself in the middle of this swirling storm.

We were climbing into the BMW when a wild-eyed young man opened a back door and jumped into the backseat. I thought I was going to have to grapple with the guy, but Jerry held up his hand to me. "Hang on, Davis. I'll handle this." He turned around and smiled at the intruder. "Not tonight, man." The kid got out and said good night.

Back at Hepburn Heights we sat before the television as if it were a fireplace; we smoked and talked about everything. "Did I tell you about the *People* magazine incident? They interviewed the drummers for weeks and then the rest of the band. I didn't want to do it. Finally I said okay, and then they asked me about my love life! Of course, when the article came out it was all Jerry Garcia and pictures of me! It was awful," he laughed.

I told Jerry that *People* magazine had interviewed me and come over to my apartment to take pictures, including a humiliating shot of me lapping up milk with our cat. And then they woke me up on the phone at 8:00 the next morning to ask about Dan Aykroyd's love life. Of course, no article appeared at all. We laughed. The next day we started writing.

Phil Lesh showed up and invited me to visit his house. As he was driving me there, he asked if I understood what this stuff was that Jerry was smoking, and did I understand what was going on? He begged me to be sure that Jerry didn't use any needles.

Kreutzmann told me that sometime before, he had come over to the house to confront Jerry, who wouldn't answer the door. So he had rolled a few large pieces of sawed-up tree down the hill to boom against the side of the house. A message from a drummer.

In Rock Scully's *Living with the Dead,* Scully recounts that when the whole band showed up and Jerry was posed with the ultimatum: choose between us and the Persian, Jerry said, "Sorry, but I'll go with the Persian." Jerry called their bluff.

Rock and Nicki Scully lived upstairs at Hepburn Heights. Rock had been with the band since the beginning, and now, as road manager, a lot of his time was spent scoring drugs for Jerry and himself. The band and crew fired him and Jerry did not intercede because he was angry that Rock had brought a doctor over to examine him.

Jerry took me and his daughters, Annabelle and Trixie, to dinner at a Persian restaurant in the Bay Area. As we were seated and starting to look at the menu, the bandleader for the four Persian musicians who were performing spotted Jerry from their modest stand. The bandleader shielded his eyes from the lights, grabbed a microphone and announced in his accent, "Ladies and gentlemen—the great Jerry Garcia is here tonight! Jerry Garcia—come up here! Jerry Garcia everybody!"

Jerry smiled and dutifully walked up and accepted a set of finger cymbals. They played music and Jerry accompanied skillfully on the little bells, while dancing like a trained Russian bear.

Even I had the occasion to say, while we were deep in the first draft, "You know, this stuff is probably going to make you sick when we're right in the middle of all this" and he turned to me very soberly and said, "All right, let's have this conversation, but just this once . . . the fact is, I'm surprised I made it this far. Plus, I don't care, and that's the truth. Why can't I do this if I want to? Now . . . do you want some or not?" I did.

> Jerry: "Hey Davis, you got any snorts?"
> I: "Yes, but I haven't chopped it yet."
> Jerry pointing to the base of his nose: "Don't worry about it. I got a grinder right here."

The man's lungs were congested and his sinuses abused. He was also overweight and he had sleep apnea from hell. Phil Lesh in his memoir, *Searching for the Sound,* recalled:

> At that time Jerry was still the voracious reader and cultural explorer I had always known. When I heard that in June 1985, the San Francisco Opera would mount a production of Wagner's Ring, my first thought was to invite him to attend with us.
>
> Jerry made it for the first three operas . . . [*ellipsis mine*] but on the third night, for "Siegfried," in the final scene of act 2, our hero, after killing the dragon Fofner and winning the Ring, discovers that, having drunk the dragon's blood, he can understand the language of birds. He holds a brief conversation with a wood bird, and just at the most tender part, as Siegfried is singing about the loss of his mother, from behind me comes a sound—part chainsaw, part the rooting of a wild boar for truffles. Oops—Jerry has fallen asleep and begun to snore. Micky leaps to

the rescue, jabbing him with a salad fork while shaking his shoulders and urging him, half asleep, back to the foyer.

Once, I came in while he was sleeping in his chair. I sat down and gently asked, "What are you dreaming about?" His eyes opened and he smiled, "Little green men."

Without freeze-drying the wonderfully cosmic *Sirens of Titan* story line, there is a sequence where tens of thousands of "Martians" attack earth in flying saucers. The Martians are abducted human beings who are slaughtered by the people of Earth as they emerge from their saucers, wearing army surplus gear. This pathos unites the Earthlings in a global epiphany, starting a new religion. I asked Jerry what might be the musical score beneath such a monumental scene—Mars the Bringer of War, in Holst's *The Planets*? Jerry: "Oh my God, no. Dixieland rag with kazoos!"

Bea, one of the central characters of *The Sirens of Titan,* has been an unwilling participant in all this cosmic manipulating and spends her last thirty years living a bizarrely comfortable life on Titan, writing reams of bad poetry. Garcia and I spent a few days amusing ourselves writing bad poetry for her. As it turned out, we shared considerable talent for bad poetry. Submitted for your disapproval, two bad poems by Garcia/Davis from their screenplay:

> *A little girl with pony stands,*
> *O'er looking Rumfoord's Sea.*
> *The giant birds of blue they soar,*
> *While crying "Hello, there, Bea."*
> *Air and food and money,*
> *Are no longer her concern.*
> *Simple pleasures milk and honey,*
> *With daily labor earns.*

> *I know what it is to be a tool,*
> *In the hands of a shoddy craftsman,*
> *While artisans poor,*
> *Dissect the floor,*
> *To the plans of shoddy draftsmen.*

> *Yes he loves to dance on your brain,*
> *While your face he is a slappin'.*

He smiles when he says you soon will know,
The worst that can happen.

We actually finished a first draft in January 1985. A week later, Jerry was supposedly on the way to rehab when he was busted for smoking a controlled substance off aluminum foil in an unregistered BMW in Golden Gate Park; in his briefcase were twenty-three empty bindles with traces of heroin and cocaine.

Several months later I had returned, and Jerry drove me to downtown San Francisco near where his mother once ran a bar. He took me into Colossal Studios and introduced me to his filmmaker friend, Gary Gutierrez, who was working on storyboards and illustrations for *Sirens*. They were beautiful. We started thinking about pitching to some studios in Hollywood. Whom did we want to play the lead, Malachi Constant? Bill Murray? And the other role of Rumfoord, the Space Wanderer, was kind of a Ken Kesey figure . . . maybe John Lithgow . . . hmmm.

In Manhattan, at the Landmark Tavern on Eleventh Avenue and Forty-eighth, I bought lunch for Bill Murray and an old-school, chain-smoking Hollywood executive from Columbia, Shel Schrager. Mr. Schrager suggested I should direct the film. Never having directed—and being diminutive in character—I immediately dismissed the notion. I was still young and should have seized the opportunity. Anyway, we set up a meeting in L.A.

The night before this meeting, in June 1984, I had attended the Hollywood premier for *Ghostbusters*. So when I picked up Jerry and his manager, Richard Loren, at the airport, I had a ghost-shaped swag bag in the back window of my '62 Comet (Rent-a-Wreck). Jerry and I stayed at the Chateau Marmont, in that house by the pool. He gave me a five-minute guitar lesson, at my behest, showing me how to keep the thumb moving when fingerpicking.

Robert Greenfield's oral biography of Jerry Garcia, *Dark Star,* quotes Gutierrez: "It was Tom Davis and Bill Murray, and Jerry and me, and a bunch of attorneys and this guy from Universal [Michael Ovitz], sitting around this huge table, and during this very serious discussion about the deal, there was Bill Murray making his mouth like a billiard pocket at the edge of the table and Tom Davis was rolling gumballs across the table, trying to get them in Bill Murray's mouth."

That evening I left Jerry in the passenger side of the Comet as I dashed into a convenience store on Santa Monica to get aluminum foil, some Bic lighters, vodka and OJ, and Yoo-Hoo chocolate drink (for Jerry). When I came out, a homeless hippie was talking to Jerry, whose window was rolled down.

>Homeless Hippie: "Man—you sure look like Jerry Garcia."
>Jerry: "Yeah. I get that a lot."

At the Burning Man festival of September 2006, I saw Jerry's wife, Carolyn "MG" or "Mountain Girl" Garcia, and told her I was writing this chapter about *The Sirens of Titan* and Hepburn Heights. She told me she was recently going through some stuff from the era and found a note written in Jerry's scrawl:

1. **Script development and writing—T and J— $100,000++**
2. **Salaries, payoffs, etc.—$20,000**
3. **Money for drugs—$30,000 per month.**

Jerry and I both quit the stuff after he went into and came out of a diabetic coma in 1986. This started a marvelous new blossoming of the band that produced a hit record, *In the Dark*. Eventually we both did heroin and coke again, though I never used a needle, and he never used one in front of me. I entered a methadone program in 1994 and stayed in it for three years. Jerry died his first night in rehab in 1995, at the age of fifty-three. He was almost exactly ten years older than I. Big Steve told me that in the autopsy, they found half of his enlarged heart was blocked off, and that he had been in a lot of pain toward the end. However, it wasn't the heroin that did him in. It was the cheeseburgers, chocolate cake, and cigarettes.

I showed the manuscript of this book to my good friend Jon McIntire, former manager for the Grateful Dead:

>Jon: "I read that chapter on Garcia—Hepburn Heights—you went right for the heroin, didn't you? Nothing about the spiritualism or the transformational quality of the music. Don't you know how hurtful that stuff can be? Your book is the worst thing since *Going Down on Janis*!"

So I sent the manuscript to Carolyn Garcia:

Carolyn: "I really liked your book, and I liked *you* even more after reading it. Of course we always loved you, but I didn't know you were such a little acid head!"

I: "I know. Everybody thought I was a coke dealer for the longest time."

Carolyn: "All this amazing stuff happened to you—and you hardly ever mention your feelings."

I: "That's deliberate—my technique is understatement."

Carolyn: "I know, but I don't even know how you feel about the Grateful Dead."

I: "But I've got them running all through the book—I mean, they were my band—they spoke to me; they spoke for me . . . they always will. Robert Hunter is my favorite poet."

Carolyn: "So put that in."

I: "Okay . . . let me ask you something—that long, detailed description of the preparation of the dope—was that hurtful for you to read?"

Carolyn: "I wasn't hurt by that but I worry a little bit about you—I mean, do you want to be that 'drug guy'? It was pretty serious—why don't you take a Magic Marker and censor out key words so it'll read like 'then we took the *blank* and put it in the *blank*'—so you won't know what it is (laughs)? Can I show your book to Annabelle?"

Jerry and Carolyn's daughter Annabelle sent me a marvelous cartoon scenario about my manuscript:

Annabelle: "You were in all these places with all these wonderful people at just the right time. I don't know if it works like that anymore."

I: "Of course it does. You're one of those wonderful people. Let me ask you something—was there anything that you found sensitive or hurtful—like that description of the dope preparation in Hepburn Heights?"

Annabelle: "No. That chapter was like summer vacation for me. Summer was when I got to be with Dad, and when you visited, you guys seemed to have so much fun, I wondered what you were talking about. I'd like to read more of that."

I: "Really? I was hoping you would help remember some of that stuff for me."

HEPBURN HEIGHTS, THE DEN OF EQUITY

22
MORE AF

(In a disagreement with his wife): "Honey, I'm going to really put my foot down on this one—is that okay?"
—Al Franken

Franken and Davis did a lot of Nixon satire, so when the Senate Watergate hearings were broadcast live five days a week for three months in the spring and summer of 1973, we didn't miss a minute. The weather in L.A. was getting hot and we had no air-conditioning, so we wore boxer shorts and T-shirts. We had a black-and-white television in the living room and a small one in the kitchen, so we could cook.

Senator Sam Ervin was the colorful chairman, kind of a Foghorn Leghorn character. "I'm just an ol' country lawyer from Dixie," he would say, but he was a master of constitutional law. What became a dark crisis for the country became high comedy for us.

Senator Howard Baker: "What did the president know and when did he know it?"

The evil twins of Haldeman and Ehrlichman being hoisted on their own petards. John Dean—the snitch—saving his own skin or the honest one coming clean?

> Dean: "I told him, 'There is a cancer growing on the presidency.'"

To this day I bake chicken the Franken way, seasoned thoroughly and placed on a "chicken rack," along with carrots and onions, to keep them suspended above the dripping fat at the bottom of the aluminum foil tray. Al said his gravestone should say, "He ate his share of broccoli." He made a great Bolognese because we were always eating spaghetti. It took me years to figure out why Al used *so* much fresh garlic, other than that he really loved lots of garlic: thinking that a "clove" of garlic was actually the whole "head" of garlic, Al had been using ten times the prescribed amount from recipes he had been reading. We'd reek for days afterward.

When Haldeman aide Alexander Butterfield took the stand, we both observed how agonized he looked. Then he revealed the existence of the tapes, and Al and I danced around the apartment, whooping and cheering as if the Vikings had just won the Super Bowl. I don't know that we ever had more fun than that. And we had plenty of fun.

During our six-week gig in the lounge at Harrah's in Reno, Franni and my live-in girlfriend Lucy drove up from L.A. to visit. We all went out to a Chinese restaurant. For dessert we had pistachio ice cream and fortune cookies. My fortune read, "You will be married soon." I crumpled it up and began pouring everybody more oolong tea from a fresh pot.

> Al: "My fortune said to trust your instincts—what did yours say, Honey?"
>
> Franni: "Ah . . . it says, 'You will get good news from far away.'"
>
> Al: "How 'bout you, Lucy?"
>
> Lucy: "I like mine: 'You will be a success at whatever you choose.'"
>
> Al: "What's yours, Tom?"
>
> Tom: "Ah—it was the same as Lucy's."

Al: "Really? Let's see it."

Tom: "Geez, I threw it away."

Al: "No—there it is crumpled beside your cup. I'll get it."

As he reached for the crumpled fortune, I "accidentally" poured some steaming oolong on his hand. He leapt up from the table with a yelp and threw his cloth napkin at me so hard, it bounced off my chest.

"Why did you do that?!" he demanded rhetorically as he shoved his hand into a water glass. But he'd forgotten about the cookie's message.

From: Tom Davis
Date: Wednesday, 25 April 2007 9:38 AM
To: Al Franken
Subject: Memoir

What was your exchange with Spiro Agnew at the NBC elevators in 1975?

From: Al Franken
Date: Wednesday, 25 April 2007 8:30 PM
To: Tom Davis
Subject: Re: Memoir

It was in the makeup room at Tom Snyder's studio. Agnew was being made up and I sat in a chair next to him. I think that's the sixth floor. Perhaps Conan's studio. It was a total misfire. I turned off the tape recorder just before I talked to him and I quoted to him something Nixon said (the protesters were bums) and attributed it to him and asked "aren't you a bum?" (for taking bribes). Then he got to say "I didn't call them bums." "You didn't?" "No, that was Nixon." Later Snyder's producer called Lorne and asked him not to let his people come down to six and bother his guests.

Halfway through the first year of *SNL*, Lorne invited all the writers to join him to see Monty Python in a rare live stage performance, opening for the Eagles at Madison Square Garden. Backstage after the show, there was an event tent with tables and chairs and lavish catering. Al and I filled our plates and sat down at a table next to John Cleese.

Al: "Hi, I'm Al Franken. I've always thought you were the funniest Python."

Cleese pointed at Eric Idle a few chairs away.

Cleese: "Tell that to *him*."

In November '76, Al and I were in a pickup touch football game in Central Park. Al ran a deep post route and our QB threw it as far as he could. Al made a diving catch in the end zone, but in the process wiped out badly on the gravelly, overworn field. But he hung on to the ball. As our team ran up to congratulate him, he was rubbing his head but smiling. When we lined up to kickoff to the other team, I saw a confused look on his face and he was standing there like he didn't know what to do. Uh oh.

I: "Al—you okay?"

Al: "Ah . . . I think so. I just wasn't sure where I am . . ."

I: "Al—who's the president?"

Al: "Ah . . . (little laugh) . . . Nixon?"

He was almost two presidents behind. I realized he'd suffered a concussion. I explained to the other guys, handed Al our football, and began leading him back toward Eighty-sixth and Riverside.

Al: "Hey Tom—just tell me something—what happened?"

I: "I think you must have hit your head on a rock and gotten a concussion."

Al: "How did I do that?"

I: "You made a diving catch in the end zone for a touchdown."

Al: "Great—so we won?"

I: "Yes."

Al: "That's great . . . so what happened?"

Now I was worried.

I: "What do you mean? I just explained it to you."

Al: "Don't get angry with me—just tell me what happened, okay?"

I realized he was on a loop of memory that was lasting about fifty seconds. So to try to help him recall, I started telling the story exactly the same way each time, and paused to encourage him to volunteer the details through repetition. By the time I got him home, I was exasperated and experiencing some anger that he had sacrificed his body for a touch football game. Suppose he was going to be like this for the rest of his life? I flashed on the *Brain Tumor Comedian* bit and winced. Franni saw the look on my face. By the time we got Al to sit down in the living room, she had heard me explain the story twice to Al. She was really worried.

Franni: "Okay—we're taking him to the hospital."

Al: "The hospital? Would someone please tell me what's going on?"

There was a cassette tape player on the table. There was no blank tape, so I covered up the holes of a Steely Dan cassette with cellophane tape and recorded three back-to-back explanations to an increasingly frustrated Al Franken. He sat between Franni and me in the backseat of a taxi, and when he'd demand to be told what was happening, I'd play him the tape. He would listen with rapt attention and amusement, and thirty seconds after the tape ran out, he'd ask, "So what happened?" Franni went in with him for the examination while I gratefully stayed in the waiting area. Fifteen minutes later I overheard two technicians who came from the examination room, one telling the other "and then he says, 'so just tell me—what happened?'"

I rode with them back to the apartment but then bailed on them. I lived downtown now with Emily, and I couldn't take anymore of Al's loop. Carla was there to give Franni support. I was told Al's faculties returned around noon the next day.

From: Tom Davis
To: Al Franken
Sent: Tuesday, 1 May 2007 1:45 PM
Subject: Memoir

Bill Clotworthy and Jane Crawly—Standards and Practices what was the thing about "horny"?

From: Al Franken
To: Tom Davis
Sent: Tuesday, 1 May 2007 5:49 PM
Subject: Re: Memoir

Jane Crowley was the Margaret Dumont of standards and practices. Once we wrote a sketch that had the word "horny" in it. She was scandalized and said we had to take it out and that we should substitute the word "sexy." I said to her they didn't mean the same thing. She said they did. And I illustrated by saying: "A dog humping your leg is horny, he isn't sexy." And she relented.

Dick Schaap
Editor

October 29, 1976

Mr. Al Franken
Saturday Night Live
WNBC
30 Rockefeller Plaza
New York, New York 10019

Dear Al:

Well, look at it this way: you've blown membership
in the Fellowship of Christian Athletes, but you made
a lot of people laugh. I really appreciate it. The
other cocksucker was funny, too.

Please come back.

Better yet--how 'bout writing an article for SPORT?

Best,

641 Lexington Avenue, New York, New York 10022 (212) 935-4758

When Franni gave birth to Thomasin Davis Franken in 1980, Gilda threw a baby shower for her and invited all the girls from the cast and office staff. She was married to guitarist G. E. Smith and they had a beautiful apartment in the Dakota on Central Park West. I was in G.E.'s den with his massive guitar and amp collection, next to the girls' gathering. He and I were peeking through a crack in the door when Al entered the party as the proud father, bearing the precious bundle wrapped in a baby's blanket. The girls clasped their hands and made a collective sound of cooing motherhood. Then Al tripped over the edge of a rug and fell, slamming the baby's head against the corner of an oak table before falling to the floor and bouncing on top of it. Now the collective sound from those women was a blood-curdling, primal dead-baby scream. I'll never forget it. Then Carla entered with the real baby and Al revealed he had a doll. Everyone laughed. They had to.

Al and I were at Carrie Fisher's new house at the top of Laurel Canyon in 1981. She had told us to bring swimsuits because she had a sauna and a pool. None of her other guests were interested, but I led Franken into the sauna, and then we went out to the pool. I stuck my hand in and was surprised how cold it was. It was winter, even in L.A.

Al: "How's the water?"

I: "It's a bit cool."

Then I dived in and swam around languorously, pretending the water wasn't frigid, which I could do because, being half descended from Swedes, I like cold water.

I: "Actually, it's a lot warmer out here in the middle, Al."

Al: "Oh, okay."

Al takes a leap for the center of the pool and I saw his body recoil as he entered the icy fluid. He surfaced, gasping in agony and holding the back of his neck with one hand.

Al: "God—it's f-freezing! You told me it was warm—now I've got a crick in my neck!"

His neck was sore for a week.

In 1982, Belushi and Aykroyd bought a second Blues Bar after being evicted from the first one on Hudson Street. This one had been known as Mickey's Bar, at the corner of Greenwich and Murray, near the World Trade Center. After John died, Danny wasn't around much—he was busy making movies in Hollywood. But he gave me carte blanche with the bar. I had a party band, and I threw parties there. During one of the breaks during one such party, I was out on the sidewalk talking with my pot dealer, Captain J. Al walked up and Captain J introduced us to an acquaintance who had just escaped from federal custody. The guy's pickup-camper parked at the curb was equipped with blinding flash beams on the rear bumper in case he was chased by police. The guy did a double take at "Al Franken."

© 1983 CHUCK PULIN

Guy: "Is your father Joe Franken?"
Al: "Yes."
Guy: "In Hopkins, Minnesota?"
Al: "Yeah."
Guy: "Wow. I bought an American Express card and had private detectives get all the information in Minneapolis—I rented small aircraft all over South America with that card."

A year before, Al had been walking home from the Pick and Pay on Eighty-seventh and Broadway with a *New York Times* and a bagel in his mouth when a mugger put him in a headlock hold and got his wallet. The Amex was in his father's name.

Captain J's acquaintance was apprehended a week later.

In the early 1980s, General Mills introduced a sugar-laden breakfast cereal for children named "Frankenberry." The box had a pink Frankenstein monster's face that bore coincidental (I think) resemblance to Al's face. Al would show the audience the cereal box and complain bitterly that General Mills had used his likeness without his permission. "Look at this—that's my mouth, that's my nose, those are my glasses. And the top of its head—that's my ass! I'm going to sue!"

We were making each other laugh with an idea for a movie star-

ring Al's parents, Joe and Phoebe. In 1983, they really had a time-share in St. Thomas, Virgin Islands. We fantasized that they had a time-share on the island of Bonarco, where native leftist guerrillas take them hostage, and the two of us go to save them. In the process there are chases and violence, like Al's old man shooting an Uzi at narco-terrorists, and Al and me getting captured by a village of voodoo cultists, whom we recruit to spring Joe and Phoebe. Very silly, but we decided to go to the real Caribbean to write it.

We went first to Negril, Jamaica, to a nice touristy hotel on the beach. I bought pot from a Rasta who kept his stash in the nearby trees. We interviewed him with our hand-size Sony cassette recorder and Al asked him what he would do if someone cut off his dreadlocks.

"He would feel my machete een hees chest, mon."

Then Al was out on the beach talking to a beautiful native girl. He tried teaching her how to throw a Frisbee. It took him an hour before he finally figured out she was a hooker. She couldn't believe it.

That night I walked into a bar filled with white American girls with black Jamaican boyfriends, and I had to back out of that place. Time to leave Negril.

We drove a rented car into the Blue Mountains and met really nice people. Then in Ocho Rios, with the waterfalls and the ocean, we met a cool hippie chick who invited us to have dinner with her Jamaican artist friends. She led us along a jungle path and then we followed her single file, wading across a thigh-high bay. Three quarters of the way across, Al shouted in pain—he'd stepped on a sea urchin. I had to laugh because I was following him and I was scared now, too. But we made it to shore and were welcomed into the home of intellectual Jamaicans who could really cook, drink beer, and smoke ganja. We had a wonderful exchange, and then we had to return before the sun set. Hippie chick led us back, and I swear Franken stepped on the same fucking sea urchin again! We dropped off the car in funky Kingston town and flew to St. Thomas.

Joe and Phoebe's time-share had all the amenities, including a full kitchen and a television. There was a nice bar on the beach. Al had one rum punch; I got plastered. In the moonlight I skinny dipped out to a swimming platform and then back. The next day everybody on the beach was talking about the really big barracuda that lived under the swimming platform where I had been trolling.

Al was married with a child, but I was single again. It was mostly a community of retired Americans, but there was one gorgeous girl on the beach in a bikini and a straw hat. She was from Chicago, and we had a romantic exchange before Al and I flew to Haiti to research voodoo.

At the Port-au-Prince airport there were armed soldiers everywhere. Visitors were separated from returning natives, who were all loaded down with merchandise. We were whisked through customs, and taking Al's brother Owen's advice, we jumped into a cab and checked into the Hotel Oloffson. Sitting high on a hill, this old, elegant hotel was where journalists, diplomats, and savvy tourists stayed within its luxurious confines. I expected James Bond to walk into the bar, where competent mixologists used fresh fruits and shaved ice to make delicious concoctions. The pool had water flowing from the mouth of a sculpture of a porpoise. Al got the Marlon Brando suite; I got the Barbara Walters. After dinner, we befriended a guy who used to be a producer for NBC at 30 Rock. He loved Haiti and shared some of what he knew. Cocktails in hand, he walked us out into the night and down the hill to the cemetery where Papa Doc's tomb was guarded by two soldiers with automatic weapons. They waved us away. Baby Doc was calling the shots now.

The next morning, our taxi driver from the airport was outside the Oloffson front door. We told him we were interested in seeing some voodoo practiced.

> Jean: "*Certainement.* But after sunset. Now we go see sacred falls and river, the beach, shop downtown."

After our dinner that evening, we jumped back into Jean's colorful taxi and he drove us out of the city as the sun set. Soon the two-lane road turned into a single, unpaved affair with a jungle canopy that allowed only a narrow view of the stars.

> Al: "You know—we didn't tell anybody where we're going."
> I giggled: "I know. Where *are* we going?"
> Finally we turned into a driveway with a large, opened wrought-iron gate. We pulled up to an old vine-covered two-story house with a few floodlights illuminating the driveway and door.
> Jean: "You go in. I stay here with the car. Have a good time."

Two attractive women in colorful dresses and scarves on their heads led us out to the back where there was a porch with some patio tables and chairs facing a small stage where a goat was tethered. The Oloffson was a million miles away as they brought us iceless rum and lime-syrup drinks. The only other person in the "audience" was a middle-aged black guy in a U.S. Army staff sergeant's uniform. His eyes bulged, he was grinning so hard. "I'm from St. Louis, and I *love* voodoo shows!" I turned to Al.

> I: "*We* might be the show."
> Al: "Us and the goat."

Several men and women emerged from a beaded curtain. A candle in the top of a large wax-covered bottle was lit, and colorful powders scattered around it. Two guys started wailing on congalike drums, and the girls danced and gyrated and began speaking in tongues. I snapped several pictures with my Polaroid. Our waitress was one of the possessed dancers; as she twirled past our table she grabbed the photos and disappeared through the curtain. Next, a thin middle-aged man (in Haiti this means about sixteen) took to the center of the floor, sprayed lighter fluid on a wooden board, and lit it afire. As the flames started to die down, he ferociously bit off and chewed chunks of the board. I'll bet the real trick was the next morning. Then, a shirtless young man possessed by a spirit came in brandishing a machete, which he tapped on the concrete floor to demonstrate its authenticity. To our relief, the rope around the goat's neck became untethered, and it wandered off into the underbrush. But now the young man put the tip of the blade to his stomach, and then bent it back with his hands, nearly in half, without piercing his skin or disemboweling himself. We left a huge tip.

When Jean dropped us off at the Oloffson, he got a huge tip, too. We completed our script, *Bonarco,* and shopped it around Hollywood. Nobody liked it but us.

From: Tom Davis
To: Al Franken
Sent: Saturday, 5 May 2007 2:11 PM
Subject: Memoir

When did we do "The Comedy Team That Weighs the Same" on Letterman? What was the weight and how did we accomplish that? Tom

From: Al Franken
To: Tom Davis
Sent: Sunday, 13 May 2007 10:47 PM
Subject: Attach: The Comedy Team That Weighs the Same

I actually can't remember what year it was, but it had to be around '82, '83 and we were booked on the Letterman show a number of weeks in advance. We decided to do something a little different for this appearance—something conceptual, and about three weeks out, I turned to you and said, "How much do you weigh?" You said, "I don't know. Probably about 170."

I said, "I weigh about 178. Maybe I could lose a few pounds and you could gain a few and we could go on as the Comedy Team That Weighs the Same."

We immediately started laughing and came up with the idea of wearing robes on the show and then getting weighed wearing just bathing suits on a big scale with one of those circular clock faces with a red hand that spins and then stops at your weight.

I immediately started watching what I ate and working out. About a week later—two weeks out from the show—I was down to about 175 and I asked you if you had weighed yourself. You told me you hadn't and I got a little miffed. So, that night you weighed yourself and you called me to tell me you were at 163 pounds. Now I was even more miffed, because this meant I was going to have to lose more weight while you had yet to make any attempt to gain weight. This was somewhat typical of our partnership. I tended to be more, shall we say, focused.

Also, your being a basically skinny person your entire life, it turned out you had absolutely no idea about what to eat to gain weight. I had to explain to you what foods were fattening and your job was to eat a lot of them, which you soon started complaining about. Meanwhile, I was having steamed fish and salads with no dressing.

About a week out, I was down to 172 and you were only up to 165. Worse still, you were scheduled to go to an outdoor Grateful Dead concert up in Saratoga over the weekend, which meant you were probably going to take acid and probably lose a few pounds. I told you to eat a big breakfast before going to the concert. "What can you eat for breakfast that's fattening?" you asked.

"Waffles! Pancakes! Bacon! Sausage!"

The week of the show we would go to lunch and I'd be starving myself, eating nothing but steamed vegetables while I had to listen to you complain about eating stuff like corned beef hash with a malted. As the day approached, I had gotten down to about 170 and you up to about 167. I knew from my wrestling days that we were in range.

The day of the show, I calculated that we'd both be able to be at slightly over 168. I just didn't eat and I made you eat stuff and we monitored our weight on the scale the Letterman people had gotten for us. As the show started, we were still about a pound apart, but right before we went on, I went to the bathroom and you drank a glass of water. We were both at same weight. We were, if only for one brief shining moment, the Comedy Team that Weighs the Same.

The appearance went great. We entered barefoot, in our robes. David asked us if there were any other comedy team that weighed the same. You, I think, said that Stiller and Meara claimed to weigh the same, but that we doubted it was true. Then I said that Laurel and Hardy evidently weighed the same at one point, but that was just at the very end of Ollie's life. That got something of a groan, but also a big laugh.

Then David asked us if we had any funny stories from being the Comedy Team that Weighs the Same. You said something like: "Dave, Al and I were at a carnival in Mamaroneck yesterday, and you know the guy who can guess your weight? Well, when he saw us coming, he couldn't believe it."

Then the big moment came. The weigh-in. We took our robes off, revealing fairly skimpy Speedos. I can't remember who got on the scale first, but when the second got on and the red dial went to exactly 168 pounds and four ounces, the crowd went nuts.

In January 1987, Al joined Al-Anon. This experience inspired him to write a screenplay with Ron Bass (*Rain Man, Gardens of Stone*) titled *Significant Other,* and starring Andy Garcia and Meg Ryan. Ron was once a big showbiz lawyer who was nice and represented us once or twice.

> Al: "We were walking out of a meeting and [studio executive] Jeff Katzenberg says, 'Oh by the way, we're changing the title to *When a Man Loves a Woman*—but don't tell anybody because we haven't gotten the rights from Percy Sledge yet.' The next day an NBC affiliate flies me to Baton Rouge on behalf of the show [*SNL*]. They have a car pick me up at the airport driven by some guy who was a film nut. Apparently they shot *Sex, Lies, and Videotape* there, and ever since, this guy follows show business on his computer, so as he's driving he's talking about Tom Hanks and Debra Winger working with Alan Pakula and so forth. He takes me out to lunch at this restaurant whose walls are covered with celebrity pictures and then he asks me about my movie, *Significant Other,* and I tell him, 'It's not *Significant Other* anymore—they're calling it *When a Man Loves a Woman*. And the guy says, 'Really, because Percy Sledge comes in here for lunch all the time—and he sits at *that* table.'

23

THE BREAKUP

Anything that can be said can be gainsaid.
—Homer, *The Iliad*

Phoebe, Al's mother, had told him since birth that he was brilliant and wonderful. A little confidence goes a long way; a lot of confidence goes even longer. Al always had confidence in himself, and there was real evidence of brilliance and some wonderfulness. My parents always loved me, but there was some doubt about my intelligence and lack of assertiveness. I struggled with math and was nonaggressive in athletics. It wasn't until I left home and school that I discovered my own gifts.

But Phoebe knew Al was smarter and more aggressive than I, and being goyish, I would probably have issues with drink. One day in 1969, Al and I were sitting at her kitchen table, deciding what name to call our comedy team. I was arguing that it should be "Davis and Franken" because "Franken and Davis" could be misconstrued as "Frank and Dave." Al recognized this logic and agreed. Then Phoebe walked up to the table and said, "It's Franken and Davis, and that's that." Al was devoted to his mother, and the ruling was final, but for the next twenty years lots of people saw a comedy team called Frank and Dave.

The fact is, Franken and Davis was never a very successful comedy team. We were sometimes brilliant and uniquely funny, but we rarely improvised within our act. We were popular at colleges, but we never got our own television show or movie. Even at *SNL*, we were substitutes for those times when four minutes needed to be filled before the "Good nights," and Lorne indulged us to keep us happy as writers.

We had always been fifty-fifty partners, but that started to change in 1980 when Al took off with the *Al Franken Decade* commentary at the *Weekend Update* desk, parodying *The Me Decade* that the '80s was touted to be. I knew I was in trouble when he asked me if I wanted to help him write the *Al Franken Decade* movie. At the same time, Franni became pregnant and Al no longer got high.

I asked Mimi Raleigh to marry me in 1990. She accepted and we started to think about plans and the future. "Let's do inventory and see how much we've got," she said. That's when I discovered that the Franken & Davis 'Bogus Productions' books were all screwed up and our business manager had done us a great disservice. Al had always told me

MIMI RALEIGH © 1990 TOM DAVIS

how much better a businessman he was than I, and I had believed him until that moment. Al couldn't believe me over our business manager, and the dissolution of our partnership became a messy divorce. Meanwhile, I asked Al to be my best man. He recalled I gave him the ring at the Monday pitch meeting. At the reception dinner, he concluded his speech with, ". . . good luck, Mimi—he's your problem now."

Most ironically, a year before we had agreed to be "Alumni of the Year" for our high school alma mater—something they had been asking for years. We couldn't get out of it, so Al and I showed up visiting student classes, accepting framed document awards, and finally performing (for the last time) in the place where we had started. As an old teacher was introducing us as "the two boys whose dreams came true," Al and I were backstage arguing; as we took the stage we were saying, "Fuck you," "No—fuck you!" It was a great show, but when it was over our deep friendship was put in a trunk at the back of a dark closet. After I left *SNL,* I saw him three or four times in the next ten years, usually at an *SNL* funeral or reunion show.

One night in early 2004, I was watching *Jeopardy!* when the statement was revealed, "He was the comedy partner of Al Franken," and everyone was stumped, including Ken Jennings, the greatest *Jeopardy!* champ ever.

In the summer of 2004, I was standing in line at a supermarket with a cartload of groceries. I was about to look at a *Cosmopolitan* magazine to see what new sex tips they might be suggesting, when I saw Franken's face on the cover of *The New York Times Magazine,* talking into a radio microphone that had LIBERAL on it like call letters. I'm sure whoever wrote the article was fresh out of college, but when they devoted a few paragraphs to Al's history, it said he had gone to high school with Mark Luther, and then nothing much happened to his career until *SNL,* where he wrote with Jim Downey. There was a picture of his parents with Owen, Al, and me standing behind them, but beneath the picture, the caption read, "Al with his parents, Joe and Phoebe, his brother Owen, and a friend."

Franken's Air America radio show was brilliant. I would listen to it often as I wrote this book. Al called me up several times to come on his show and do some Bob and Ray–type bits, and it was like riding a bicycle. I was glad to see him. He flew me out to Minneapolis to help him at a couple of fund-raisers, where we dusted off a few old Franken and Davis routines and managed to do some new bits as well. It was a joy.

Martin and Lewis lasted only ten years. If you were to compare us, I would be Dino and Al would be Jerry. With Simon and Garfunkel, Al would be Paul and I would be Artie. Sonny and Cher—Al would be Cher.

I love Al as I do my brother, whom I also don't see very often.

Phoebe was right. Al is destined to do great things, and I am thrilled he has reclaimed Paul Wellstone's seat in the U.S. Senate, and serves his country representing the state of Minnesota.

SHOW # 90   HOST: STEVE MARTIN   (FOR AIR) (REVISED)

AIR: APRIL 22, 1978

<u>SHOW RUNDOWN:</u>

COLD OPENING/BLUES BORTHERS
OPENING MONTAGE (VT)
OPENING MONOLOGUE/PICKPOCKET
HEY YOU/PARODY COMM'L (VT)
THE FESTRUNK BROTHERS
    Commercial # 1

MEDIEVAL SURGEON/BARBER
    Commercial # 2
       ESSEX HOUSE PROMO (VT)

DANCING IN THE DARK
    Commercial # 3
    UPDATE PROMO
    STATION BREAK

UPDATE
    Commercial # 4

KING TUT
    Commercial # 5

LOVE STORY
INTRO LARAINE
WEIS FILM (VT) "Swan Lake"
TROFF 'N BREW
    Commercial # 6
       EAST WIND LIMO (SL)
       STATION BREAK

NERD SCIENCE FAIR
    Commercial # 7

INTRO STEVE
BLUE BROTHERS "I DON'T KNOW"
    Commercial # 8

NEXT WEEK IN REVIEW
    Commercial # 9

GOODNIGHTS
& CREDITS

<u>CUT:</u>

TATTOO PARLOR
NICK SPRINGS

TOM DAVIS   278

24

THE BEST *SNL* SHOW EVER: WHERE DO YOU GET YOUR IDEAS FROM?

You're only as good as your last show.
—Lorne Michaels

I was standing by the coffee and doughnuts, at the nexus of all the action at *Saturday Night Live*. There were the doors to Studio 8H, the control room, the host's and the musical guest's dressing rooms, and the avenue from wardrobe, design, and props. On a Saturday afternoon's camera blocking, there are usually a lot of anxious-looking people buzzing through this space. Today, they weren't anxious—they were excited. Steve Martin was hosting. He'd come to host the show and brought this ridiculous song he'd written, called "King Tut." It was silly and stupid—and wonderful. It was Steve's fifth show in two years, April 22, 1978.

Lorne had told design and wardrobe to knock themselves out, and they had succeeded. The set for Tut was lavish, glittering gold and filled with hieroglyphics; it revealed the *SNL* band, and Steve, the Pharaoh who sang his song. The rehearsal with costumes was effortless, but as one of the black chick singers came into the nexus, Jay Otley, our gentlemanly Standards and Practices guy, had costume designer Franne Lee in tow, and he stopped the young woman. "Franne—look—you can clearly see her breasts." The beautiful singer was, indeed, wearing a see-through, golden chiffon top.

> Otley: "You can't have topless women on network TV."
> Franne: "Yeah, but look at 'em—they're gorgeous. All right, we'll cover 'em up, if you want. It was worth a try."

That's the kind of show it was.

I had my plate full, as usually happened when Steve hosted. I was working on three sketches that made it past Wednesday's read-thru: a Bill Murray *Nick the Lounge Singer (Nick Springs), Troff 'n' Brew,* and *Theodoric of York.* As *SNL* writers, we were responsible for the production of our own sketches. Each piece was camera blocked (rehearsed for the director and cameramen) once on Thursday or Friday, then again on Saturday afternoon, when every sketch was rehearsed in costume and with props. The script was always being revised, and changes had to be given to the control room, and then to cue cards. The props were never right the first time. The Property guys had been working there since 1950, and they didn't read scripts. Of course, most people can't read a script and get the jokes. These old-timers, Willie and Henry, were sweet, and glad when we worked with them. If I had written in for a flying saucer on filament string at the end of a pole, they would let *me* operate the ridiculous, un-wieldy prop (unheard of with today's Union guys).

On the preceding Tuesday after dinner, Bill Murray, Dan Aykroyd, Paul Shaffer, and I had gone out on the obligatory barhopping it took to write one of Billy's lounge singer sketches. I carried the long legal pad and several regular Bic pens. Having already done "Nick Summers" and "Nick Winters" in previous shows, and since it was March, "Nick Springs" was an obvious choice. We decided Nick would perform on a small corner stage in a bar at the Poco-mount Hotel, a honeymooners' spot in the Pocono Mountains (Emily, and I had just gone there to the Covehaven Hotel, to re-search an editorial piece she was writing for *Penthouse* magazine). Billy wanted to have a small mirror ball and other disco decorations, and a rhythm machine to do "I Thank You" with the drum solo. Paul loved that. Danny would enter near the end, as his character, Native American Jimmy Joe Red Sky. He always carried in some kind of dead animal he'd found, in this case a wet squirrel from the swimming pool filter. For Nick to work the lounge crowd, we wrote in Laraine Newman as a

woman with a man other than her husband. She is mortified at Nick's attention as he sings "Love to Love You Baby." Then Gilda Radner, as a newlywed with poison ivy, causes Nick to launch into a ripping rendition of "Poison Ivy." To end the sketch, Nick liked to sing songs with no lyrics, this time the theme to *Close Encounters* ("... First encounter ... YOU ... next encounter ... ME ... Third encounter ... LOVE ... the *Close Encounters* Theeeeme!").

Earlier that same Tuesday, Danny and I had dined at Charley O's at the corner of Forty-eighth and Rockefeller Place. It became the inspiration for our sketch *Troff 'n' Brew,* a watering hole for the business lunch crowd. It featured cattle-feeding troughs filled with chili, and round, galvanized-steel watering basins supplied by a constant stream of beer from a spigot near the bottom of a voluminous vat. While people discussed business and gossip, they bent over and put their faces into the food, and then literally lapped up the brew. Steve had to have vegetarian chili, so we had buckets of it for his mark at the

THE BEST *SNL* SHOW EVER

trough. The sketch ended with a PA announcement: "Troff 'n' Brew is closing for a half-hour hose down. Please pay and exit up the main ramp."

We wanted waitresses, Gilda and Laraine, to spray off people's faces with a hose, but the director, Davey Wilson, was worried about water on the studio floor, so we ended up with smaller spraying devices, and the water didn't read on camera to my satisfaction. I couldn't argue with him, though.

An accident had happened the week before, which became the inspiration for *Theodoric of York*: Al Franken and I had written a hockey sketch for the host, Canadian actor Michael Sarrazin. The idea involved actors wearing roller skates to get the ice skate look. The POV (point of view for the camera) was from the back of the penalty box, so you couldn't see the feet. There was an "extra" role of the referee, which we gave to fellow writer Don Novello. Both Al and I can skate (we're from Minnesota), but it was our sketch, and we had to watch over the entire production, on the studio floor and in the control room. During camera blocking on Friday, Don, who had no meat on him and was not a great skater, fell on the studio's concrete floor. He couldn't get up, and it became apparent that he'd broken his hip. I visited him on Monday at St. Vincent's Hospital on Seventh Avenue and Eleventh—my neighborhood. He lay flat on his back, with his leg in a cast suspended at a forty-degree angle by a rope and pulley with a large weight at the end. He was in so much pain that I had to laugh. He laughed with me, but weakly, in part because he was pissed at me for finding his replacement in the sketch even before he had been lifted off the studio floor. Such was my almost military mind-set toward the show. I apologized. But looking at Don in that hospital made me flash on how primitive this medical procedure would seem in the future.

Then I thought—let's do a sketch about medieval medicine. I walked home to 288 West Twelfth and looked through some encyclopedia (for you younger readers, an encyclopedia is a hard-copy search engine—Google it). Emily went to the library on Sixth Avenue and Tenth to find books on the subject while I prepared to go to work, eating some leftovers, drinking a beer, and snorting some cocaine. She was back in twenty minutes and had struck gold—this stuff was hilarious. I took it to the office and pulled in Al Franken and Jim Downey. The three of us usually did at least one piece together each week. Jim and Al

DON NOVELLO © 1978 TOM DAVIS

were brilliant and exacting jokesmiths, and no matter how agonizing the all-night sessions, we could crack each other up. This frequently got the script funny enough to survive read-through on Wednesday.

```
MEDIEVAL SURGEON/BARBER Steve/Gilda/Dan/ FRANKEN
DAVIS/DOWNEY/John/Laraine/Bill/Don Pardo (V.O.)

(NO ENGLISH ACCENTS, PLAY LIKE MARCUS WELBY)
(OPEN ON: FOURTEENTH CENTURY STONE
CHAMBER WITH WINDOWS AND A DOOR OPEN
ONTO THE STREET FEATURING A GUTTER
FULL OF FILTH)
(THERE ARE TWO MEDIEVAL CHAIRS, A
TABLE FILLED WITH FOURTEENTH CENTURY
SURGICAL EQUIPMENT, ALSO A SPECIAL PULLEY DEVICE.)
(STEVE IS DRESSED AS A FOURTEENTH-CENTURY BLOODIED
BARBER-SURGEON, AND GILDA IS HIS ASSISTANT.)
(ENTER DAN AS A MERCHANT WITH LONG HAIR AND BEARD)
        (SLIDE: YORK, ENGLAND, 1303 A.D.)


                    DAN:
            Hello, Theodoric of York . . .
            well it's springtime and I've
            come for my haircut and
            bloodletting.
```

STEVE:
Hello, William, son of Malcolm
the Tanner. Have a seat.
Brungilda, you start on William's
hair, and I'll open a vein here.

GILDA:
Yes, Theodoric.

(GILDA PICKS UP LARGE SHEARS, BEGINS
CUTTING DAN'S HAIR; STEVE PLACES
A BOWL UNDERNEATH DAN'S ELBOW
AS DAN GRASPS A POLE TO MAKE HIS VEINS STICK OUT.)

STEVE:
How's that baby I delivered
last Christmas when your wife
died?

DAN:
Oh. She's deformed.

STEVE:
Oh. That's right I remember now.

(STEVE TAKES A MEDIEVAL SCALPEL AND
"CUTS" DAN'S VEIN [INGENIOUS TUBE
SYSTEM]. DAN BLEEDS INTO BOWL.)

DAN:
Ahhh . . .

DON (V.O.)
And now it's time for another
episode of . . .

(TITLE SLIDE:
Theodoric of York, Medieval Barber)

DON (V.O.)
. . . Theodoric of York,
Medieval Barber!

(MUSIC: BAD MEDIEVAL FEATURING PERCUSSION AND FLUTE)

STEVE:

There you go.

(ENTER JANE AS ENGLISHWOMAN CARRYING HER ALMOST UNCON-
SCIOUS DAUGHTER, LARAINE, WHO COLLAPSES INTO THE SECOND
CHAIR.)

STEVE:

Looks like I have another
patient. I'll be back in a
minute to see how you're doing.

DAN:

Right. Thank you.

STEVE:

Hello, Joan, wife of Simkin
the Miller. Well how's
my little patient doing?

JANE:

Not so well, I fear. We
followed all your instructions;
I mixed powder of stag horn,
gum of Arabic, with boiled
sheep's urine, and applied it
in a poultice to her face.

STEVE:

And did you bury her up to her
neck in the marsh and leave
her overnight?

JANE:

Oh yes. But she still feels
listless as ever, if not more.

STEVE:

Well, let's give her another
bloodletting. Brungilda—

GILDA:

Yes, Theodoric.

STEVE:
Take two pints.

GILDA:
Yes, Theodoric.

JANE:
Will she be all right, Barber?

STEVE:
Well, I'll do everthing humanly
possible. Unfortunately, we barbers
aren't gods. You know, medicine is
not an exact science, but we are
learning all the time. Why just
fifty years ago, they thought
a disease like your daughter's was
caused by demonic possession or
witchcraft. But nowadays we know
that Isabel is suffering from an
imbalance of bodily humors
perhaps caused by a toad or
a small dwarf living in her
stomach.

JANE:
Well, I'm glad she's in such
good hands.

(BILL, SLIMY SERF WITH COMPOUND FRACTURES
ON BOTH LEGS, SPLINTERED BONE STICKING OUT
OF LEOTARD, IS WHEELED IN IN SMALL WOODEN
CART BY JOHN, HIS HUNCHBACK FRIEND)

JOHN:
Is this Theodoric, Barber of York?

STEVE:
Say, don't I know you?

JOHN:
Sure, you worked on my back.

STEVE:
What's wrong with your friend here?

JOHN:
He broke his legs.

BILL:
I was at the Festival of the
Vernal Equinox and I guess I
had a little too much mead and
I darted out in front of an
oxcart. It all happened so fast
they couldn't stop in time.

STEVE:
Well, you'll feel a lot better
after a good bleeding . . .

BILL:
But I'm bleeding already.

STEVE:
Say, who's the barber here?

BILL:
Okay. Okay. Just do something
for my legs.

STEVE:
Well, the three of us'll get
you up on the jibbet here,
(INDICATING THE PULLEY DEVICE)
and if you don't feel better
tomorrow we'll just cut them
off.

(STEVE, GILDA, AND JOHN PUT BILL ON JIBBET)

BILL:
Okay. I'm sure I'm gonna
feel better tomorrow.

STEVE:
Okay. Now this is gonna
hurt. What we're doing is
separating your broken bones.
Okay, Brungilda, put a few
leeches on his forehead.

THE BEST *SNL* SHOW EVER

(GILDA PUTS SOME SLIMY PIECES OF LIVER ON BILL'S FORE-
HEAD)

                         BILL:
         Thank you.

(STEVE GOES UP TO DAN WHO IS ASLEEP AND
STILL BLEEDING. STEVE GRABS A LITTLE
WHISK BROOM AND BRUSHES OFF HIS COARSELY
CUT HAIR)

                         STEVE:
         When was the last time you
         came in for a worming?

                         DAN:
         I guess I'm due, but I
         don't have the time today.
         Here's five pounds and a
         goose.

(DAN HANDS HIM A SMALL BAG WITH HEAVY COINS
IN IT AND A DEAD GOOSE WE HAVEN'T SEEN, FROM
UNDER HIS COAT)
(STEVE HOLDING A GOOSE GOES OVER TO LARAINE
WHO IS ALMOST DEAD)

                         STEVE:
         So how's the little patient doing?

                         JANE:
         She's worse. She's looking pale.

                         STEVE:
         Well, if she's not responding
         to treatment, I'm afraid we'll
         have to run some more tests.
         Brungilda, bring me the Caladrious bird.

                         JANE:
         Caladrious bird?

                         STEVE:
         Yes. The Caladrious bird is placed
         on a stand beside the patient. If
         the bird looks at the patient's

face, she will live, but if it
looks at her feet, she will die.

(GILDA BRINGS BIRDCAGE)
(STEVE OPENS THE CAGE AND TALKS TO BIRD)
Okay now, Freddy, c'mon out.

(BIRD FLIES OUT OF CAGE)
I don't know how to interpret that.
Did you see, Brungilda?

GILDA:

No.

STEVE:

Well, I guess take another pint.

GILDA:

It's too late, there is no more.
She's dead.

(JANE BREAKS DOWN)

JANE:
Dead, dead! I can't believe it!
My little daughter dead!

STEVE:
Now, Mrs. Miller. You're distraught,
tired; you may be suffering from
nervous exhaustion. I think you'd
feel better if I let some blood.

JANE:
You charlatan! You killed my
daughter, just like you killed
most of my other children. Why
don't you admit it? You don't
know what you're doing.

STEVE:

(À LA MIKE MCMACK)
Wait a minute. Perhaps she's right.
Perhaps I've been wrong to blindly follow the
medical traditions and superstitions of
past centuries. Maybe we barbers

should test those assumptions
analytically, through experimentation
and a "scientific method." Maybe this
scientific method could be extended to
other fields of learning: the natural
sciences, art, architecture, and navigation,
leading the way toward a new age, an age of
rebirth, a Renaissance.

(THINKS A MINUTE)
Nah!

               DON (V.O.)
Be sure to tune in next week for another
episode of . . .
(SUPER:Theodoric of York, Medieval Barber)
When Theodoric turns to Brungilda and says
. . .

            STEVE:
A little bloodletting and some boar's vomit
and you should be fine.

(MUSIC: STING)
(FADE)

During dress rehearsal, one of the funniest things I ever saw happened: the "Caladrious bird" was tied to a string, and when Steve got him out of the cage, the bird flew around and around, effectively tying Steve and Gilda together. The audience laughed for the longest time.

The Nick Springs piece didn't make it to air, but was done with great success in the show after next. Another piece that got cut was a really funny *Tattoo Parlor* written by Danny, Rosie Shuster, Steve, and Laraine. Steve played the idiot customer, Danny was "Jason" with a ponytail, and Laraine was his old lady, "Sunset." They smoke a joint to relax their customer and listen to his tattoo desires. Steve decides to trust their judgment and hours later, looking at his back in a mirror, he is horrified to see a large tattoo of WAR IS UNHEALTHY FOR CHILDREN AND OTHER LIVING THINGS. There is also a bad flower and a peace sign on his hip, alongside an image of a showerhead with spray, and the words SHOWER WITH A FIEND.

From the book *Saturday Night,* by Doug Hill and Jeff Weingrad:

> But there were many nights when everyone seemed to be on. One of them was the Steve Martin show of April 22, in the third season, which some on the show consider the single best *Saturday Night* ever.
>
> Steve Martin, who himself became *Saturday Night*'s greatest hit as a host (the ratings usually jumped by a million or more homes when he appeared), shares the opinion that this may have been the best show ever. "It was like the peak of *Saturday Night,*" he said. "It was the peak of me."

Nice review. It was one of the few shows where everybody went to the after-party happy. Every other show, there was always someone who had all their stuff cut. It was hardly ever a good time without somebody getting hurt. This show was submitted to the Television Academy of Arts and Sciences for Emmy consideration.

My recollection was that we lost to a Carol Burnett special. But in June of 2006, I was walking with Al Franken along a street in Minneapolis recalling this story, and he said, "No. Don't you remember? We didn't even know who we were up against until we got in our seats and looked at the program. Anne Beatts saw it first and cackled loudly (Michael O'Donoghue once described her laugh as a chicken falling down an elevator shaft); she said, 'Look! We're up against a Steve and Eydie special!'—Steve Lawrence and Eydie Gorme. Then I saw that Steve and Eydie were seated right in front of us, and Steve turned around and stared at Anne. Of course, when they won, they got up and turned to us with self-satisfied smirks and made the trip to the stage. We had to smile and applaud."

This is why there is the show business saying: "Ignore your bad reviews, and the good ones, too."

I say you're only as good as your best show.

PROMOTIONAL POSTCARD FOR '78 GRAND MARQUIS

25

THE GRAND MARQUIS

Life is a cosmic joke with death as the punch line.
—Bob Marks

© 2008 LINDSAY BRICE

I had to have it. For twenty years a promotional postcard for the 1978 Grand Marquis has been up on my bathroom wall. There's a guy standing beside it who actually resembles me in 1978, the peak of my show business career. I promised myself that if I ever saw that car in good shape and for sale, I would buy it.

My bathroom walls are almost completely covered in newspaper clippings and photographs, postcards, snapshots, and drawings. There's an obituary section in which I have friends, heroes, and antiheroes, like Ray Goulding and Axis Sally. There's a postcard of

Saturn next to a picture of a mule diving from a thirty-foot platform into a pool at the state fair in Birmingham. Man Ray is posited next to Keith Richards and Alfred Hitchcock. The clippings include an article about global warming from 1988 and one about the "new" Mir space station, a *New York Times* front-page lead article "EARTH-SIZE STORM AND FIREBALLS SHAKE JUPITER AS COMET DIES," and then there is a section that includes articles such as these:

CONCERN OVER MORAL VALUES LED TO FAMILY MURDERS, LAWYER SAYS—Elizabeth NJ, April 2—John E. List, a man of rigid religious principles, became so alarmed by the threat to the salvation of his family posed by societal changes that started in the 1960s that he killed them "with love in his heart," his lawyer told a jury today.

The lawyer, Elijah J. Miller Jr., in his opening statement in List's murder trial, conceded that his client shot his wife, mother, and three children to death in their Westfield house in 1971, but he asked the jury to try and understand the defendant's religious conviction that the only way to save his family from the immoral influence of "rebellion, war, drugs, and fragmented families" that he saw everywhere was to kill them.

"Let there be no mistake, John Emil List killed his family," Mr. Miller said, adding that he would try to show that "these killings are something other than murder."

ELEPHANT KILLS MOPED RIDER: New Delhi—A wild elephant trampled a school teacher riding a moped and sat beside the man's body until chased away by police.

NOSE NEWS: As a gesture of goodwill, Japan is returning 20,000 noses lopped off of Korean soldiers and civilians during a 1597 invasion. The noses—and heads of Korean generals—were taken as spoils of war. Now buried at the *senbitsuka,* or 1,000-nose tomb near the Japanese town of Bizen, they will be returned later this year. They are expected to find a final resting place in South Korea's Cholla province, where damage from the sixteenth century Japanese invasion was greatest.

BAKERY PLANT WORKER KILLED IN MACHINERY: A worker at a bakery plant was killed early yesterday when an agitator in a giant mixing bowl he was cleaning was accidentally turned on.

BLUE RIDGE, GA.: Police searching for cocaine dropped by an airborne smuggler found a ripped-up shipment of the powder and the remains of a bear that apparently died after eating twenty pounds of the drug.

DRUNK HEAVYSET WOMAN SMOTHERS YOUNG CHILD, BUFFALO, NY: A one-and-a-half-year-old boy was accidentally smothered on a couch by a fat woman who had spent the night drinking with his mother. Linda Parsons, 21, had placed her son, Chance Goforth, on the couch while she and five friends drank in her apartment Thursday night, police said. One by one, her friends left or found a place to sleep. One of the guests, a heavyset young woman who apparently was drunk—picked the couch, police said. On Friday morning, Chance was found dead, his air supply apparently cut off by the woman's thigh.

QUADRIPLEGIC ACCUSED AS KILLER—HOUSTON, SEPTEMBER 9 (AP): A quadriplegic has been charged here with murdering his wife of two weeks by using his mouth to yank a string that was attached to the trigger of a handgun. Witnesses told police that the wife had placed the string in his mouth just moments before. The thirty-seven year-old victim, Bertha Maye Burns, was slain Monday night at a bar where she and her wheelchair bound husband, James B. Burns, forty, had been talking. Police described the weapon that killed her as a nine-millimeter pistol mounted on a small board that Mr. Burns had across his lap. A string ran around two screws in the board, they said, with one end of the string running to the trigger. A shoebox that had covered the entire apparatus was removed before the shooting. Mr. Burns was upset because his wife was planning to live in California and also because he suspected her of infidelity, the police said. "According to witnesses, they were sitting in there talking in quiet tones," said police detective A. J. Topel. "She then got up and put the string in his mouth, and he jerked his head back and the gun went off." A police sergeant, J. C. Mosier, said Mr. Burns, who was left quadriplegic when shot several years ago by a previous wife, had told the police he had wanted his wife to kill him, but that "she talked me into killing her." However, the sergeant said, Mr. Burns also told police that he had jerked his head back only by accident. And in an interview Tuesday with the *Houston Chronicle,* Mr. Burns said: "Somehow the string got pulled. Somehow she pushed my head back." In the interview, Mr. Burns could not explain why three bullets had hit his wife.

Franken and I bought a house in upstate New York in 1985. It was an investment we could use. I discovered an antiquarian bookstore nearby and became friends with the owners, Howard Frisch and Fred Harris. Howard had grown up in Washington Heights, near the old polo grounds of northern Manhattan. He became a bookseller in the early '30s. He lived down the block from Edna St. Vincent Millay in the West Village. In 1962, he and Fred opened their bookstore upstate and became full-time residents. When Howard was eighty-seven, he took a fall in the shower. An ambulance arrived with two very young paramedics who were concerned he might have had a stroke, so they asked him the standard questions to see if he were compos mentis.

> Medic: "Do you know what your name is?"
> Howard: "Howard Frisch."
> Medic: "What year were you born?"
> Howard: "1916."
> Medic: "And who's the president?"
> Howard: "Woodrow Wilson."

Soon Howard became wheelchair-bound, and announced a "sea change was coming." He moved into the Eden Park rest home in Jefferson Heights near Catskill. He had his room lined with his favorite works of literature—Pascal, Milton, Shakespeare, but there he deteriorated both mentally and physically, so not only could he no longer hold a book, he couldn't concentrate long enough to finish a thought, and on bad days, speech was impossible. When Fred left town, I would visit Howard a few times a week. He had been concerned before that he would not live to see my book published, so I thought I would read to him from my manuscript as I was writing the first draft. During one of these sessions, he seemed to be suffering from a paroxysm of some kind, and I went to the head nurse who had been working there for more than twenty years, a wonderful Irish lady, Alice, who could understand Howard when no one else could.

> I: "Alice—Howard's having a bad day. I'm not so good at this dying-process thing, so if there's anything I could be doing, tell me."
>
> Alice: "Don't read to him from your book anymore—it drives him crazy."

Just before Christmas 2006, I was driving up to Jefferson Heights to visit Howard, and there it was—a 1978 Grand Marquis just like the one on my bathroom wall. Perfect condition; sixty thousand miles; cream-colored leather seats, big as a navy launch, and a FOR SALE sign taped inside the driver's window.

In the Franken and Davis Show at Dudley's in 1976, I did a silly monologue in a character inspired by my reading of Bertrand Russell. I took the stage in a smoking jacket and pipe and addressed the audience in an English accent like Robert Morley. I talked about the technique of wit on a metaphysical plane, and the transcendence of tragedy into comedy.

"I am reminded of the novel *Johnny Got His Gun,* which is told from the perspective of a young man who is a mute quadriplegic as a result of massive injuries suffered at the end of World War I. The book ends as he is finally able to communicate to a nurse by tapping in Morse code on his bedpan. He taps out the words, "Kill me," and the nurse says, "No." I think the nurse should have said, "No. Why don't you write a book?""

UNAPOLOGIA

Peter, Dan Aykroyd's father, called me on the phone: "Tom – I've just finished reading your memoir and I think it's wonderful." Pete had listened to the set of CDs I'd sent him a few days before. He has macular degeneration, which has made book reading nearly impossible. "It was a fun journey through an important epoch in America that sprang from the ethos of the '60s."

"Thanks for saying so – that's exactly what I was trying to do – let my readers have a taste."

"You described in detail a myriad of drugs that you ingested – what sort of affect do you think that had on you?"

"Good question, Pete. The subject of experimental drug taking is just as controversial as it ever was. There was, indeed, an ethos that I embraced so that to downplay it would be less than frank. Timothy Leary and Jerry Garcia didn't just experiment – they WERE the experiment, and I'm very proud to call them my friends. Some people will find my book and me repulsive or dismissible, but that's part of the fascination for me as an author: when all is said and done, am I still likeable as a person? Who shares my laughter? If my brain is damaged, do you still like the part that functions? I know you love me, Pete."

"Yes I do, and I'm happy to have been a father-figure to you. Now, I know how strongly you feel the book speaks for itself, but I think you should take what you just told me and put it in your paperback edition as an 'Apologia,' like Thomas Aquinas."

—Tom Davis, August 12, 2009

BOOKS I READ WHILE WRITING MY OWN,
WHICH HAD SOME INDETERMINATE INFLUENCE

Beatts, Ann, and John Head. *Saturday Night Live*. Avon Books, 1977.

Belushi-Pisano, Judy, with Tanner Colby. *Belushi: A Tribute*. Rugged Land, 2005.

Brillstein, Bernie, with David Rensin. *Where Did I Go Right? You're No One in Hollywood Unless Someone Wants You Dead*. Little, Brown & Company, 1999.

Brynner, Rock. *The Ballad of Habit and Accident*. Wyndham Books, 1980.

——*Empire and Odyssey: The Brynners in Far East Russia and Beyond*. Steerforth Press, 2006.

Constanten, Tom. *Between Rock and Hard Places: A Musical Autobiodyssey*. Hulogosi Communications Inc., March 1992.

Dylan, Bob. *Chronicles: Volume One*. Simon and Schuster, 2004.

Eszterhas, Joe. *Hollywood Animal: A Memoir*. Vintage Books, 2004.

Farley, Thomas, and Tanner Colby. *Chris Farley Show: A Biography in Three Acts*. Viking, 2008.

Gad, Irene. *Tarot and Individuation: Correspondences with Cabala and Alchemy*. Nichols-Hays, 1994.

Hill, Doug, and Jeff Weingrad. *Saturday Night: A Backstage History of Saturday Night Live*. Vintage Books, 1987.

Kerouac, Jack. *On the Road*. Penguin Group, 1991.

Kimmel, Steve. *You Are Who You're With*. Unpublished.

Larson, Edward J. *A Magnificent Catastrophe: The Tumultuous Election of 1800, America's First Presidential Campaign*. Free Press, a division of Simon and Schuster Inc., 2007.

Leary, Timothy. *Interpersonal Diagnosis of Personality*. John Wiley & Sons, 1957.

Leary, Timothy, and R.U. Sirius. *Design for Dying*. HarperCollins Publishers, 1997.

Lesh, Phil. *Searching for the Sound*. Little, Brown & Company, 2005.

Loos, Anita. *Kiss Hollywood Goodbye*. Viking Press, 1974.

Mace, Nancy, M. A., Peter Rabins, M.D., M.P.H., *The 36-Hour Day*. John Hopkins University Press, 2006

Martin, Steve, *Born Standing Up,* Scribner, 2007.

McNally, Dennis. *Desolate Angel: Jack Kerouac, the Best Generation, and America*. Random House, 1979.

——*A Long Strange Trip: The Inside History of the Grateful Dead*. Broadway Books, 2002.

Milkowski, Bill. *Jaco: The Extraordinary and the Tragic Life of Jaco Pastorius, "The World's Greatest Bass Player."* Backbeat Books, 1995.

Millay, Edna St. Vincent. *Collected Lyrics.* Harper Books, 1943.

Parish, Steve. *Home Before Daylight: My Life on the Road with the Grateful Dead.* St. Martin's Press, 2003.

Perrin, Dennis. *Mr. Mike: The Life and Work of Michael O'Donoghue.* Avon Books, 1998.

Russell, Bertrand. *Understanding History.* Philosophical Library, 1957.

Scully, Rock, with David Dalton. *Living with the Dead: Twenty Years on the Bus with Garcia and the Grateful Dead.* Cooper Square Press, 1996.

Wolfe, Tom. *The Electric Kool-Aid Acid Test.* Farrar, Straus and Giroux, 1968.

MY FAVORITE FILMS

1. *My Dinner with André,* Louis Malle, 1981
2. *The Man on the Flying Trapeze,* Dave Fleischer, 1934
3. *Mr. Hulot's Holiday,* Jacques Tati, 1953
4. *Saps at Sea,* Gordon Douglas, 1940
5. *The Big Lebowski,* Joel Coen, 1998
6. *Nights of Cabiria,* Federico Fellini, 1957
7. *Day for Night,* François Truffaut, 1973
8. *The Third Man,* Carol Reed, 1949
9. *Our Man in Havana,* Carol Reed, 1959
10. *The Captain's Paradise,* Anthony Kimmins, 1953
11. *Dr. Strangelove or; How I Learned to Stop Worrying and Love the Bomb,* Stanley Kubrick, 1964
12. *2001: A Space Odyssey,* Stanley Kubrick, 1968
13. *Citizen Kane,* Orson Welles, 1941
14. *The Day the Earth Stood Still,* Robert Wise, 1951
15. *GoodFellas,* Martin Scorsese, 1990
16. *Get Crazy,* Allan Arkush, 1983
17. *Bedazzled,* Stanley Donen, 1967
18. *Gandhi,* Richard Attenborough, 1982
19. *Chinatown,* Roman Polanski, 1974
20. *The Tragedy of Macbeth,* Roman Polanski, 1971
21. *The Tragedy of Othello: The Moor of Venice,* Orson Welles, 1952
22. *The Grapes of Wrath,* John Ford, 1940
23. *The Gold Rush,* Charles Chaplin, 1925
24. *Quest for Fire,* Jean-Jacques Annaud, 1981
25. *Sunset Boulevard,* Billy Wilder, 1950
26. *Body Double,* Brian De Palma, 1984
27. *The Abominable Snowman,* Val Guest, 1957
28. *Wild Strawberries,* Ingmar Bergman, 1957
29. *Who's Afraid of Virginia Woolf?,* Mike Nichols, 1966
30. *House of Games,* David Mamet, 1987
31. *Anatomy of a Murder,* Otto Preminger, 1959
32. *Rope,* Alfred Hitchcock, 1948